ETHICS AND GLOBAL POLITICS

ETHICS AND GLOBAL POLITICS

The Active Learning Sourcebook

Edited by
April Morgan,
Lucinda Joy Peach,
and Colette Mazzucelli

Kumarian
Press, Inc.

Ethics and Global Politics: The Active Learning Sourcebook
Published 2004 in the United States of America by Kumarian Press, Inc.,
1294 Blue Hills Avenue, Bloomfield, CT 06002 USA

Copyedit by Nancy Burnett, Golden Cypress Publication Services
Index by Barbara DeGennaro
Proofread by Beth Richards

The text of this book is set in 10/12.5 Sabon

Production and design by Victoria Hughes Waters
Hughes Publishing Services, Worcester, MA

Printed in the United States of America by Thomson-Shore, Inc.
Text printed with vegetable oil-based ink.

♾ The paper used in this publication meets the minimum requirements of the American National Standard for Information Sciences—Permanence of Paper for printed
Library Materials, ANSI Z39.48-1984

Library of Congress Cataloging-in-Publication Data

Ethics and global politics: the active learning sourcebook / edited by
April Morgan, Lucinda Joy Peach, and Colette Mazzucelli.
     p. cm.
Includes bibliographical references and index.
     ISBN 1-56549-187-4 (pbk. : alk. paper)
     1. International relations—Moral and ethical aspects—Study and
     teaching—Activity programs. 2. International relations—Moral
     and ethical aspects—Problems, exercises, etc.
I. Morgan, April II. Peach, Lucinda J. III. Mazzucelli, Colette.
     JZ1306.E84 2004
     172'.4—dc22

                                       2004007399

13 12 11 10 09 08 07 06 05 04   10 9 8 7 6 5 4 3 2 1   First Printing 2004

TABLE OF CONTENTS

ACKNOWLEDGMENTS

During six weeks of Summer 2001, several of us involved in this project participated in a faculty development seminar entitled, "Supranationalism: The Ethics of Global Governance," sponsored by the National Endowment for the Humanities (NEH) and directed by the Carnegie Council on Ethics and International Affairs (CCEIA) at Columbia University in New York. A seed unknowingly planted earlier by Ayappa Bidanda germinated there in the form of this volume. We thank him, NEH, CCEIA, the International Studies Association, Pat Freeland, Jim Lance, Guy Bentham, and Erin Brown for their support. David Reidy, Robert Denemark, Mark Boyer, Mary Caprioli and the reviewers offered helpful comments. We are also grateful to our students for bringing these modules to life and for bringing life to our classrooms.

INTRODUCTION

As Martin Marty has noted, exclusivity is inefficient in effective communication.[1] An effective communicator must know at least two states of mind: his or her own, as well as at least one other's. This book presents spaces, incentives, vocabularies, and techniques for students to explore many states of mind engaged in global politics. This is crucial for those interested in international conflict and cooperation, because in order to know what we think is right we must know ourselves, and to deal with others we must know at least something of what they think is right.[2] Dialogue may not settle who's right and who's wrong, but this knowledge-accumulating process is a precursor to everything else in world affairs. This sourcebook is an attempt to begin to get serious about enabling students to communicate across political and ethical frameworks that tend to collide with one another in contemporary world affairs. It seeks to foster fundamental skills necessary to understand and navigate a diverse world—ethically.

This volume's contributors employ a range of active learning techniques in their explorations of ethics in international politics. One benefit of this approach is that it prioritizes students' opinions. Active learning's emphasis on the meanings students attach to what they discover rewards those who come to know their own ideas as distinct from the preformulated answers of their professors, governments, parents, peers, and so on. Every activity in this book, therefore, challenges students to define themselves in relation to a real-world problem. In the process, they encounter opportunities to make others less foreign. They thereby experience learning as a series of dialectics, including those between past and present, themselves and others, and the learning environment and the real world. Mastery of these dialectics offers the potential to experience learning as a lifelong endeavor.[3]

Part I introduces some basic information about diverse approaches to life and ethics generally relevant to international relations. Part II presents opportunities for students to apply these values, as well as their own or others they select when grappling with some of global politics' more intractable problems. Activities thrust students into controversies surrounding blood diamonds, terrorism, Iraq 2003, corporate social responsibility, just war theory, peacekeeping, intervention, disability rights, truth commissions, nuclear weapons, environmental degradation, and the drama of it all. Applying different values as the goals to be achieved when problem-solving helps students develop an ear for the particular multiplicity of voices and issues that constitutes international politics.

This book also attempts to move students beyond the words to the deeds of world affairs. It propels them to go to the sources of and interact with the values, beliefs, and decisions that determine our global environment. We hope that these experiences prompt them to appreciate the stakes they already have in international events and to act accordingly in and outside the classroom.

Organization of the Book

Toolkit 1 explains how and why to use this sourcebook. It also seeks to locate the volume within the synergy among international politics, ethics, and pedagogy for the benefit of professors leading classrooms on related topics. It focuses in particular on how these issues intersect within what has traditionally been called the discipline of international relations, although the interdisciplinary nature of the sourcebook argues against the extrication of phenomena from their larger, multidimensional contexts. Thus it is also about making problematic what strictly positivist approaches to international relations may prefer to make simple and straightforward. Although students may certainly read it, unlike the rest of the book, students are not intended to be part of its target audience. Toolkit 1 therefore differs from the deliberately student-oriented pieces in the volume. For example, although it poses a list of debriefing questions and highlights key concepts you may choose to introduce in any subsequent active learning exercise, it provides no exercises or handouts.

The rest of the volume places active learning opportunities front and center. These opportunities take one of two forms:

1.) *Toolkits*, the second and third of which introduce students to values in different ways. In Toolkit 2: Kant, Mill, and Sound Ethical Arguments, Kristin Andrews shares how she teaches undergraduates the ethical perspectives of Immanuel Kant and John Stuart Mill. She also demonstrates how she assists students in the construction and evaluation of effective decision-making arguments. In Toolkit 3: The United States Is Not the Globe, Helena Meyer-Knapp and Lucinda Joy Peach bring forward a selection of community values found around the world to challenge the assumption of universality of Western ethics. Both toolkits contain activities for students to apply and reflect on.

2.) *Active Learning Modules 1–10* challenge classes to construct ethical solutions to real problems in global politics. In doing so, they apply the values and lessons they discovered in the toolkits or others (those they choose or those they are assigned to represent). Thus the toolkits and modules can be used independently or in conjunction with one another. The ten active learning modules cover (A.) the use of armed force in conflict, as well as (B.) other questions of social justice. They revolve around active learning techniques, which place different degrees of responsibility on students. For example, in Module 6: Blood Diamonds in Africa, Peter Lucas demands a great deal of his students by having *them* construct multimedia curricula on resource wars. Using Web links, film, and class discussion, Gabriel Palmer-Fernandez (Module 2: Just War Theory and the 2003 War Against Iraq) asks his students to grapple with the changing nature of armed conflict in view of just war theory, and then to determine whether the 2003 war in Iraq was just or unjust.

Other contributors take a more proactive role in defining the boundaries of their learning contexts by assigning roles for students to research and represent. Meredith A. Heiser-Durón's module on the 1999 NATO intervention in Kosovo (Module 4: German, Polish, and Czech Support for the 1999 NATO Intervention in Kosovo: How Does the Power of Norms Interact with the Norms of the Powerful?) and Craig Warkentin's exercise on the relationship between international terrorism and global civil society (Module 5: Flies in the Ointment: International Terrorists and Global Civil Society) utilize this tactic.

And, while some activities ask students to grapple with the legacy of classic turning points in world history, as April Morgan (Module 1: What's So Unique About the Nuclear Era?) does regarding the US decision to use atomic bombs in 1945, others such as Nancy Flowers and Janet E. Lord (Module 9: Drafting a Convention on the Human Rights of People with Disabilities: A Treaty-Negotiation Simulation) involve students in an ongoing process in which the outcome is not yet known.

Geography is another variable these teachers manipulate for pedagogical effect. Julie Mertus (Module 8: Truth Commissions) and Vivian Bertrand (Module 7: The Pursuit of a Green Global Conscience: A Debate in Distributive Justice and Global Environmental Governance) transport components of their issues into new, perhaps more familiar, geographic contexts. This technique pushes back against the tendency to distance ourselves from problems by rationalizing that they take place somewhere else.

Organization of Active Learning Components

Toolkits 2–3 and Modules 1–10 include teaching instructions and materials to photocopy and distribute to students. Specifically, each is divided into the following sections: **About This Toolkit/Module** explains the activity's purpose and how the author uses it to achieve specific educational goals in the context of a particular class. The **Miniglossary** previews two or three key concepts prominent in each module by presenting baseline definitions of each. **Step-by-Step Directions** walk educators through implementation, breaking activities into necessary preparations and in-class steps. **Student Handouts** separate student material from the surrounding pedagogical discussion. These handouts are designed to be as photocopy-ready as possible to assist in direct distribution to students, so that no additional typing is necessary. The **Debriefing** section suggests ways to help students analyze and critically evaluate what they learned in the activity. This often takes the form of discussion questions you may pose to prompt reflection. This component is designed to help students make explicit, thoughtful connections between the activity and your learning goals.[4] The **Selected Bibliography** highlights a few of the most useful supplementary sources the module's author recommends to help you and your students take this exercise one step further. This material is divided into in-print and online sources.

Teaching Tips

These activities are intended to complement an existing syllabus and teaching style, rather than to replace either. We suggest introducing one or two modules into a course, studying the effect, and tweaking them as necessary in future applications. For their authors, these modules work well "as is"; they may also be modified to suit other teaching personalities, audiences, recent events, and course goals. As you would with any recipe, adjust ingredients and procedure, given particular tastes, resources, and aims.

Ensure that students have sufficient time for debriefing. Students often feel cheated if not given adequate time to reflect upon their experiences or analyze them from several angles, on more than one level, and at different times. For example, the 15 minutes directly following a dramatic presentation is often giddy; students may need to burn off a "high" by talking about events on a somewhat superficial level, before they can connect those happenings with global politics and course themes. Thus the initial post-activity discussion frequently can be a fairly loud exchange of perceptions, as students compare and contrast what they saw, heard, knew, felt, and decided based on the stimuli presented. Within the group, this retelling of the story from a series of angles forms the basis of the class's shared oral history of the event and creates a resource they can all refer back to later as part of their collective memory, regardless of their individual roles and perspectives.

If time runs too short for a thorough, same-day debriefing discussion, a one-minute reaction paper can channel, soak up, and document initial reactions before they are lost. For the last minute (or two or five) of class, students write about whatever they are feeling about what happened during class that day. You might ask, "What's your immediate reaction to what happened here today?" They turn in this informal, personalized feedback on the way out the door. This type of unloading or venting assignment gives *everyone* a chance to have his or her say—not just those who are prone to speak in class—and encourages everyone to take a "first cut" at looking back over events. During the next class, interesting passages or points from the reactions can be used to segue into a more extensive and deeper discussion that goes beyond initial reactions. You might facilitate discussion by saying, "In looking over your reaction papers, I noticed that...how does this connect to...?"

Further settling and distancing is usually required before students can access deeper levels of critical analysis and reflective judgment. Time away from the hubbub of class that permits quiet introspection and short thought pieces or journal entries provides important reflection opportunities that assist students in constructing meaning around events and pondering what else could or should have happened. It's where the "second cut" begins. This is the chance for the learner to discover what wisdom comes to him or her from this situation.

Many of the modules in this volume call for such brief follow-up assignments. These papers are usually intended to be low-risk grades (such as simple checkmarks for completion), which do not comprise a significant or potentially threatening portion of the overall grade. Knowing they cannot be held hostage to their overall grades by your evaluation of their individual reflections can embolden students to prioritize their developing convictions around the material. Another advantage of such assignments is that they *hold everyone accountable* for thinking more deeply about the module, regardless of how prominent their roles were and how much (or little) they spoke in class.

In other words, such assignments are intended to be anything *but* busywork. Rather, they are spaces you carve out and turn over to students, who then fill them with what *they* find of value in the activity. By requiring such assignments, reading them, commenting on them, grading them, referring to them, sharing passages from them (with the student's permission, of course), you show that you value what *students* make of events and who *they* are in relation to the material. Later, these miniassignments may also serve as exam preparation notes that remind students of the lessons they taught themselves.

Teachers who use the reaction and/or reflection paper technique show that they are sincere about wanting to fulfill active learning's promise of valuing what students make of a subject or experience. Synthesizing student feedback (whether it's oral or written, reactionary or reflective) is authentic work, and indicates that teachers aren't merely adopting active learning modules because they want a day off or a light workday. Moreover, students typically enjoy reaction and reflection papers, because they're *all about them*; they get to use the first-person voice in relation to class topics—a voice that is banned from many classrooms—which gives them an immediate stake in any activity and makes writing flow more naturally than when they attempt to adopt a mythological, objective standpoint outside themselves.

Within appropriate professional boundaries, go with the flow. This is true in several ways. First, you may choose to break into an activity in order to point out *a change in circumstances* that has the potential to affect others. One colleague tells of a student who walked over to another group in the middle of an international negotiation, picked up an unprotected water pistol that represented the other country's ICBM stash, and took it back to her group, thereby taking the other state out of the nuclear club in one simple action. The professor saw that not everyone appeared to notice or grasp the significance of what had transpired (it was done casually, slyly), so she broke into the negotiations by asking, "Did everyone see what just happened here? LeKisha stole A's nuclear arsenal. What does that mean? That the balance of power shifted from Group A to Group B."[5] Awareness of the implications of this shift altered negotiating strategies and thus ultimate outcomes. It also showed how even seemingly subtle shifts in a dynamic social matrix can have substantial impacts.[6]

Second, *each active learning module targets specific, intended learning opportunities, but these are by no means finite.* Students often bring fresh insights to these activities. If active learning is to be taken seriously in its quest to value what students make of the material presented and constructed, creativity is to be respected even when it falls outside your expectations and assumptions. Otherwise successful active learning opportunities can be deflated when new, suggested ways of doing and thinking are scoffed at as untenable. Pressing students to refine ideas is not out of bounds, however, nor is an analysis of practicality or desirability.

Third, *the relaxation of passive learning's boundaries is not intended to relax other essential, professional boundaries.* Whatever pedagogical techniques we employ, we remain responsible for our classrooms. This point may appear so obvious as to be trite or unnecessarily stodgy, but in the course of an impassioned activity, cooler heads don't always prevail—especially when it comes to characterizations of others' beliefs. Sometimes it can be helpful to remind the class of the appreciation between a participant's given role and established stakes versus his or her personal beliefs and political positions. *The ideas students give voice to are not always their own; they may be trying out others' voices.* Some modules call for students to project the ideas of those who have been flatly labeled evil in the real world. Yet how well and how convincingly participants represent others' beliefs can determine their grades, regardless of how unpopular some of the ideas they express in the process may be.[7] This does not mean that those perspectives and their outcomes cannot be criticized. Quite the contrary, those who are critical of such views may realize the unfairness of holding student actors responsible for expressing ideas they do not agree with, even as they speak them.

Fourth, *test Web links prior to assigning a module.* If a site listed is inoperable, use a search engine or the library to locate a suitable substitute.

Fifth, *have fun.*

April Morgan
January 2004

Endnotes

1. Many times over the years, Dr. Martin Marty has given a speech entitled "Awash in a Sea of Pluralism" that includes this observation, as when he spoke to the students of Oberlin College on April 10, 2003. Although more scholarly definitions abound, I simply say that communication occurs when someone is heard or known, in whatever way this happens.

2. Marty, 2003.

3. This is consistent with John Dewey's model of experiential learning. See John Dewy, *Experience in Education.* (New York: MacMillan, 1938.)

4. See Toolkit 1 for more detail on debriefing.

5. I thank Mary Caprioli for sharing this incident with me.

6. For an active learning module that highlights the dynamic nature of an ongoing series of events, see Module 4: German, Polish, and Czech Support for the 1999 NATO Intervention in Kosovo: How Does the Power of Norms Interact with the Norms of the Powerful, in which developing situations and new conditions are broadcast as background to diplomatic negotiations.

7. See, for example, Module 3: The Drama of International Relations, about the incorporation of theatrical works to illustrate and articulate, in grand style, classic themes in global politics.

PART ONE

PERSPECTIVES ON ETHICS AND GLOBAL POLITICS

TOOLKIT 1

International Relations Theories and Pedagogical Approaches*

April Morgan

International relations (IR) is a highly pluralistic discipline. This is true in at least two primary ways. First, the spectrum of theoretical approaches to IR contains well over a dozen schools of thought with competing assumptions about the way the world is structured and how we as professionals ought to study it.[1] Second, global politics is cocreated through the interactions of various sectors of a sociopolitical matrix that contains at least sixteen major religious traditions, nearly two hundred states, tens of thousands of international organizations, and more than six billion individuals. The inherent structural complexity of the milieu which exists at the intersection of these two pluralistic dimensions encompasses virtually all aspects of life on Earth, and thus distinguishes it from other fields of study that examine more narrowly defined subjects. Identifying a pedagogical approach to effectively present such a wide spectrum of worldviews can be daunting. In the face of this challenge, this essay argues that a constructivist pedagogy which prioritizes active learning is particularly well-suited to teaching across the range of perspectives inherent in the practice and study of international politics. Two key reasons are:

1. its capacity to highlight how subjective, intersubjective, and contested understandings play an important role in determining outcomes in the ivory tower, as well as in the real world.
2. the compatibility between underlying theories of knowledge that inform constructivist pedagogy and the newer generation of IR theories, including subaltern realism, social constructivism, constitutive theory, and postmodernism.

Toolkit 1 therefore proposes presenting key elements of international relations through active learning techniques in order to promote enhanced understanding of behavior and analysis of a variety of actors with often competing philosophical frameworks. Toward those ends, it analyzes active learning as: 1.) the pedagogical gold standard; 2.) a particularly apt method of teaching across contending theories of IR; 3.) a useful way to address repopularized normative concerns in international affairs; 4.) an aid in development of a global theory of mind (GToM), a psychological concept related to understanding others' perspectives. It concludes with 5.) a short discussion of debriefing questions based on the theoretical material presented in this essay that teachers may use to augment the module-specific debriefing materials contained in the other sections of this volume.

The Gold Standard in Education

Active learning's modes of instruction go beyond familiar ways of *receiving information,* such as listening, transcribing, and reading, to include methods of *building meaning* through problem-solving, creating products, role-playing and, of course, conceptual analysis, evaluation, synthesis, and critique.[2] Whereas a teacher's role in passive learning is that of the sage on the stage, in active learning that role shifts to being the guide on the side. Here, the teacher selects, produces, and supports the learning process, but the students themselves do the actual work of discovering and constructing meaning. Active learning focuses on doing something with the material and/or experiencing it in the moment.

As a means of increasing knowledge, the success of active learning techniques has been interpreted quantitatively by the National Training Laboratories in Bethel, Maine in an analysis that measured and contrasted average retention rates across a variety of teaching styles. The results are presented in Figure 1.

As we move away from passive observation activities (information delivery modes on the left end of the x axis) toward increasingly active learning techniques (on the right end of the x axis), we see a corresponding increase in students' average retention rates. An especially significant jump in retention occurs when students participate in the presentation of material themselves, rather than absorb presentations produced by others. Hence, while watching a demonstration produces a 30% retention rate on average, cocreating the presentation through either group discussion or teaching others more than doubles the average retention rate.[3]

Similarly, according to Alexander Astin, "literally hundreds of studies of college undergraduates have shown clearly that the greater the student's degree of involvement, the greater the learning and personal development."[4] This fundamental finding—that there is a statistically significant correlation between the ways we learn and the retention of what we learn—

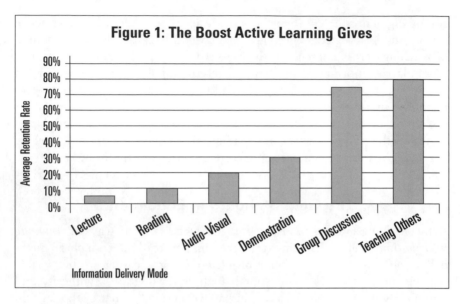

Source: Environment for Learning Study, 1997

is consistently upheld across investigations as well as over time. In fact, active learning has been referred to as "the most distinguished of all instructional practices due to the amount and consistency of research" about it.[5] Such results clearly empower students to "feel their own agency with respect to knowledge," which is the heart of active learning's connection to constructivism.[6]

The common denominator in the studies cited above is that the evidence is unequivocal: Greater learning and development occur when students are actively engaged. This can occur through a variety of means, which extend beyond the active learning techniques discussed here. This consistent finding confirms that what students get out of their education is to a significant degree a product of how much of themselves they put into the experience. Hence, schools seeking to promote academic achievement would be prudent to support the creation of learning environments that encourage high levels of student involvement, including active learning techniques.

Teaching Across Competing Theoretical Perspectives

Active learning is not only proven as a highly successful instructional technique, it is also flexible enough to teach across a range of diverse perspectives, which makes it especially useful to those who want to learn about global politics. This is because IR is characterized not only by theoretical hyperpluralism, but also by fundamentally competing assumptions—rather than merely varying points of emphasis—across philosophical frameworks.[7] This classic tension between opposing approaches to the study of international politics is captured in many tales of the first of the modern discipline's Great Debates, the battle between realism and idealism in the early twentieth century.

Textbook writers frequently articulate this essential tension by depicting idealists and realists as in strong disagreement "on almost every subject."[8] This dichotomy is often depicted in a simple chart that treats these differences as polar opposites. Such charts, for example, often contrast classical realism's assertion that humanity's negative characteristics (such as hunger for prestige, greed, and competitiveness) can only be constrained by prudence or a hierarchical international power with idealism's belief that human nature is more flexible and capable of being molded for good ends by laws, institutions, and education. Similarly, these graphics tend to counterpose classical realism's emphasis on states as the central units of analysis in international politics with idealism's tendency to expand this focus to include nonstate actors such as international organizations.

Nonetheless, despite the differences that divide classic theories of international politics such as realism and idealism, both may be taught successfully in an active learning context. In fact, these alleged opposites may be taught using the very same exercise.[9] One excellent example of this is the teaching supplement Professor Richard J. Harknett created for W.W. Norton entitled, "The Fate of Melos."[10] This exercise is set circa 415–421 BC, as Athens is rumored to be preparing to force Melos to become part of the Delian League by virtue of a threat to invade and conquer if submission is not forthcoming. This scripted, role-playing simulation of crisis decision-making debates within the Melian and Athenian communities directs students to take up either the Athenian or Melian side of the conflict as each society determines foreign policy in a tight bipolar balance of power. At the end of the scripted debate, students assess the information presented which articulated their community's values, and settle on a course of action.

There are many passages in the Athenian Assembly debate which articulate a classically realist perspective such as:

> **Hobbses:** ...[I]n the affairs of states, what matters is power. The strong do what they can and the weak do what they must. This is the law of international affairs.

> **Athenian in Assembly Crowd:** What of justice and morality?

Hobbses: The true standard on which justice rests depends on the presence of an equality of power to compel...In the relations of states, independence is preserved through Strength. If we do not compel Melos to join us, what will both enemies and subjects think? If we allow a weak island state to remain free, when all other islanders have joined us through compulsion or respect of our great naval power, will this not reveal a weakness on our part? What example will this set? Might not other subjects think it possible to escape from our empire? If we reveal weakness, then we should expect that by the law of nature our security will be placed at risk...Shall we pursue an unnatural course in which we cast aside the dictates of power in favor of some abstraction, fully aware that our subjects and enemies, given sufficient power, will follow the dictates of power?[11]

The Melian Council, on the other hand, voices the concerns of many idealists, as in this declaration:

Wilses: In the affairs of states, those who infuse the dictates of power with justice will find a truer security for themselves. The pursuit of power without the moderation produced through a universal sense of right and wrong can only lead to constant war. And in constant war, there is no true security.

When one falls into danger, there should exist some sense of fair play and just dealing. The enormous power that Athens plans to set against our small state eliminates the possibility for just debate in which the righteousness of our position might counter the failings of the Athenians' argument. They do not plan to deal with us in a just manner. But should we resort to their brutal view of the world? In doing so, do we not disgrace our ancestors who provided our freedom and encourage further aggression against others?[12]

When students read the Athenian side of the dialogue, they recognize values debated such as power, independence, and the morality of requiring the Melians to join the Delian alliance as characteristic of realism. In my experience, most students develop a gut feeling at that point, revolving around whether or not these values are the appropriate criteria upon which the ultimate policy decision should rest. They thus begin to define the point they occupy somewhere along the spectrum between idealism and realism, to recognize who they are in relation to one historical axis of the field at large, and to crises of this particular nature.

VARIATION FOR ADVANCED OR SOPHISTICATED STUDENTS: THE INCOMMENSURABILITY THESIS

When they get to this point (in this activity or in their learning in general), where some students identify and/or portray themselves as realists alongside others who project idealist values, students may embody their versions of the incommensurability thesis in international relations. Popularized first by Thomas Kuhn and Paul Feyerband and more recently incorporated into IR theory, one prominent interpretation of the incommensurability thesis holds that "contending paradigms are not only incompatible, but actually have 'no common measure.'"[13] As Mark Neufeld interprets the consequences of this thesis, because different paradigms have different terminologies, are built upon different values, and serve different political masters, positivism strives:

> by means of separation of subject and object, to derive a "neutral observation language" which will allow for a point by point comparison of rival paradigms. In this context, it is important to note the possibility of a reasoned assessment of empirical claims. Indeed, it is not going too far to assert that for positivists this assumption is at the core of reason itself.[14]

But, reflectivism[15] (reflexivism) contends that knowledge is embedded in "paradigm-specific, knowledge-defining standards," which are inherently linked to competing social and political agendas. If so, then some theorize that no such neutral observation language between differing paradigms may be possible.[16] Neufeld argues that positivists struggle against acceptance of the incommensurability thesis, because this would require them to accept Karl Popper's "Myth of Framework," which holds that "'we are prisoners caught in the framework of our theories; our expectations, our past experiences, our language,' and that as a consequence, *we cannot communicate with or judge those working in terms of a different paradigm*."[17]

This is consistent with Ole Waever's discussion of the incommensurability thesis in IR as a matter of debate *form*: "The paradigms could not have a real, normal 'debate.'[18] They could not be tested against each other since they basically did not speak the same language." Instead, several paradigms operate simultaneously.[19] Similarly, when faced with one another's differing terminologies, agendas, values, and beliefs, students have the opportunity to ask themselves if reasoned assessments across IR theories and global cultures are possible.

Expecting undergraduates to take up and consider this highly abstract question may seem unrealistic to some, but they are capable of engaging the question at an introductory level. For example, in looking back at "The Fate of Melos" simulation, students can ask, If Melos values justice above all else and Athens values its security above all else, which worldview is superior? Moreover, *how* do students seek to answer this question? Sophisticated students can then discuss whether or not they agree with IR scholars, such as Patomaki, Wight, and Waever, who believe that we have moved *beyond* incommensurability, that it is not the "inevitable, final pattern of international relations."[20] In addition, students can grapple with the post-structuralist impulse to deconstruct the question by considering what commensurability among and within paradigms would entail by evaluating Waever's position that "total communication *never* occurs."[21] Finally, they may choose to assess his argument that the preferable, contemporary mode of relating to schools of thought within IR is according to a "division of labor" where none assumes the position of grand theory and each does a different job, such that they are not in competition.[22]

Grappling with this type of problem may also boost postformal reasoning skills. While information processing, formal reasoning, and critical thinking enhance a learner's ability to solve puzzles, even these advanced cognitive skills "are not always best suited to addressing the real-world problems of adults," because the latter are typically characterized by "conflicting or incomplete information, unspecifiable parameters, and a number of possible solutions, none of which may be verifiably correct."[23] When confronted with "ill-structured" or "wicked" problems, such as pollution, crime, and poverty (all of which also exist at the international level), logic may be insufficient; tentative solutions may need to be "constructed," rather than "discovered."[24] In these situations, reflective judgment appears necessary. This requires complex reasoning and judgment skills, as well as intellectual creativity and the ability to reason along a multilevel continuum. When achieved, it manifests itself in the capacity to see more than one side of a controversial issue and to propose possible solutions. Surely it serves students and society when learners are prepared to grapple with such intractable real-world problems.[25]

Throughout this and other activities, student and role-given beliefs interact with exogenously determined values and identities; awareness of this mix becomes part of the lesson plan in the debriefing question-and-answer period. Although this is difficult to measure in quantitative terms, this awareness of and engagement of self and other can serve as the foundation for the construction of individual student meaning in this scenario. Students are usually full of ideas about what they think "The Fate of Melos" simulation means, in terms of several different Big Pictures ranging from the Cold War to the Golden Rule. This activity gives them the chance to phrase these ideas in the vocabulary of international relations.

Thus this active learning exercise enables students to experience, articulate, and act on both realist and idealist assumptions, despite their strong differences separating their underlying assumptions. Naturally, this connection between realism and idealism and active learning is not limited to this exercise; anytime students apply realist or idealist values (their own or someone else's) to a crisis simulation, active learning simulates that philosophical framework. It is a testament to the robustness of active learning that this same exercise also provides educational opportunities for a host of other key concepts in IR, such as power, justice, constructivism, postmodernism, bipolarity, balance of power, anarchy, sovereignty, feminism, rationality, zero-sum vs. variable-sum games, and more.

Of course, the field today contains many additional schools of thought alongside classical idealism and idealism. The next section explains why and how active learning is also compatible with the new generation of IR theories, given the similar assumptions between their underlying approaches to knowledge and their emphases on norms.

Active Learning and the Repopularization of Normative Concerns in IR

At its most basic, international relations is about understanding conflict and cooperation between people across community boundaries. To the layperson, conflict may imply actual violent behavior, such as hitting your brother on the head with a plate. But, in world affairs, conflict includes a state of mind in which people possess antagonistic attitudes or mutually incompatible goals, whether they act on them or not.[26] If, for example, the Palestinians and Israelis both want Jerusalem for themselves or seethe with fear and hatred for one another, even if they never act on these attitudes and goals, conflict exists.[27] Thus it is important for students of world affairs to learn about the existence of contradictory beliefs, norms, and attitudes across national communities as significant contributing factors in the social matrix of war and peace, alliances versus rivalries, and prosperity amid deprivation. The following brief theoretical overview of IR since the first Great Debate may help to explain why the field has been delayed in its embrace of such subjective considerations.

In the 1950s and 1960s, as the modern discipline came of age, prevailing scholars drew a particularly sharp distinction between positive and normative analysis, focusing on the former and, according to critics, in effect minimizing the latter.[28] Jim George identifies E. H. Carr's evolution as a realist as symbolic of this larger trend. George tracks Carr's movement from an original position that believed that morality and power were "from the onset inexorably linked"[29] to one that separated fact and value, and came to rest in a worldview that "privileged fact *over* value, is *over* ought, and object *over* subject."[30]

The most prominent example of this positivist and determinist tradition is structural realism. Structural realism requires ignoring differences and emphasizes very abstract similarities. Leading structural realist Kenneth Waltz would have us believe that a state is a state is a state, one billiard ball just like another. As long as there is no higher power common to all states, the anarchical system will be predisposed to war. Structure is thus determinative of a conflict-prone international environment. According to Waltz, a theory of international politics:

> ...as a general explanatory system, cannot account for particularities... [T]he theory does not tell us why state X made a certain move last Tuesday. To expect it to do so would be like expecting the theory of universal gravitation to explain the wayward path of a falling leaf. A theory of one level of generality cannot answer questions about matters at a different level of generality.[31]

Waltz works from a rung high atop the theoretical ladder of abstraction; in their subjectibility to formal anarchy and its consequences, all states are alike.[32] To determine how a particular state will react—or the path a specific falling leaf will take, so to speak—is not an appropriate focus for a theory of international politics in *his* eyes. However valuable it may be to know the content of a particular state's belief structure in *some* fields of inquiry, it does not belong in IR theory as *Waltz* frames the discipline.

One consequence of this conclusion was that as a theory and as a behavioral methodology, structural realism drowned normative issues in a sea of science. Dissatisfied with this result for different reasons, scholars across the range of IR theories reclaimed and rearticulated the background political philosophies that inform contemporary IR theories and imbue them with more expansive treatments of norms as part of what makes international relations "hang together."[33]

Perhaps the first to do so were realists who sought to distance themselves from and to defend realism against unsubtle, overly simplistic, and programmatic summaries that failed to appreciate the way moderation, prudence, and order inform realist analyses. As Joel Rosenthal has pointed out, "Critics have taken the realists' insistence on maintaining the separation between 'ethics' and 'politics' to mean that the realists saw no place for morality as a standard of judgment in international relations...[N]othing could be farther from the truth."[34] While some have characterized Waltz as a moral skeptic,[35] neorealist Robert Gilpin explains the relationship between the realist's focus on security and moral values this way:

> This is not to say that power and security are the sole or even the most important objectives of mankind; as a species we prize beauty, truth, and goodness. Realism does not deny the importance of these other values, although particular realists may...What the realist seeks to stress is that all these more noble goals will be lost unless one makes provision for one's security in the power struggle among social groups.[36]

This approach is consistent with the views of classical realist Hans Morgenthau, who declared that the realist is always "aware of the moral significance of political action."[37] According to Morgenthau, "Self-preservation both for the individual and for societies is...a moral duty."[38] As Raymond Aron pointed out, in an anarchic world where optimal choices may not exist, politicians sometimes make compromises without which the outcome would be "even worse, more brutal, less reasonable."[39] Thus Harbour concludes that realists of all stripes engage in "moral choices" consistent with consequentialist arguments that evaluate likely outcomes in terms of their ability to protect a state's citizenry and to maintain order even when they do not engage in "extended ethical analysis."[40]

The landscape of IR theory has continued to widen since the 1980s as scholars from many schools of thought have sought to further explore normative issues and to expand the theoretical spaces in which they are studied.[41] This exploration has generally taken one of two forms: 1.) an investigation into *how norms are formed* in global politics and what their effects are; or 2.) proactive engagement in *setting new standards* intended to influence global politics. The latter is most radical in that, where traditional realism's instrumental rationality takes preferences for granted, many of these theorists focus on producing new norms,[42] beliefs, values, conditions, and subtle changes in preference sets that have the power to vastly alter possibilities of outcomes.[43] This group includes individual scholars whose models of the world place them at or near these points along the theory spectrum: subaltern realism, cosmopolitanism, communitarianism, critical theory, constitutive theory, and postmodernism. What academics in both categories share is that in their attempts to incorporate greater discussion of contextual normative detail into IR theory, they necessarily occupy a lower level of abstraction than Waltz's structural realism. They appear to agree with R. J. Vincent that some theorists seeking to distill an essence of global politics boiled away much of its substance, which they seek to put back in.[44] In this way, all are more "bottom-up" theories.[45] Thus values, ethics, norms, subjectives, and unobservables are increasingly being deemed relevant and appropriate subjects of study again, especially as sociologists, philosophers, psychologists, theologians, ethicists, and even linguists—professionals trained to work with these often messy concepts—join political scientists in debating international politics, the role of morality in foreign policy, and the quest for global justice through international institutions.[46]

What are the results of these new trends in contemporary IR theory? At a minimum, heightened epistemological awareness prompts scholars to articulate normative implications of their theories and to acknowledge the political agendas their preferred theories serve, whereas previous scholars may not have explicitly acknowledged or discussed these dimensions of their works.[47] Then there are those who emphasize the roles of particular norms in specific spaces of socially constructed reality. At its most proactive, recent IR theory includes more explicitly prescriptive, extended ethical discourse that seeks to promote change. Four examples demonstrate this attention paid to normative issues and contextual detail in different ways along the IR theory spectrum.[48]

First, in his argument in favor of a new approach called "subaltern realism," Mohammed Ayoob combines what he identifies as the enduring elements of classical realism—statism, survival, self-help—with historical sociology's effort to take into account the effect of time and space on outcomes to debunk the claim that all states are the same.[49] He details how the situations of Third World states in time and space differentiate their experiences from those of First World states, and argues that their perspectives have traditionally been largely excluded from dominant theories of international relations. To those who teach and research international politics, Ayoob *urges setting aside theoretical parsimony,* because while this may create elegant theory,

> ...it perpetuates inequality by providing the opportunity to the more powerful to exclude and occlude the interests and experiences of those who have less power and less voice.

Acknowledging the complexity in human affairs—less "theory" and more "perspectives"—opens up avenues for accommodation and adaptation that permit the subalterns to enter the world of ideas, concepts, and yes, theory.[50]

Thus Ayoob's brand of realism advocates less "mindless 'scientism,' which attempts to find law-like generalizations on the model of the physical sciences, and [argues] for more explicit reliance on the exercise of judgment...."[51]

Ayoob's identification of this theory (which relies strongly on elements of social constructivism and Marxianism or globalism) as at least partly realist in orientation is illustrative of many post-positivists' goal not to negate structural realism, nor "lay down an injunction" against the deployment of its enduring assumptions.[52] Rather, many seek to question whether it *alone* is sufficient to capture the fullness of creative human potential in global politics. Moreover, the transplantation here of theories, methods, and values developed elsewhere is an example of the deterritorialization of the borders between IR theories and the increasingly nomadic nature of IR theorists.[53]

Second, analysts of *Verstehen* or the interpretative school of social science reject positivist assumptions, which assert that social reality is knowable without direct involvement of the investigator. Drawing on the works of Peter Winch[54] and Wilhelm Dilthey,[55] these social constructivists hold that social science ultimately revolves around understandings observers give to actions and interactions between people.[56] In order to know any part of social reality, they argue that an event needs to be understood from the subjective and intersubjective perspectives of the people involved in whatever is being studied. Isolating and recording mere events such as a uniformed man's walk down a red carpet after alighting from an airplane as rifles fire overhead are not sufficient to make sense of these actions and interactions. To appreciate the meaning of diplomatic proceedings, observers must understand the practice from the points of view of those involved: diplomats, pilots, soldiers, etc....Observers would need to know what politicians value, what a diplomat is and does, what an honor guard is, what the connection between military and politics is, what red carpets symbolize, and how all of these and many other factors constitute shared understandings that comprise the social dialogue of international diplomacy.[57] To obtain this information, *the observer must at some point interact with participants* to gain insights and arrive at the correct interpretation of actions based on correct analysis of the meaning of the act through the eyes of those being investigated as built upon *their norms*, rules, and principles.

Third, Mervyn Frost's constitutive theory of individuality is premised upon the assumption that before normative theory can answer questions such as, "What *should* we as a country do?" it must first evaluate the moral standing of relevant social institutions, such as family, states, and international organizations, in order to assess *which values should be primary*.[58] Before we can ascertain what *ought to be done* in a particular situation, Frost claims that we need to know whether freedom should be more valuable than equality, for example. Is justice more important than both of these? Where do human rights fit in? Theories which properly analyze relationships that *ought to hold* between institutions can then indicate what institutions, such as the state, might *do* vis-à-vis other actors.[59]

Frost's theory is constructivist given its emphasis on the primacy of shared beliefs; he concludes that, although there may be no agreement on a wide range of normative quandaries in international politics, there is widespread agreement that the preservation of the state system is good, that intervention in domestic affairs is normally wrong, and that peace is usually better than war. From this consensual background, however, he argues that we can *construct answers* to the more contentious normative dilemmas in international politics *where agreement does not yet exist*.[60] Thus Frost's constitutive theory differs from the *Verstehen* school of social constructivism in that at some point, not only must the observer interact with participants in order to understand participants' subjective and intersubjective understandings, in the former, he or she must also *accept* or *evaluate* those beliefs in order *to propose a solution* intended to produce a moral outcome. The successful professional is not merely one who correctly interprets facts to explain what has been, what is, and what will likely be, but one who also makes judgments and proposals based on these interpreted facts in order to further more desirable worlds.

Fourth, postmodernism encourages us to enter The Matrix—to borrow from a recent movie title—of social practices that constitute reality, and to Reload it with alternative ideas and experiences in order to interrogate the classic, dominant story we tell ourselves about the way the world works.[61] Jim George advocates *treating theory as discourse rather than as an account of external reality* to open theoretical orthodoxy's "deep silences, omissions, and points of closure," so that we may create a space for "alternative ways of thinking and acting in relation to global issues."[62] The reloading of alternatives creates a discourse that "makes 'real' that which it prescribes as meaningful."[63] "A discourse then is not a way of learning 'about' something out there in the 'real world'; it is rather a way of producing that something as real, as identifiable, knowable, and therefore meaningful."[64] *Engaging in discourse is therefore never a neutral process*; it is always imbued with the power and authority (or lack thereof) of the "namers and makers of reality—it is always knowledge *as* power."[65] By presenting alternative readings of great texts, postmodernists reveal the discipline of international relations as a process in which certain knowledge is privileged, challenges to tradition are marginalized, fragile assumptions are exposed and attempts to go beyond "that which is" are ridiculed—even as something new is already taking shape (at least through the efforts of those engaged in the discourse). Thus, whereas both social constructivism and postmodernism acknowledge that "none of us can 'float' above or detach ourselves" from the global political existence we observe, postmodernism also urges recognizing that "to one degree or another, we as modern peoples are intrinsic to the problem as well as crucial to any solution."[66]

These theories share the following characteristics, which exemplify the new generation of IR theories:

1. They take distinctions between agents seriously; this includes agents of political thought as well as practice: First World states vs. Third World states in subaltern realism; social scientists vs. participants in and creators of reality in social constructivism; problem-experiencer vs. problem-solver in Frost's constitutive theory; supporters of orthodoxy vs. advocates of disruption in postmodernism.
2. They prioritize analysis of the roles of norms in international relations theory and practice. Some theorists do this in order to identify and understand "what is" and how this came to be, while others go beyond this to propose what "ought to be" as well.
3. At some point, each of these theories favors judgments *over* facts and "the implied and embedded standards, criteria, *norms* and *principles* that *make judgments possible and give them privileged status.*"[67]

Thus these theories not only allow for, but require greater detail and less abstraction in, their models and methods. In this sense, they are more "bottom-up" theories and methodologies that emphasize interaction between observer and observed, which lend themselves well to active learning strategies encouraging students to become *a part of* the material. Frost's constitutive theory and postmodernism may most fully realize the potential of constructivist approaches to learning, because they encourage and support evaluation and action beyond understanding "what is." Both invite students to think outside the "iron cage" of given theories by creating a space to consider what an event, theory or dilemma in global politics means to them and, if dissatisfied with the status quo, to enter into constructing new ways of thinking and acting, in order to bring into being the world as *they* think it ought to be.[68] The priority these theories afford observer response connects to the research on active learning, which concludes that educational outcome depends to a large degree on how much of themselves students put into what they study. The combination of the two therefore ought to create significant and rich learning opportunities.

More broadly, active learning is compatible with the contemporary IR theorists' move to transcend strictly objectivist and positivist approaches to international relations, because it can easily be employed to help students become acutely aware of their own beliefs; experience how these beliefs can interact with others in the creation of a common reality (even when they may be trying to restrain this influence); evaluate the desirability of this shared outcome through assessment by any number of ethical yardsticks; and provide them with the opportunity to construct solutions to contentious ethical dilemmas. Role-playing simulations such as "The Fate of Melos" are perhaps the most obvious examples of how active learning can achieve these goals. There, students first experience the way the values they are instructed to take as given in the context of the assigned role influence the social construction of domestic and international political reality. A good time to tell students what we think actually happened after this hypothetical debate comes in the post-decision discussion; it tends to provoke a strong reaction. This then sets up the class to evaluate the consequences of Athenian and Melian decisions from whatever perspectives they like (inside or outside their assigned roles), thereby prioritizing pluralism, norms, and ethical treatments in the study and practice of international politics.

Thus active learning instructional techniques remain an effective way to teach across a wide range of competing perspectives. Active learning's incorporation into the IR classroom may be now especially apropos, given its compatibility with newer brands of IR theory that emphasize the role of norms in the social construction of reality. Yet, despite the fact that norms are now a growth industry[69] in professional research, even those who are ardent supporters may hamper their return to the classroom, because they lack the tools and training to teach across contending cultural approaches. The next section expands upon one way to do this and the potential benefits of doing so.

Toward a Global Theory of Mind (GToM)

One way to expose students to intercultural conflict and cooperation between actors is to assist them in developing a theory of mind (ToM).[70] Achievement of ToM introduces students to contexts from which *others* may be approaching the same situation. One interpretation of this theory holds that there can be no morality without empathy—i.e., the ability to put yourself in someone else's shoes.[71] Theory of mind is said to be achieved when one can empathize with another's perception of reality, as in this statement: If I hit my sister or take away her favorite toy, she will be hurt, sad, and possibly afraid; therefore, she may strike back at me. This thought process promotes socialization and helps people understand what motivates others and how what others value affects their beliefs and actions. According to developmental psychologists, it is something most children begin to achieve around the age of four or five as a result of their interactions with family members and playmates.[72]

Failure to develop ToM is sometimes associated with autism. Technically, autism is characterized by "a failure to develop normal social relationships, or to cope with the social environment, even in the cases where intelligence is in the normal range."[73] In layperson's terms, it has been suggested that autistic children give the impression of treating others as if they were objects, because they are unable to consider the mental states of others. British psychologists Simon Baron-Cohen, Alan Leslie, and Uta Frith tested the hypothesized relationship between autism and ToM by using what has come to be called the Sally-Ann variation of Heinz Wimmer and Josef Perner's original false belief test.[74] In this experiment, in order to accurately predict others' behavior, the subjects who were tested had to be able to appreciate that others may have been under the influence of a false belief.[75]

In the Sally-Ann false belief test, a child is shown two dolls, one named Sally and one named Ann. Sally has a basket; Ann has a box. The child observes Sally putting one marble into her basket. Sally leaves. In Sally's absence, Ann takes the marble out of the basket and puts it in the box. When Sally comes back, the child is asked, "Where will Sally look for her marble?" In their experimental study, Baron-Cohen, et al. found that 80% of the autistic children tested guessed that Sally would look for her marble in the box (where Ann had moved it, unbeknownst to Sally).[76] The children failed to adjust behavioral predictions for others' false beliefs, and thus failed to demonstrate ToM.[77]

Baron-Cohen, et al. hypothesized that those without ToM tend to treat what knowledge they themselves possess (that the marble has been transferred from the basket to the box) as equally accessible to others as a basis for predicting others' actions (even though the new location becomes available to the child when Sally is absent).[78] Most nonautistic children four and older (including those with Down's syndrome) usually pass this test—theoretically because they have developed the understanding that people act on the basis of mental models, models that may be true or false. Thus ToM is said to require a shift in thinking from *our perception of facts* to what other agents *believe to be fact*. Further, ToM indicates an ability to accurately predict others' behaviors, whether the models of the world on which they base their actions are true or false.

Applying the concept of ToM in the IR classroom sows the seeds of *international* socialization, even for those who have never traveled outside the United States and may never do so. It empowers students to empathize with actors beyond their immediate peer groups and larger cultural communities in a way that helps them predict behavior and see others as more than objects.[79] Global theory of mind (GToM) is thus a cultural skill helpful to any observer of global politics seeking to integrate actor-specific detail into his or her thinking. However, it may be a prerequisite to prescriptive ethical theory (such as constitutive or postmodern theory), if Kristin Andrews is correct in saying there can be no morality without empathy: "The first step in making an ethical decision is to learn as much as possible about the beliefs and desires of those people who are involved in the situation. It is very easy to act immorally toward those people whose beliefs and desires you do not understand...you cannot respect a person's autonomy if you do not know what her projects are."[80] Without GToM, how does the observer know if citizens of Rwanda would benefit more from a book, a sandwich, a vaccination, a gun, or a dollar apiece? In addition, giving this cultural skill a name and creating spaces in which students can develop it gives something that is already happening in many IR classrooms added value. What makes GToM different from some existing approaches that rely on personal experience in theory-building is that GToM is a skill which doesn't necessarily assume the determinative influence of any particular motivation, desire, or project for international actors in decision-making. Applying this capacity allows the researcher to investigate—starting from a virtually blank slate—another's state of mind or horizon of beliefs.

Placing students in the positions of non-US actors and asking them to make decisions on others' behalves can assist in achieving these goals. Interactive role-playing, for example, encourages students to recognize the self-specific rationality of others' positions, even when those positions are diametrically opposed to their own understandings of fact. It is also consistent with Alan Leslie's observation in 1987 that in role-playing or pretend play, "we are permitted to portray the world in contrary-to-fact ways...We are allowed such license...when we refer to the content of another's belief."[81] Play thus supports development of the capacity to appreciate others as agents with independent minds and distinct models of the world, and underlines the fact that this conception of rationality refers to a choice that most efficiently attains a given goal, rather than the perceived reasonableness of goals. Getting students over this hurdle is a crucial goal of any undergraduate class in international relations, because it reminds students that their country's way is not necessarily the only way; that other rational choices exist *given others' models of the world;* and that when countries pursue policies not in alignment with our own, this can be technically rational from someone else's perspective, even if it is not desirable given our perspective. By applying the concept of economic rationality to the process of achieving given goals, students have the opportunity to begin to empathize, understand, and find meaning in contradictory points of view.

For example, prior to "The Fate of Melos" simulation, I poll students on their preferred theoretical models of international relations. At least a few initially identify themselves as idealists and roundly condemn realism as immoral or amoral for the promotion of policies that at face value appear to them to be unsavory. Typically, when these same people subsequently find themselves participating in the Athenian Assembly's debate, in which survival in an anarchic environment is presumed to be the primary goal, they suddenly grasp that, at least for some classical realists like Hans Morgenthau, realism is neither amoral nor immoral; rather, its actions are dictated by the desire to survive within the constraints of an anarchic environment. It becomes moral for states to do what they must in order to survive. The possible subjugation of Melos is then seen as a rational means to an end predetermined to be moral, *given Athens' model of the world*. Students who experience this process do not change from idealists to realists—nor should they; rather, they take the first steps toward development of a global theory of mind in that they begin to empathize with, understand, and find meaning in contradictory points of view. They are less likely at this point to disregard those with whom they disagree as stupid, crazy, or evil, and are more likely to regard them as sane, despite their differences.

I contend that IR students who fail to achieve this minimal understanding of what motivates global actors are akin to autistic children who are perceived as treating people as objects. Implications of GToM also extend to interstate relations. State policies can be viewed internationally as excessively unilateralist, because of the perception that elite decision-makers see other actors only as means to preferred ends, rather than as sovereign entities with distinct realities, values, and policies.[82] Thus the perception that a state's policy-makers lack development of GToM provides one potential explanation of unilateral international behavior.

It should be emphasized that the goal here is not to push students toward either compromise or cooperation, nor is it to encourage anyone to change worldviews.[83] As is appropriate in an IR course, activities like "The Fate of Melos" can help enlarge students' worldviews by providing additional information about others and the wider world. They may also promote self-knowledge by prompting students to consider who they are in relation to this other.[84] In any event, what students make of new data is ultimately up to them. As we well know, whether they are in the process of developing GToM or not, some students will at times construct bigoted, racist, sexist, homophobic, genocidal worlds no matter what cards they are dealt to play with. Attainment of GToM simply creates a situation in which students' capabilities to hear where others are coming from may be amplified; it also facilitates understanding of why others are so directed and supports prediction of what actions may be taken as a result of given motivations (which serves to enhance political science's explanatory and predictive powers).

Pondering international relations this way requires a commitment to exploring methodological pluralism and epistemological opportunism. The sum of this pushing and pulling at different levels of analysis across cultures, issues, and theories brings to life in the classroom a simulation of the social matrix in which all of IR discourse and practice exist. Whatever the outcome, students who question and tinker with the "problem field"[85] of international relations tend to appreciate anew the inherent difficulties of problem-solving in this field, which satisfies another classic learning opportunity in IR.

Through the development of theory of mind and its application to a host of global issues in an active learning format, students can simulate the construction and analysis of international politics theoretically, ethically, and practically. Through active learning exercises, they represent agents of international politics where their choices determine outcomes. Their selections engage the agent-structure debate by empowering them to decide for themselves if individuals are more than structural "dopes" of the larger system.[86] Hence, theories, methods, norms, beliefs, and empathy become tools students learn to wield in decision-making simulations as they develop their own agency.

This approach emphasizes several key themes prominent in the theory and practice of world affairs: the incommensurability thesis, the role of values and value conflicts in international policy-making and international negotiation, the social construction of world affairs with particular attention paid to theory, practice, and ethics, and the problem-field that contains all of this. Students can take advantage of any or all of these learning opportunities to incorporate meaning into their study of international relations by engaging in "describing, arguing, self-discovering, world-disclosing, difference recognizing, policy proposing, state constructing, interpretation criticizing, collectivity mobilizing, historical sense making, lesson drawing, explanation seeking, and consequence inferring activities."[87] In short, by combining key elements of the current generation of IR theories with active learning, what students make of the world matters and helps them define human purpose and value relevance among other things.

Conclusions

As long ago as 1984, the National Institute for Education targeted active learning as its number one priority in higher education reform. Yet, throughout the 1980s, studies continued to report that passive learning occupied as much as 80–95% of class time, regardless of class size.[88] Where it has been adopted, active learning remains concentrated in disciplines such as biology, engineering, physiology, optometry, education, and social work.[89] Paradoxically, recent research suggests that the more abstract the topic—such as ethics and theories of world affairs—the more useful active learning techniques may be;[90] yet it is in these areas where active learning's absence is most prominent.

Despite evidence of some change, stubborn barriers evidently still retard adoption of active learning techniques (and thus also suppress learning potential). The most widely heard barrier is surely time pressure, which can take one of several forms. First, faculty frequently argue that they simply have too much content to cover as is, without the adoption of new procedures. Second, although Adrianna Kezar finds that the literature "shows a distinct movement toward a renewed emphasis on the importance of teaching" in academia, she notes that "support for faculty teaching is not being countered by a release from responsibilities for research; teaching is simply added on."[91] Third, although the teacher's in-class effort in active learning classes may be comparatively lighter than in a lecture format, the preparation time needed to create even one successful active learning module can be prohibitive. This sourcebook is designed to address these barriers by presenting a series of prepared and pretested active learning opportunities related to the exploration of certain ethical dimensions of global politics.

Although experimentation always comes with a risk, it has paid off handsomely for some. English professor Jane Tompkins has characterized her discovery of active learning as a remedy for the pedagogical distress most academics experience at some point in their careers, if not chronically. She says:

> One main aim of a de-centered classroom is to get the instructor into a position on the feedback loop where she will be drawing on the students' energy instead of expending her own fighting it. A pedagogy that pays attention to students' moment-to-moment reactions, that takes account of where they are and uses their desire and their curiosity instead of stomping on them is not irresponsible—it is *realistic*.[92]

At a minimum, students who learn about global politics through active learning come to know *experientially* why conflict is so very prevalent in international relations and just how difficult global cooperation can be to achieve. On average, previous research indicates that students taught using active learning will retain the material longer than those taught without any use of this technique. The most successful active learning may inspire students to take proactive measures in the real world to help bring into being the world as they would like to see it. This would make them true agents of international relations.

Advanced Debriefing Questions

Debriefing questions related to the material found in this toolkit are designed for students who demonstrate mastery of theoretical dimensions as they relate to specific active learning experiences, rather than for those who are still struggling with the relevance of basic theoretical premises. Therefore they are intended to be selectively added to the debriefing activities contained within each module. While some may express skepticism that undergraduates can grapple with these issues, the active learning experiences which precede debriefing serve as students' immediate frames of reference. These experiences have the potential to make what would normally be abstract material real enough to be accessible for analysis and discussion. If nothing else, dropping one or two of these questions into discussion may provide a challenge to the most advanced students in a group who want the challenge of taking their thinking one step further.

- Does this activity indicate that theories (of international politics, ethics, and religion) are innocent apolitical projects? Why or why not? Whose projects were served here? What are they? At whose expense are they promoted?
- Where does theory come from: research programs or intuition? What good is it, if any?
- Are students like you, observers like the press, and professors like me truly outside and apart from these problems or, in fulfilling our roles, are we also participants? Why is social science, and perhaps international relations in particular, slow to own the polygamous marriage between ideology, science, ethics, and pedagogy?
- Which theories and concepts seem to be the most politically well-packaged, even if they are not necessarily the best theories per se? What are the apparent results of this? Can this advantage be countered?
- Beyond the obvious crisis, what other agendas may also have been pursued, or what other games may also have been played, during this simulation (either under the table or above board)? Is it possible to isolate one dimension or issue from its interconnections to the rest of the social matrix, problem-field, or reality in which we exist? If not, why might some theorists present issues as separate from the larger contexts in which they are embedded?
- What are the implications of this activity's outcome for the production of social knowledge beyond this particular event? For example, what stories *won't* be told as a result of this decision? What will the impact of that silence be?
- What are the potential drawbacks of trying to achieve global theory of mind (GToM) in international negotiations involving more than

one other actor? Are these barriers that can be overcome or merely managed? How can either be done and at what cost?

- Are marginalized voices truly included inside IR classrooms like this one?
- Do you perceive international politics as poised at a stalemate between incommensurable perspectives or cultures? What are the implications of such a possibility?
- What are the prerequisite conditions for genuine dialogue across competing worldviews? Must conversationalists be roughly equal in status in order to avoid stereotyping? Why should (and would) the powerful debate the ideas of the less powerful? How much genuine dialogue do you see between opposing philosophical frameworks? Is perfect communication possible? How would you know if it occurred?
- How do we define what works in global politics? Who gets to validate what works? Do we need a court of ethics in global politics to make these assessments?
- How do we handle a pluralistic set of assessments about what works? How do we formulate evaluations when there is more than one winner and one loser, as well as variable gains and losses which are not easily quantified, let alone easily expressed transculturally?
- Where does this leave us? Where do we go from here? Based on what you perceived here and what it suggests to you about international politics beyond this room, how can we do better in the real world?

Selected Bibliography

In Print

Starhawk, "The Boy Who Kissed the Soldier," *The Sun* 332, August 2003: 14–20. Is this an example of one developing global theory of mind (GToM)?

Related Web Sites

www.wwnorton.com/irseries/site/welcome.htm Richard Harknett, "The Fate of Melos" (W.W. Norton, 1999). Click on "World Politics in Action" and "Fate of Melos."

Endnotes

*Toolkit 1 is adapted from A.L. Morgan, "Toward a Global Theory of Mind: The Potential Benefits of Presenting a Range of IR Theories Through Active Learning," *International Studies Perspectives*, no. 4 (2003): 351–370. © 2003 International Studies Association.

1. Stephen Walt, "International Relations: One World, Many Theories," *Foreign Policy,* no. 110 (1998): 29–46.

2. This discussion of the nature of active learning draws on a presentation by the Northern Arizona University Office for Teaching and Learning Effectiveness (1998).

3. Carl Benware and Edward Deci, "Quality of Learning with an Active Versus Passive Motivational Set," *American Educational Research Journal* no. 21 (1984): 755–765.

4. Alexander Astin, "Involvement in Learning Revisited: Lessons We Have Learned," *Journal of College Student Development* 37, no. 2 (1996): 124.

5. David W. Johnson and Roger T. Johnson, "What We Know About Cooperative Learning at the College Level," *Cooperative Learning* 13, no. 3 (1993): 17.

6. Jane Tompkins, "Jane Tompkins Responds," *College English* 53, no. 5 (1991): 604.

7. Because of the ongoing debate about whether paradigms exist in the study of international relations and my desire not to contribute to this controversy, I avoid this term except where reference to original sources requires clarification of the author's language and intention.

8. Frances Harbour, *Thinking About International Ethics: Moral Theory and Cases From American Foreign Policy* (Boulder: Westview Press, 1999), 14.

9. Of course, disagreement exists as to just how different competing schools of thought in international relations are. Despite differences, similarities certainly also exist.

10. Richard Harknett, "The Fate of Melos." W.W. Norton Teaching Supplement available online at www.wwnorton.com/irseries/site/welcome.htm. Click on "World Politics in Action," and then "Fate of Melos."

11. Harknett, "The Fate of Melos."

12. Harknett, "The Fate of Melos."

13. Mark Neufeld, *The Restructuring of International Relations Theory* (Cambridge, UK: Cambridge University Press, 1995), 43. See also Thomas S. Kuhn, *The Structure of Scientific Revolution* (Chicago: Chicago University Press, 1962).

14. Neufeld, 44.

15. Neufeld, 44.

16. However, it is worth noting that many philosophers disagree about the best way to use the concept of incommensurability. For example, some point out that Kuhn identifies common criteria in science that traverse paradigms such as accuracy, consistency, scope, simplicity, and fruitfulness, which provide, in Kuhn's words, a "shared basis for theory choice." Thomas S. Kuhn, *The Essential Tension: Selected Studies in Scientific Tradition and Change* (Chicago: University of Chicago Press, 1977), 322.

17. Neufeld, 44. Emphasis mine.

18. Ole Waever, "The Rise and Fall of the Inter-paradigm Debate," from Steve Smith, Ken Booth and Marysia Zalewski (eds.), *International Theory: Positivism and Beyond* (Cambridge, UK: Cambridge University Press, 1996): 149–185. See page 158.

19. Waever, 161.

20. Waever, 170.

21. Waever, 171.

22. Waever, 173–174.

23. Earnest T. Pascarella and Patrick T. Terenzi, *How Colleges Affect Students: Findings and Insights From Twenty Years of Teaching* (San Francisco: Jossey-Bass, Inc. Publishers, 1991), 122.

24. Pascarella and Terenzi, 122.

25. Paul Feyerabend asked: "…[I]s it not more realistic to assume that fundamental changes, entailing incommensurability, are still possible, and that they should be encouraged lest we remain forever excluded from what might be a higher stage of knowledge and of consciousness?…The attempt to break through the boundaries of a given conceptual system and to escape the reach of 'Popperian spectacles' (Lakatos) is an essential part of such research (and should be an essential part of any interesting life)." Paul Feyerabend, *Against Method: Outline of an Anachronistic Theory of Knowledge,* from Michael Radner and Stephen Winokur (eds.) *Analyses of Theories and Methods of Physics and Psychology,* Vol. IV (Minneapolis: University of Minnesota Press, 1970), 17–130, at 86–87.

26. Paul Viotti and Mark Kaupi define conflict as "disagreement; the opposition or clash of units. Conflicts may be nonviolent or at varying degrees or levels of violence…" Paul Viotti and Mark Kaupi, *International Relations Theory: Realism, Pluralism, Globalism, and Beyond,* 3rd ed. (Boston: Allyn and Bacon, 1999), 473.

27. Robert Lieber points out that "the competition of national interests, including power, ethnicity, ideology, and the characteristics of individual leaders and regimes[,] provides an impetus toward conflict…" Robert

Lieber, *No Common Power: Understanding International Relations*, 4th ed. (Upper Saddle River, NJ: Prentice Hall, 2001), 265.

28. Chris Brown, *International Relations Theory: New Normative Approaches* (London: Harvester/Wheatsheaf, 1993), 8.

29. E. H. Carr, *Twenty Years Crisis: 1919-1939* (London: Macmillan & Co., 1962), 95–96.

30. Jim George, *Discourses on Global Politics: A Critical (Re)Introduction to International Relations* (Boulder, CO: Lynne Rienner Publishers, 1994), 78.

31. Kenneth Waltz, *A Theory of International Politics* (New York: Random House, 1979), 118, 121.

32. Waltz, 122.

33. Wilfred Sellars defined philosophy as the study of "how things, in the broadest possible sense of the term, hang together, in the broadest possible sense of the term." Quoted in Richard Rorty, *Consequences of Pragmatism* (Harvester/Wheatsheaf, Hemel Hempstead, 1982), xiv.

34. For example, in *Ethics in International Affairs*, Andrew Valls declares that, "A central tenet of realism, long the main school of thought in international relations theory, is that morality does not and should not apply to international affairs. It does not because, as an empirical matter, international actors are not motivated by moral considerations, and it should not because when moral concerns do intrude into international events, the results are usually worse than if they had not done so." Andrew Valls, *Ethics in International Affairs* (Lanham, MD: Rowman & Littlefield, 2000), xiv.

35. Harbour, 36.

36. Robert Gilpin, "The Richness of the Tradition of Political Realism," from *Neorealism and Its Critics*, edited by Robert Keohane (New York: Columbia University Press, 1986), 305.

37. Hans Morgenthau, *Politics Among Nations. The Struggle for Power and Peace* (New York: McGraw-Hill, 1993), 13.

38. Hans Morgenthau, *In Defense of the National Interest* (New York: Alfred A. Knopf, 1952), 38.

39. Raymond Aron (trans. by R. Howard and A. Fox), *Peace and War: A Theory of International Relations* (Garden City, NY: Doubleday, 1966), 318–319.

40. Harbour, 34–37. Mark Amstutz differentiates between morality and ethics. He notes that morality "describes what is good, right, or proper" whereas ethics is a process of reasoning that identifies and applies relevant moral criteria, not only to likely outcomes, but also to goals, means, and

intentions in specific problem-solving contexts in order to create a moral outcome. Mark Amstutz, *International Ethics: Concepts, Theories, and Cases in Global Politics* (Lanham, MD: Rowman & Littlefield, 1999), 2–4, 13, 27.

41. Many appear to be motivated and strengthened by continuing criticism of realism, which takes this theory to task for its "narrow conception of morality," "limited palette of moral values," and judgment of "consequences rather than means or intentions per se." Harbour, 34.

42. Political philosophers in particular, including Charles Beitz, Thomas Pogge, Allen Buchanen, and David Reidy have argued that the full domain of normativity includes decisions based on etiquette, religion, and reasonableness (John Rawls' term for a moral point of view that cannot be reduced to rational self-interest), as well as rationality. According to this way of thinking, normative propositions come in many forms. Straightforward claims to the effect that "doing X is instrumentally rational if one desires Y" are normative claims. But they're not moral claims. They're claims of prudential rationality. Claims to the effect that "doing X is required by shared norms of etiquette or shared religious norms" are also normative claims. But, again, they're not moral in this strict sense. Within this realm, what distinguishes moral claims from other normative claims is that moral claims are generally thought to be universal in their application over their relevant domain; to be public in the sense of being publicly known, publicly enforced (even if only through social criticism), and publicly justified; and to override other normative considerations. The last point is perhaps the most important. A claim that is normative in the moral sense has normative force sufficient to outweigh the normative force of claims that are normative in the sense of being merely instrumentally rational or grounded in shared religious or etiquette norms. When scholars recognize prudential rationality as the only normative standard, they foreclose moral possibilities other theorists are currently exploring.

43. Walter Carlsnaes, "The Agency-Structure Problem," *International Studies Quarterly* 36 (1992): 250–251; and Yaacov Y. Vertzberger, *The World in Their Minds: Information-Processing, Cognition, and Perception in Foreign Policy Decision-Making* (Stanford: Stanford University Press, 1990), 113.

44. R. J. Vincent, *Human Rights and International Relations* (Cambridge: Cambridge University Press, 1986), 121.

45. Martin Hollis and Steve Smith, *Explaining and Understanding International Relations* (Oxford: Clarendon Press, 1990), 8.

46. Steve Smith, "The United States and the Discipline of International Relations," *International Studies Review* 46 (2002): 67–85.

47. IR scholar Don Puchala cited this as one of the clearest outcomes he sees of the new generation of normative IR theory. Don Puchala, round-table presentation on "What Is Dead and What Is Still Living in IR's Third Debate?" Feb. 28, 2003 at the national conference of the International Studies Association on "The Construction and Cumulation of Knowledge," Portland, Oregon, February 26–March 1.

48. This is not to suggest, however, that each theory occupies one discrete point along a finite spectrum of mutually exclusive theories.

49. Mohammed Ayoob, "Inequality and Theorizing in International Relations: The Case for Subaltern Realism," *International Studies Review* 4, no. 3 (2002): 27–48.

50. Ayoob, 48.

51. Ayoob, 28.

52. Richard Ashley, "The Achievements of Post-Structuralism," from *International Theory: Positivism and Beyond*, eds. Steve Smith, Ken Booth and Marysia Zalewski (Cambridge: Cambridge University Press, 1996), 244.

53. Ashley, 244.

54. Peter Winch, *The Idea of a Social Science* (London: Routledge and Kegan Paul, 1958); and Peter Winch, *Ethics and Action* (London: Routledge and Kegan Paul, 1979).

55. Wilhelm Dilthey, *Selected Writings*, H. P. Rickman, ed. (Cambridge: Cambridge University Press, 1979).

56. John Ruggie and Friedrich Kratochwil, "International Organization: The State of the Art on the Art of the State," *International Organization* 40 (1986): 753-776; Alexander Wendt, "Anarchy is What States Make of It: The Social Construction of Power Politics," *International Organization* 46 (1992): 391–426; Robert Keohane, "International Institutions: Two Perspectives," *International Studies Quarterly* 32 (1988): 379–396; Anthony Clark Arend, "Do Legal Rules Matter?" *Virginia Journal of International Law* 38, no. 2 (1988): 107–153; Friederich Kratochwil, *Norms, Rules, and Decisions* (New York: Cambridge University Press, 1989); Martha Finnemore and Kathryn Sikkink, "International Norm Dynamics and Political Change," *International Organization* 52, no. 4 (1998): 887–917; Ted Hopf, "The Promise of Constructivism in International Relations Theory," *International Security* 23, no. 1 (1998): 171–200.

57. Mervyn Frost, *Ethics in International Relations: A Constitutive Theory* (Cambridge: Cambridge University Press, 1996).

58. Frost, 4.

59. Frost, 4.

60. Frost, 9.

61. The movie referred to is *The Matrix: Reloaded*. George uses postmodernism to point to the works of Foucault, Derrida, Barthes, Baudrilliard, and Lyotard—works which, when fully engaged with theory as practice, represent "the most acute critical perspective in the critical social theory spectrum." George, 39, footnote 79.

62. George, 10.

63. George, 30.

64. Bradley Klein, *Strategic Discourse and Its Alternatives* (Center on Violence and Human Survival Occasional Paper No. 3, New York: John Jay College of Criminal Justice, 1987), 4.

65. George, 30.

66. George, 231.

67. R. D'Amico, "Going Relativist," *Telos* 67 (1986): 135–145. Italics mine.

68. Max Weber, *The Protestant Ethic and the Spirit of Capitalism* (Boston: Unwin Hyman, 1989).

69. Chris Brown, *International Relations Theory: New Normative Approaches* (London: Harvester/Wheatsheaf, 1993).

70. Martin Davies and Tony Stone, eds., *Folk Psychology: The Theory of Mind Debate* (Oxford: Blackwell Publishers, 1995).

71. Martin Davies and Tony Stone have edited a volume in which this complex interdisciplinary debate is presented in thoughtful detail. The debate springs from a paper written by David Premack and Guy Woodruff in 1978 that asked, "Does the chimpanzee have a theory of mind?" One side of the debate does not assume that empathy is required for theory of mind. "The idea here is that having a theory of mind is having a body of information about cognition and motivation that is applicable to others, just as much as to oneself. Given such a body of generalizations, one can use premises about what another individual knows or believes, in order to reach conclusions about that individual's actions, for example...On the other side of the debate are those who say that basic theory of mind abilities are better thought of as grounded in a capacity to empathize (or simulate, or identify in imagination) with another." Used in this second way—as I do—theory of mind allows the user to predict what an actor will do by engaging in empathy. Davies and Stone, 1.

In her discussion of empathy in higher education, Kathryn Miller says that we need to get "past the idea that empathetic communication is touchy-feely business that demonstrates weakness. In fact, empathic communication is disarmingly powerful." Kathryn Miller, "Empathy in Higher Education: Not Just for Counsellors Anymore," (Washington, DC: American Association of Higher Education Bulletin, 2002), online at www.aahebulletin.com.

72. Davies and Stone.

73. Davies and Stone, 39.

74. Simon Baron-Cohen, Alan Leslie and Uta Frith, "Does the Autistic Child Have a Theory of Mind?" *Cognition* 21 (1985): 37–46.

75. See also Simon Baron-Cohen, "Autism and Symbolic Play," *British Journal of Developmental Psychiatry* no. 5 (1987): 139–148; Simon Baron-Cohen, "Autism: A Specific Cognitive Disorder of 'Mind-Blindness'," *International Review of Psychiatry* no. 2 (1990): 79–88; Uta Frith, *Autism: Explaining the Enigma* (Oxford: Basil Blackwell, 1989); Uta Frith, "Autism," *Scientific American* 268, no. 6 (1993): 78–84; Alan Leslie, "Pretense and Representation: The Origins of 'Theory of Mind'," *Psychological Review* 94 (1987): 412–426.

76. Baron-Cohen, Leslie and Frith, 42.

77. This is in contrast to 86% of the children with Down's syndrome and 85% of the clinically normal children tested who chose the basket (Baron-Cohen, et al., 1985). Moreover, according to Gordon and Barker, "even those [autistic children] who had attained the mental age of 9 typically performed at the 3-year-old level on false-belief tasks. Despite being 'smarter' than the other subjects [who were 4 or 5 years old], the autistic children appeared to suffer from a specific deficit in at least this aspect of psychological competence." R. Gordon and J. Barker, "Autism and Theory of Mind Debate." *On Demand Newsletter* (Cave Creek, AZ: Cross Roads Institute, 2002).

78. Baron-Cohen, Leslie and Frith, 42–43.

79. Kristin Andrews of York University (2001) applies the empathy interpretation of ToM to the World Trade Organization (WTO) to measure its moral agency in an essay entitled, "Institutional Moral Development: Will the WTO Ever Grow Up?"

80. Kristin Andrews, Toolkit 2, page 56.

81. R. Gordon, "Developing Commonsense Psychology: Experimental Data and Philosophical Data" (Paper presented at American Psychological Association's Eastern Division Symposium on Children's Theory of Mind, Dec. 27, 1995).

82. However, as Gordon (2002) points out, the theory does not require that those without ToM perceive themselves as superior to others, even if others perceive them as excessively self-centered.

83. Donald Kennedy discusses the role of educators in teaching values vs. teaching about values. He holds that one purpose of teaching is to support students in gaining access to competing ideas about values, analyzing them, and comparing them. "[T]hat is the way to form one's own values securely." Kennedy goes on to note that letting students work this out for themselves "requires almost exquisite restraint on the part of the teacher/scholar—a careful curb on the natural desire to display one's own convictions." Donald Kennedy, *Academic Duty* (Cambridge, MA: Harvard University Press, 1997), 66–67.

84. Kennedy refers to evidence that students about to enter college or university list among their top objectives development of a philosophy of life. Knowledge of self would seem to be central to achievement of this goal. Kennedy, 60.

85. Heikki Patomaki and Colin Wight, "After Postpositivism? The Promises of Critical Realism," *International Studies Quarterly* 44, no. 2 (2000): 213–237.

86. Walter Carlsnaes, "The Agency-Structure Problem," *International Studies Quarterly* 36 (1992): 249.

87. Hayward Alker, "The Humanistic Movement in International Studies: Reflections on Machiavelli and las Cases," *International Studies Quarterly* 36, no. 4 (1992): 347–371.

88. Thomas McGovern, *Handbook for Enhancing Undergraduate Education in Psychology* (Washington, DC: American Psychological Association, 1993): 183–214.

89. G. Levin et al., "Preclinical Exposure in a Baccalaureate Program in Pharmacy," *American Journal of Pharmaceutical Education* 60, no. 2 (1996): 183–214.

90. Sara Swenson and J. Rothstein, "Navigating the Wards: Teaching Medical Students to Use Their Moral Compasses," *Academic Medicine* 71, no. 6 (1996): 591–594.

91. Adrianna Kezar, "Higher Education Trends (1997–1999): Instruction" (Washington, DC: *ERIC: Clearinghouse on Higher Education,* ERIC Document Reproduction Service No. ED435348).

92. Jane Tompkins, "Jane Tompkins Responds," *College English* 53, no. 5 (1991): 604. Emphasis mine.

Kant, Mill, and Sound Ethical Arguments

Kristin Andrews

About This Toolkit

When making decisions, ethical considerations often come into play. However, people often find it difficult to explain and justify their ethical commitments. The intent behind this toolkit is to help students clarify their moral beliefs by teaching them to think clearly, and to show them how to identify both their motivations and their theoretical commitments. The toolkit consists of a reading, with activities designed to introduce concepts that will help students develop their moral reasoning abilities, and an active learning exercise, which will allow them to apply their newly learned skills. It is based on theories of ethics developed in Western philosophy.[1]

When introducing ethics to an undergraduate audience, I first emphasize the importance of logical thinking. Although the ability to clearly articulate one's justification for a position is important in many areas, for ethics it is particularly useful to realize the difference between a taste—something that doesn't need justification—and a grounded moral position. Although we don't ask our friends and neighbors why they prefer coffee ice cream to strawberry, we might ask them why they are opposed to the death penalty, for example. The philosophical study of ethics is based on logical argument, and so the first third of the toolkit introduces the student to key logical concepts. I have found that after using these concepts, students report an increased ability to discuss and debate issues, and their initial disinterest in logical reasoning transforms into excitement about their new abilities. (Students appear especially pleased at how these concepts allow them to better discuss and defend ideas when talking with their parents.)

The second third of this toolkit introduces students to different ethical theories in Western philosophy. Theory is described in the reading as the definition of the word "good." Students are encouraged to think of their own definitions of the term, and they are introduced to different ways the word has been defined. The central ideas of two influential philosophers,

Immanuel Kant and John Stewart Mill, are also summarized. As is relevant for a lesson on ethics and international relations, the issue of cultural differences is emphasized in this section.

Once the tools have been introduced to the students, they are given the opportunity to use them in an active learning exercise on Navy sonar testing, which has been criticized for harming marine mammals. The background is presented and discussion questions are introduced. I also include an analysis of the example that students can read and discuss.

After engaging in these activities, students should be able to articulate the relevance of argument for ethical reasoning and define terms such as *valid* and *sound*. They should also have considered to what extent they are Kantians or Utilitarians (or neither), and what they think the term *good* means.

Miniglossary

Consequentialism A kind of moral system that judges the goodness of an action based on the consequences of the action.

Deontology A kind of moral system that judges the goodness of an action by how well the act corresponds to a set of universal laws.

Utilitarianism A consequentialist moral theory according to which the total amount of happiness is what is relevant in assessing the consequences of an action.

Kantianism A deontological moral system according to which the universal law derives from the rationality of human beings.

Step-by-Step Directions

Make enough copies of Student Handout 1, "Kant, Mill, and What Makes a Sound Argument" for everyone in the class. Give students this reading with the instruction that it is to be done out of the classroom. The text includes activities that students can begin thinking about alone, but that are also brought up in the classroom. These activities and brainstorming questions are distinguished from the text and appear in a box. Answers to some questions are in the Appendix.

I spend at least one hour of class time on logical reasoning. For students to fully grasp the structure of valid arguments, they need to construct some of their own. After a 15-minute lecture on the main points of Toolkit 1, I ask students to construct a valid argument on a subject relevant to the focus of the course. At this point, the content of the argument isn't important; rather, you are looking for arguments with good logical form. In addition to the group discussion on validity, students can work in pairs, in which each student is required to write a valid argument on a specified topic. Then, within the pair, the students exchange arguments and offer constructive criticism. These topics can be the ones listed in the final box of the section (i.e., prayer in school, death penalty, euthanasia, freedom of religion, animal testing, infanticide, abortion, public healthcare). Finally, I have two students act out the dialogue on abortion and, as a large group, the class works though the discussion questions.

A full introduction to this toolkit would take at least two hours of class time, but some instructors will choose to skip discussion of the theories I present as weak and focus only on Utilitarian and Kantian ethical theories. Each of the four views discussed will take at least one-half hour of class time, with 10 minutes for presentation of material and 20 minutes to work through the activities. Another one-half hour should be spent on discussing the compatibility of cultural differences with objective ethical theories.

The exercise on sonar testing included in Student Handouts 2 and 3 is an in-class activity. I divide the students into groups of about five people and give each group one copy of the handouts. One member of the group is chosen to take notes. Then the background material is read aloud. I have found that it works well to have each group member read one paragraph. This helps break the ice in the group and seems to encourage students to more fully participate in small group activities. The students are then asked to consider a series of questions about the potential problems, and the secretary records the conclusions the group reaches on each question. If there is disagreement, all conclusions are recorded. The students work through the opinion piece and questions in the same manner. If time remains, they can return to the first set of questions after considering the opinion piece. During this period, I circulate among the small groups and engage with them as if I were a member of the group.

After about 45 minutes, the groups join together to share their conclusions with the rest of the class.

Student Handout 1:
Kant, Mill, and What Makes a Sound Argument

You wonder if you should call the number on the screen and help the young African boy get an education. You read about the debate between Europe and the United States over military intervention, and wonder who is right. What you're doing in both these cases is asking an ethical question. We ask ethical questions in order to help us understand how we should live. For example, we might ask ourselves, *Should I give to charity?* or *Who should I vote for?*

The study of ethics can be seen as primarily an attempt to answer two questions: What *should* I do? and What *can* I do? The first question deals with our moral obligations, those behaviors we must engage in if we are to act ethically. The second question focuses on moral prohibitions. Just as there are some things we must do, there are also some things we must not do. Ethics is there to help us generate answers to both of these questions.

In the Western philosophical tradition, ethics has always been seen as a practical pursuit, since the goal of ethical exploration is not simply knowledge, but action. For example, one may ask, Now that I've gotten a raise, am I obligated to send extra money to Oxfam, or can I indulge in that new plasma TV? If I gave money to charity last month, can I treat myself this month? We ask these questions because we want to be good people, and we want to do the right thing.

While we were kids, it was pretty easy to do the right thing (if we wanted to). The right thing to do was what our family told us to do. It was right to share toys and obey the teacher. It was wrong to tell a lie and to be mean to others. But then things got more complex. Maybe you can remember the first time you questioned a rule that you had until then blindly accepted. Did you catch a teacher telling a lie? Did you overhear your mother being mean to someone? Once we begin questioning some of the rules we were given as children, we have to start asking what it means to do the right thing. One of the aims of ethics is to provide tools that help us determine what to do in particular situations.

There are two sets of tools that you should take home from this toolkit:

1. Tools that help you defend your ethical beliefs (and correspondingly, help you to critique beliefs that you do not share)
2. Tools that help you identify what it means to be good

The first set of tools will help you construct arguments, and the second will introduce you to a few ways philosophers have defined the word "good." Once you have these tools in your personal toolkit, you can use them when deciding the right thing to do in a particular situation. These tools can help us see that there are shared assumptions across cultures, and that humans don't live in radically different and incommensurable civilizations. These tools can also help us decide what to do in the kinds of cases we read about daily in the newspaper.

At the conclusion of this toolkit there are a few questions that you should be able to answer. Keep these questions in mind as you work through the toolkit:

- What is your definition of the good?
- Are you a Kantian? A Utilitarian? Some combination of both? Or neither?
- What is a valid argument? A sound argument? What is the importance of argument for ethics?

Tool Set 1

Goal: To recognize and construct sound ethical arguments.

1a. Arguments

Before we even start attempting to construct answers to our ethical questions, it will be very helpful to have some skill in constructing *arguments*. When philosophers say that the study of ethics is based in argument, they mean that a philosophical approach to ethics will involve asking and attempting to answer *Why?* questions. One must give reasons for believing an act is morally permissible or morally obligatory, and those reasons, at the least, must be *consistent* with others (see below).

A philosophical argument is not a fight or disagreement. Rather, in philosophy, an argument is a set of reasons for the position being defended. For example, if I believe that I should give money to world hunger relief every month (so long as I have the money I need to meet my basic needs), I might give the following argument:

Premises (reasons): Everyone has the right to food and clean water. There are some people who do not have enough food and clean water. I have the means to help at least a few people get that nourishment. Whenever someone has a right, others who can help have a corresponding obligation.

Conclusion: Therefore, I have a moral obligation to donate money to charity whenever I can in order to help feed the hungry.

If you disagree with the conclusion to this argument you have two choices:

1. You can criticize the logical structure of the argument in order to show that the reasons, if true, would not *entail* (or necessitate) the conclusion; or

2. You can argue that one of the reasons given in support of the conclusion is false. (Of course, a particularly bad argument can suffer from bad logical structure and have false premises!)

In order to test the first choice, you can ask yourself if the conclusion would be true if all the reasons given were true. That way you won't get distracted by the second choice when trying to analyze the logical structure. In the above argument, the logical structure is good, so we say that it is a *valid* argument.

A valid argument isn't good enough, however. We also want our arguments to be *sound*. A sound argument is a valid argument with all true premises. Sound arguments guarantee the truth of the conclusion. A valid argument with even one false premise won't guarantee the truth of the conclusion. For example, consider the argument:

All cats bark. Huxley is a cat. Therefore, Huxley barks.

This argument, though valid, is not sound. If it were true that all cats bark *and* Huxley *is* a cat, then the conclusion must be true (this is what it means for the argument to be valid). However, it isn't true that all cats bark, making the argument unsound, so we cannot determine whether the conclusion is true or false. It could be true (maybe Huxley is a barking fish). But it also could be false (if Huxley really is a cat, for example).

So you also need to consider the second choice and look at each premise to determine whether or not it is true. If you find even one false premise, the argument won't do. Let's look at our original argument premise by premise:

A. Everyone has the right to food and clean water.
B. There are some people who do not have enough food and clean water.
C. I can help at least a few people get that nourishment.
D. Whenever someone has a right, others who can help have a corresponding obligation.
E. Therefore, I have a moral obligation to donate money to charity whenever I can in order to help feed the hungry.

This argument has four premises (A–D). Sentence E is the conclusion to the argument. Look at each of the four premises. Do you believe that they are all true? Either way, you need to provide an argument for your belief. Suppose you think that D is false. Then you can defend your belief by constructing an argument that concludes Not-D, or "It is false that whenever someone has a right, others who can help have a corresponding obligation." There are many arguments that have been developed which can help you enhance your logical thinking skills.[2]

1b. Consistency and Contradiction

Another important point about arguments is that your beliefs, if they are all to be true, must be *consistent* with one another. A set of statements is consistent if it is possible that they are all true. They might not be all true, but consistency only requires that there could be a fantasy world in which all the statements are true. For example, the following statements, though false, are consistent: Mars is made of Velveeta *and* Scientists are concerned that Mars may be completely consumed by the mice who live there. You can think of a story that would make both statements true. In fact, all good fiction has the property of being consistent. Imagine reading a novel in which a dead character reappears without any explanation, the personality of the protagonist varies radically from page to page, and the antagonist who is described on one page as being a short bald man is portrayed brushing his golden locks in the next chapter. Such a novel probably wouldn't be very compelling and you might end up throwing it down in frustration.

Just as novelists usually aim to have a consistent story, people usually want consistent beliefs. This is because if you have inconsistent beliefs, you are guaranteed to have at least one false belief. For example {2 + 2 = 4 and 2 + 2 = 5} is an inconsistent set, and the two claims taken together are a *contradiction*. At least one of the two claims must be false. The following is also an inconsistent set, and hence a contradiction: {Simone is a cat *and* Simone is a dolphin}. This is because an individual cannot be two different species. It is also a contradiction to say: It is currently raining outside my window *and* It is not currently raining outside my window. Any two sentences of the form *P and not-P*, where *P* stands for the identical statement, will be a contradiction.

Often people make claims that look like contradictions, even though they aren't. Suppose that when I ask Aziz whether he likes the hamburger he responds, "It's good and it's not good." Even though this might at first appear to be a contradiction in the form *P and not-P*, it isn't. Why? Because Aziz is using the term "good" in two different senses, so we cannot correctly describe the sentence as *P and not-P*. If we did, we would misrepresent Aziz's point. In one sense, he thinks the hamburger is good in that it is delicious. But in another sense it isn't good, because the hamburger interferes with Aziz's low-fat diet. Given this understanding of Aziz's description of the hamburger, it becomes clear that he isn't making a contradictory or paradoxical claim.

Someone might look at the sentences {*It is currently raining outside my window* and *It is not currently raining outside my window*} and claim they can both be true. But notice that, to make sense of both sentences as being true at the same time, the words need to refer to different things. For example, it might be raining to the left of my window, but still sunny to the right.

In that case, "outside my window" would refer to a different location in each sentence. Or perhaps the word "rain" is used to refer to different kinds of precipitation. Given these interpretations of the sentences, they are consistent. But if "currently" and "rain" and "outside my window" refer to exactly the same thing in each case, it is physically and logically impossible that both sentences are true; only one could be true.

If you want to have true beliefs, then it is in your interest to avoid believing in an actual contradiction. And we usually want to have true beliefs. If I'm going to get my hair cut, I want my belief that the salon stays open until 8:00 p.m. to be true. Otherwise I would have taken the bus ride for nothing. And when I'm trying to figure out what I ought to do, it becomes even more important to have true beliefs, because I don't want to do something bad. I realize that I might not be able to determine what I ought to do, but I know that I can try my best to come up with true rather than false beliefs.

One test of whether my beliefs are all true is to ask whether they are consistent. If my beliefs are inconsistent, I am guaranteed that at least one of them is false. And since I don't have to have false beliefs, I should try to make my beliefs consistent with one another by changing or modifying one of my beliefs, as Kathy does in Kathy and Jenny's Dialogue.

KATHY AND JENNY'S DIALOGUE

Kathy: I think abortion is wrong.

Jenny: Why?

Kathy: Because a fetus is a human.

Jenny: OK, I agree with that. A fetus has human DNA, and so it is human. But I still don't see why that makes abortion wrong.

Kathy: Well, it's wrong to kill people, of course. Everyone knows that you shouldn't kill.

Jenny: Is it always wrong to kill?

Kathy: Yes, that's what I think.

Jenny: So you think that it's wrong to eat meat, too?

Kathy: I don't follow. Why are you talking about meat now?

Jenny: Well, you have to kill in order to eat meat. You said that it's always wrong to kill. If it's always wrong to kill, then it's wrong to kill a cow or a dog or a chicken for food.

Kathy: Oh, I don't mean that it's always wrong to kill period. Just that it's always wrong to kill humans. Remember, I said that a fetus is a human.

Jenny: OK then. I'm not sure why you think it's OK to kill animals, but not humans—I'm not sure what the difference is between, say, a chimpanzee and a 2-month-old baby, but let's not deal with that right now. I still want to know whether you really think that it's always wrong to kill humans. Let's think about all the cases where humans are killed. Sure, I agree that it's bad to kill a human in order to rob him, but what about other kinds of killings?

Kathy: Well, I guess there are also killings in self-defense. You know, if someone is attacking me and I can only defend myself by killing him, I think that's OK. I mean, it would be moral.

Jenny: So you don't really think that it's always wrong to kill humans.

Kathy: I'm not saying it's ideal to kill someone who attacks me, but it's OK—it is morally permissible to kill the person who is attacking me, as long as there is no other way to protect myself.

Jenny: So would you say that it is always wrong to kill a human, except in cases where one's own life is at risk?

Kathy: Yes, I'd have to say that.

Jenny: Then you must agree that abortion is sometimes permissible.

Kathy: No, I don't think so. I believe that abortion is always wrong.

Jenny: Even when the woman's life is at risk?

Kathy: Yes, that's my belief.

Jenny: Well then, you have two conflicting beliefs. You just said that it is morally permissible to kill in order to save your own life. So in a case where the woman's life is at risk, it would be OK for her to kill the fetus in order to save her own life. Either you must reject the claim that you made earlier, about killing in self-defense being OK, or you will have to accept that abortion to save the woman's life is OK.

Kathy: No, I think the two cases are different. If someone is trying to rob me and threatens to kill me, he is guilty. But the fetus is not guilty. So I can kill a robber in self-defense, because he's done something wrong to begin with. But the fetus has never done anything wrong. So I can't kill the fetus.

Jenny: OK, then you've changed your moral principle again. Now it is: It is always wrong to kill a human, except in a case where one's own life is at risk by a guilty person. But I wonder if you really believe that.

Kathy: Sure I do.

Jenny: OK, here's a story. Jake is abducted by crazed scientists who are experimenting with mind control. They study Jake's brain and learn how to control his actions like a kid controls a remote control car. He knows what he's doing, but can't control his body. He tried to keep from doing what the mad scientists tell him to do, but he cannot. The scientists are trying to see how far they can make Jake go, so they instruct him to kill you. He attacks you, and you defend yourself. Now, knowing that Jake isn't responsible for his actions and that Jake isn't guilty, can you kill him in order to save your own life? It's either him or you, no other options are available.

Kathy: That's never going to happen. This is just a science fiction story.

Jenny: Maybe so, but still, imagine that you were in a situation like this. If you don't kill him, he will kill you.

Kathy: Well, that's harder. I mean, if it's me or him...I wouldn't want to die. But Jake didn't do anything to deserve to die. He has no control over his actions. It's those evil scientists who're to blame.

Jenny: You can't get to the scientists, at least not right now. And if you get killed, you'll never be able to bring the scientists to justice.

Kathy: I guess I'd probably defend myself, and that's probably the right thing to do. I wouldn't be very happy about it, though. And I'd feel guilty. But either I'd feel guilty, or I'd be dead. And I guess I have a right to protect my life in that case.

Jenny: So?

Kathy: I know where you're going with this. Yes, then, I guess it would be morally permissible for a woman to have an abortion, if her life were at risk. But she shouldn't be happy about it.

Jenny: OK, now I want to go back to your claim that it's only OK to kill in cases of self-defense. Aren't there any other cases in which it's OK to kill humans? In our society, we kill people who kill other people—it's called the death penalty.

Kathy: Yeah, yeah, I know about the death penalty. But I don't think that it is moral to kill killers anyway.

Jenny: Do you think it's inconsistent for someone to believe in the death penalty and also share your argument against abortion?

Kathy: Well, I'm not sure. OK, yes, it is inconsistent. But someone who wanted to support the death penalty and be opposed to abortion—except, of course, in the case of the mother's life—might say that it's always wrong to kill *innocent* people, except in self-defense. That leaves open the possibility that in some other cases it might be OK to kill guilty people. But I can't support that claim, because I think it's barbaric for the state to kill humans like that.

Jenny: OK, well, I'm not going to argue with you there. But besides the death penalty, we also kill people in war. And not just guilty people. We kill children and women and all kinds of noncombatants. There's always collateral damage, as the government puts it—to make it more palatable, I think. And we accidentally kill our own soldiers. And we've accidentally bombed hospitals and food storages, and once in Yugoslavia we bombed the Chinese embassy. So, given your argument against abortion, is war always wrong?

Kathy: No, sometimes we need to go to war in order to stop a greater harm. I know that bad things happen in war and it's terrible, but what would happen if we didn't go to war?

Jenny: So you've given me a reason why some wars are permissible, but this argument seems to be in conflict with your argument against abortion. See, someone could make the parallel argument: "Sometimes a woman needs to get an abortion in order to avoid a greater harm. I know that there is some harm involved in abortion and it's terrible, but in some cases greater harm to the child and the woman would happen, if she didn't have an abortion."

Kathy: But I think that the woman is responsible for getting pregnant, no matter what, and she needs to take responsibility for her actions.

Jenny: If a woman gets pregnant through rape, it's not her fault, right? But never mind that for right now. Your argument against war is based on appeal to consequences. But your argument against abortion says that consequences are irrelevant. And your major premise in the argument against abortion can be used to argue against war, too. So either you need to accept that war is wrong, except when absolutely necessary to save your own life, or you need to modify your premise.

Kathy: I'm getting pretty confused.

Jenny: And after we figure out which you choose, we can then consider whether mercy killing or euthanasia is immoral. You know it's legal in Oregon right now. But it's inconsistent with your premise, for it is the killing of an innocent person that isn't in self-defense.

Kathy: I'm not sure what I think anymore, and my head's starting to spin. Can we finish this later?

- What is Kathy's argument at the beginning of the dialogue?
- Which premise is at issue in this dialogue?
- What are the variations of this premise that are made throughout the dialogue?
- How could Kathy make her argument consistent with the morality of some wars and euthanasia?

ARTICULATING YOUR OWN ARGUMENTS

You probably have beliefs about many of the following topics:

- prayer in school
- death penalty
- euthanasia
- freedom of religion
- animal testing
- infanticide
- abortion
- public healthcare

Take a minute to jot down your positions on these issues. Then think about the argument you could develop to support each of your positions. Finally, ask yourself if the reasons supporting your beliefs are consistent with one another.

Tool Set 2

Goal: To consider different definitions of the term "good."

2. Ethical Theories

The birth of the Western philosophical tradition is usually identified with the ancient Greeks, who started recording their musings more than 2,000 years ago. These philosophers asked about the nature of the world, space and time, the origins of humans and animals, and the meaning of life. Most relevant to us here are their questions about the nature of the good. While many of these philosophical questions have spawned other disciplines (biology, physics, and mathematics, for example), ethics remains within the domain of philosophy. This is because philosophers have not been able to reach an agreement about the nature of the good, whereas the breakaway disciplines have accepted a shared methodology and set of background assumptions. The agreement allows scientists to develop experiments, which help them discover how things work. Unlike scientists, ethicists have no experiments and few shared assumptions. Ethicists don't even agree on what is meant by the word "good."

In this section we will examine four different ways philosophers have tried to characterize the good. Each of these definitions is the basis for an ethical theory, and we can examine the strengths and weaknesses of each.

WHAT'S GOOD TO ME?

Before seeing how others have answered the question, ask yourself: How would I define "good?" What is the good to me?

Two Weak Accounts

2a. Good = God approves

According to this view, when we say it would be good to forgive debt in the developing world, we mean God would approve of our forgiving debt in the developing world. The Divine Command Theory states that right acts are those commanded by God and wrong ones are forbidden by God. Thus ethics depends on the will (and the existence) of God.

In his dialogue *Euthyphro*, the ancient Greek philosopher Plato (c. 428–347 BC) criticized this view when he introduced the following puzzle:

A. Are actions right because God commands them?

or

B. Does God command actions because they are right?

STOP TO CONSIDER

Do you find one of these options to be more acceptable than the other. Why? Take a minute to weigh the pros and cons of each.

Now let's look at both options:

A. Suppose actions are right because God commands them. Then:

- God could have commanded anything
- There could be no prior reasons for God to prefer love over hate
- Ethics is arbitrary

On the other hand,

B. Suppose God commands actions because they are right. Then:

- God's commandment is merely consistent with the goodness in the world
- The fact that God commands these things doesn't explain why they are good
- There exists a standard of right and wrong independent from God's will.

Plato's puzzle gives us reason to reject this definition of good. On the one hand, good is arbitrary; on the other, good has meaning, but that meaning is not dependent on God. Given either interpretation of the claim, we need to look for a different definition of the term.

2b. Good = My culture approves

There is a tension between two aspects of ethics. One common assumption about an ethical truth is that it is objective. That is, if it is wrong to throw an infant off a rooftop for fun, then this is true for everyone, regardless of whether they believe it is wrong or not. On the other hand, people feel they need to be sensitive to the beliefs and moral commitments of unfamiliar cultures. This tension leads some people to conclude that they should not criticize another culture for their moral beliefs, and that by virtue of having those beliefs, a culture is *justified* in having those beliefs. This extreme view doesn't seem to allow for one culture to ever intervene in the actions of another, and it is this view that we will refer to as *Cultural Relativism.*

According to this definition of "good," ethics is not objective. That is, unlike the objective claims of math, political science, or literature (claims that can be confirmed or disconfirmed by others, such as "Adam Smith wrote *The Wealth of Nations*"), ethical statements are not strictly speaking true or false. It is always true that Adam Smith wrote *The Wealth of Nations,* regardless of who makes the claim, and it will continue to be true at any time and in any place. The cultural relativist believes that ethical claims are only "true for" a particular population at a particular time. Thus if the majority of a culture believes that something is good, then that thing *is* good.

For example, suppose that the majority of the population in the United States believed in 1798 that slavery was good. Given Cultural Relativism, it follows that in 1798 slavery in the United States was good! In 2004 the majority of Americans believe that slavery is bad, so in 2004 slavery in the United States is bad. However, we aren't morally better than the Americans of 1798; there has been no moral improvement since then. In fact, moral improvement is altogether impossible. This is because the cultural relativists' view of the term "good" is purely descriptive, not evaluative. You don't use "good" to make a judgment about the value of something, but merely to describe society's attitude toward it.

Ethics is the study of what we *ought* to do. But the cultural relativist's definition of good doesn't tell us what we as a society ought to do, just what we as a society in fact do. Many people conclude that Cultural Relativism is not truly an ethical theory, because it doesn't capture our intuitions about ethics. For example, if the cultural relativist's definition of good is true, then:

- There can be no moral improvement in society. For example, the fact that women can now vote in the United States is not an improvement.
- Something can be right at one time and wrong at another.
- Someone can be bad at one time and good later. For example, when Martin Luther King Jr. began his work for human rights, he was a bad man. Today, he is a good man for the exact reasons he was once a bad man.
- There is no basis for arguing that social practices should be changed.
- You can never be sure that a particular action is right (for without taking a vote there is no way of knowing what people would think at this

moment about this particular act, and there is no reason to think that people's moral beliefs are consistent, so it can't be derived).
- You can't judge other societies. This would make military intervention always morally impermissible.

Cultural Relativism also suffers from two other problems. One is defining how the boundaries of a society are determined. Should we divide societies at national boundaries? State boundaries? Some other cultural or geographical divide? And what status should we give countercultures? Further, Cultural Relativism is particularly weak when it comes to looking at ethics and international relations, because the cultural relativist doesn't give us any suggestion about what to do when two or more societies are in conflict.

An important thing to notice about Cultural Relativism is that you don't have to be a cultural relativist in order to be sensitive to cultural differences. The term "relativism" often sets off buttons for people. Some people strongly defend something they call relativism, and others use the term as an insult. I think this is because people are using the term in different ways. It is very important for people who disagree about the value of relativism to be very clear about what they mean by the term. Here I have shown one way in which the term is used. Contemporary analytic philosophers reject this variety of relativism for the reasons given above. However, they do not reject or ignore the importance of cultural differences around the world. In fact, one can hold that different actions are ethical in some parts of the world and not in others, while still rejecting Cultural Relativism. I'll return to this point after looking at the two major ethical theories in contemporary Western philosophy.

Two Strong Accounts

2c. Good = Treating all rational agents as intrinsically valuable

This definition of the good is associated with the German philosopher Immanuel Kant (1724–1804). Kant thought that the only thing intrinsically good is good will. By that he meant that in order to be good, we must act with the right intention. That right intention involves treating all other people (or as Kant said, *rational agents*[3]) as ends in themselves, never merely as a means to an end. If Kant had his way, you'd never be anyone's stepping stone.

In order to illustrate his point, Kant told a story about two very different shopkeepers. At first, they look exactly alike. Both act the same way; when a small child comes in to buy a quart of milk, neither shopkeeper overcharges her. However, the two shopkeepers act honestly for different reasons. The first believes that it is wrong to take advantage of the relative ignorance of small children; the second believes that, while there is nothing wrong with cheating, there is a problem with getting caught cheating. So the second shopkeeper doesn't overcharge anyone, because he's afraid that people might find that he cheats his customers, and then they'll start shopping elsewhere. The second shopkeeper does the right thing, but with the wrong intention, whereas the first shopkeeper does the right thing with a good will. According to Kant, only the first shopkeeper acts ethically, for only he intends to treat all his customers as important in their own right.

There is much more to be said about Kant, and this definition of good is only one of several different definitions that he gives. Kant thought that the formulations of his definition of good (which he called the *Categorical Imperative*[4]) are equivalent, but there is much debate about that. A good introduction to Kant's moral theory can be found in his book, *The Groundwork to the Metaphysic of Morals.*[5]

Kant's approach to ethics is an example of a more general approach. His system is deontological, which means that it is based on the following of rules. There are rules about the treatment of other rational agents that must always be followed, *regardless of the consequences*. If you act with the right intention and follow the rule, then your act is a good one, even if the results of your actions are disastrous. According to Kant's approach, the road to hell cannot be paved with good intentions, because anyone who acted with good intentions would be a moral saint. Kant pointed out that we can never be certain of the future, so we ought not bet on future outcomes when deciding what to do. Instead, we need to act according to principles and ignore the individual details of the situation.

Though some people describe Kant's moral theory as akin to the Golden Rule ("Do unto others as you wish they would do onto you"), there are some important differences between the two. First, Kant realized that what you want people to do for you may differ from what those people want for themselves. For example, if you are a sadist and like being hurt by others, this doesn't give you the right to hurt others in return. Instead, we must be aware of each other's particular projects to a certain degree, and treat others appropriately given those projects. This doesn't mean that you have to find out the dreams of the kid working at Taco Bell before you order a burrito, but you shouldn't treat him as an unthinking machine either. You should treat him as a person, and realize that he is working at Taco Bell for some reason, in order to fulfill some goal, and you must be appreciative of that if you are to be a good person. Through his work, Kant asks us to appreciate others' autonomy, or right to self-determination, in all our dealings with them.

CULTIVATING TALENT

Kant said that we have a moral obligation to cultivate at least some of our talents; no matter how badly you want to, it would be immoral to spend your life hanging out in your basement playing video games. Given what you know about Kant's moral theory, what argument do you think he would give to support this view?

2d. Good = *Acting to maximize that happiness for all*

This definition of good is most closely associated with the English philosopher John Stewart Mill (1806–1873). His ethical theory, Utilitarianism, is strongly contrasted with Kant's approach. According to Mill's theory, the only thing morally relevant when assessing the worth of an action is to *look at the consequences*. A good action is one that will create the most *happiness* in the world. This doesn't mean that a good act needs to make the greatest number of people happy, nor does it follow that the actor will necessarily be happy about the consequences of the act. Rather, the greatest amount for the greatest number of people is what Mill was concerned with. Better to make one person amazingly happy (by, say, saving his child's life) than to make ten people mildly pleased (by, say, entertaining them with jokes). In this case, if possible, you should save the child's life rather than continue telling jokes to the small crowd (even if you'd much prefer to keep telling jokes).

WHY ARE YOU HERE?

What is your reason for reading this? Maybe you want to do well in the class. Why do you want to do well in this class?

Once you figure out why you want to do well in this class, ask yourself why you want that. Then keep asking "why" questions until you have reached the end. When you can no longer answer the why question, you have discovered your foundational value.

Mill argued that the ultimate thing people value is happiness. Mill believed that the chain of why questions, as exemplified in the box above, will come to an end with the answer, "Because it makes me happy"; and that the question, "Why do you want to be happy?" can only be asked by someone who doesn't understand happiness. Happiness is the only thing we intrinsically value, thought Mill.

This doesn't mean that we ought to be hedonists and spend all our time fulfilling our base pleasures. This is because Mill thought there are different qualities of pleasures, and that a person who spends all her time eating, drinking, having sex, and watching TV will ultimately not be satisfied. Such lower pleasures must be augmented with the higher intellectual pleasures of literature, art, mathematics, and music.

According to the Utilitarian, before we act we must ask ourselves who will be affected by our actions, and we must try to determine what those effects will be. We need to consider all the sentient beings, creatures who can feel pleasure and pain, who might be affected by what we do. If the act causes more harm than happiness, we cannot engage in that action. Similarly, if there is an alternative action that would produce an even higher ratio of happiness to pain, then we must engage in the second action, for the original act would be immoral.

Unlike Kant, Mill did not think there are particular rules that must always be followed. While Kant thought it is always wrong to lie, for example, Mill believed that the particulars of each situation must be taken into account, and that we have a moral obligation to lie when a lie maximizes happiness.

2e. Problems with Consequentialism and Deontology

As Kant was a deontologist, Mill was a consequentialist. Both views have their weaknesses, and contemporary philosophers continue to modify each approach in order to deal with particular problems. Kant, for example, said that if a murderer comes to your door, states her intention to kill your friend who is hiding upstairs, and asks you where your friend is, you must not lie to her. According to Kant's view, it is always wrong to lie, regardless of the details of the situation. Many people find the details of the situation quite relevant in the case of the wandering murderer, but Kant pointed out that you can't be sure what will result from either your lying or your truth-telling. It is possible that your friend climbed out the window when she heard the murderer at the door, and if you lie and tell the murderer that you saw your friend run around the corner, you would be leading the murderer right to your friend. Mill's view also has some problems that he tried to resolve. For example, suppose you find a thousand people who get great pleasure out of watching humans being devoured by wild animals. It might be a case where the amount of pain the doomed person feels outweighs the pleasure of the thousand happy people. If a thousand people isn't enough, then you can just keep inviting people so inclined into the coliseum, until you get enough to make the happiness outweigh the pain. Although Utilitarianism has been criticized by those who think it undermines an individual's liberty, this was not Mill's intent. In his book, Mill argued that people have the right not to be harmed by others or by the government. Philosophers today who are sympathetic to Mill try to make explicit how individual liberty can be preserved within a Utilitarian ethical theory.

This brief introduction to Kantianism and Utilitarianism suggests questions that we can ask in order to determine what we ought to do:

<table>
<tr><td>

KANTIAN QUESTIONS

- Am I respecting the rights and interests of the individuals who will be affected by this action?
- Am I acting out of concern for others rather than out of personal interest?
- Am I allowing individuals to retain their autonomy?

</td><td>

UTILITARIAN QUESTIONS

- Am I considering the degree of pleasure and pain for all the people who will be affected by my action?
- Does the amount of happiness for all people affected outweigh the amount of pain being caused?
- Does this action maximize the amount of happiness that is possible?

</td></tr>
</table>

3. Who must we be concerned with?

So far, in the introduction of both Kant and Mill, I have been talking about the rights and interests of people. The word "person" used in common speech is synonymous with "human," but in ethics there is reason to use the word "person" somewhat differently. That is because we don't want to bias the question about what sorts of beings deserve moral consideration. For example, if we limited our moral concern to humans, and then met up with an intelligent alien species, our ethics would give us no guidance about how to treat members of this species. Given Kant's emphasis on rational agency as criterion for moral standing, it seems clear that he would consider a creature such as Star Trek's Mr. Spock to be a person. Though Spock is not a human, as a Vulcan he certainly counts as rational.

Furthermore, there seems to be no good argument for limiting moral consideration to members of a particular species, even if that species is our own. Neither Kant nor Mill made reference to the human species as the relevant distinction between those who are and are not worthy of moral consideration. According to Mill, anything that can feel pleasure or pain has moral worth, whereas according to Kant, any rational agent is deserving of moral consideration.

It might be a physiological or psychological question about which beings are rational and which beings feel pleasure and pain. For example, Kant didn't think there were many beings who were rational. Some things he wrote suggest that he didn't even think that all humans were rational agents. On the other hand, Mill thought that all living humans feel pleasure and pain. In addition, there are some nonhuman animals who feel pleasure and pain, so we must also take those animals into account when deciding the right thing to do. Recent work in comparative psychology suggests that not only are some other animals able to feel pleasure and pain, but they can also solve complex problems.[6] Chimpanzees who learn artificial communication systems, dogs who learn to open the door where the food is kept, and pigeons who use mirrors in order to locate food might all be considered rational. In such cases, Kant's moral theory would necessitate our treating other animals with moral consideration, just as Mill's theory does.

Other things that some believe have moral worth include cultures, ecosystems, and works of art. Some of these can be seen as instrumentally valuable; that is, they are valuable because they are valued by rational agents (according to Kant's theory) or sentient creatures (according to Mill's theory). Money is an example of something that is instrumentally valuable. If not for the social contract regarding money, the pieces of paper and numbers describing our accounts would be worthless. Euros, rubles, and dollars are worth something, because we make them worth something.

Both Mill and Kant emphasized that we cannot privilege ourselves or our loved ones over others when deciding our moral obligation. We cannot choose to protect ten Americans over the lives of a hundred Afghanis, for example, for that would harm more rational agents than necessary, and it (usually) would not maximize happiness. If it turns out that other animals are also worthy of moral concern, we may no longer be able to engage in the medical testing of animals. Testing of rational agents against their will would be forbidden under Kant's view and, according to Mill's view, it would only be permissible if the benefits of the testing outweighed the amount of pain caused to the animals and those who are concerned about them.

4. Cultural Differences

In Morocco, it is immoral to touch people with your left hand. This isn't merely a question of politeness, but it is seen as an insult to use your left hand in social situations. However, in the United States there is no such moral prohibition. There are differences between the two cultures, but that fact doesn't mean that Cultural Relativism, the view that the good is merely what your culture says is good, is true. It is easy to show how these different moral practices are consistent, given the difference in situation.

In Morocco, the left hand is traditionally used for cleaning up in the toilet. In the United States, there is no such tradition. Given the health hazards associated with human fecal matter, there are good moral reasons not to use the left hand for social activities and eating. Americans and Moroccans alike share the belief that one ought to avoid making other people ill (at least in most cases), and the different moral views regarding the left hand reflect the different activities and a different environment within the cultures. Underlying many different cultural practices rests a set of moral commitments like those expressed by Kant and Mill. For example, some cultural prohibitions are based on the idea that one ought not to offend others unnecessarily. What varies from culture to culture is what offends someone. In the United States, it is seen as offensive for women to sunbathe without (at least) a bikini top on, whereas in France there is no such prohibition. It is seen as immoral (and it is illegal) for women to bare their breasts in the US because this offends many Americans. In some parts of Turkey, it is immoral for women to show their knees for the same reason: It is offensive to many Turkish people to see female knees in public. When I travel in Turkey I cover my knees, even though I am American, while in the United States I will wear shorts without concern. I change my dress when I travel, because of the general principle: Do not offend people without good reason. The principle doesn't change from France to the US to Turkey, only the situation changes.

This principle need not be a categorical one, however. For example, Mill might say that, although, in general, one ought not to offend others, in some cases it is necessary to do so. For example, it was once offensive to many Americans to let women work outside the home, smoke and drink in public, and drive cars. The offense people felt at seeing women engage in these traditionally male activities didn't cause as much unhappiness as it did for women to remain second class citizens. Kant would agree that we must sometimes offend others when the dignity or rights of rational agents (in this case, women) are being violated.

One danger when dealing with cultural differences is to assume full knowledge about the harm being done, or the relative happiness and unhappiness caused by the action. Take the case of the veiling of women in many Islamic societies. Some Westerners condemn the veil. After considering the particular situation, however, the reasons for such a condemnation may be unclear. For one, there is a difference between the governmentally enforced wearing of the veil, as is the case in Iran, and the continued wearing of the burka after the overthrow of the Taliban gave women the legal right to wear different clothing in Afghanistan. Also, such critics would be well advised to look toward their own cultures for analogous customs and ask themselves whether those customs ought to be condemned as well. In the case of women having the choice of wearing the burka or not, the critic might claim they don't really have a choice; even though it is no longer illegal to walk out of the house without the burka, the cultural prohibitions are so strong that they may be unable to throw off the veil.

But the critic must also consider the cultural prohibitions (as well as legal ones) regarding women's dress in the United States. It is illegal for women to reveal their chests, but permissible for men to do so. Should this law also be condemned? And in mainstream American culture, women face cultural prohibitions against showing unshaven underarms or a bikini line in public. There are no laws to this effect, certainly, but American women should feel just as free to leave their houses with hairy armpits as some Afghan women do about leaving their houses without the burka.

It is easy to condemn something when you know little about it. The more you learn, the more complex the situation appears. However, it can still be difficult to understand the minutia of a culture from a great physical and cultural distance. Just as one might be shocked or offended by a Moroccan's response were you to touch her with your left hand, if you were fully informed about the situation, your disdain for the prohibition might subside. Similarly, with more information, one is in a better situation to determine whether the practice is in fact harmful, and is better suited to make the case for the immorality of that practice.

James Rachels, in "The Challenge of Cultural Relativism," his excellent essay on the subject of cultural differences, gives the following example[7]: The Callatians and the Greeks disposed of their dead relatives' bodies in different ways. While the Greeks thought it was proper to burn their parents' bodies, the Callatians would eat them. The Greeks found the Callatians' behavior barbaric ("How can you eat your mother?" they cried in horror). But the Callatians thought the same of the Greeks ("How can you treat your father's body like garbage?" fumed the Callatians). You might balk at the question, "Should we eat our dead relatives or should we burn them?" because neither option may sound optimal. Perhaps you think your ancestors deserve a "proper" burial.

Here are obvious differences in cultural practice, but are not the two cultures closer than they think, given the honor they both bestow upon their ancestors? Rather than looking only for differences between cultures, we must also dig a bit more deeply and look for similarities, because what might at first look like an irreconcilable difference may be a deeply felt agreement on another level. Once the similarities have been identified, you can also identify the arguments for the different claims, and recognize where the arguments diverge. This can help us determine whether the disagreement is an ethical one or simply a matter of taste. If it is an ethical disagreement, it is all the more important to look at the arguments on both sides of the issue, because the better the argument, the more likely the conclusion. This is the power of argumentation.

When dealing with ethics in international relations, these issues of cultural difference become all the more important. Both Mill and Kant emphasized the importance of knowing the individuals whose lives are affected by your actions; and when dealing with people from a culture very different from your own, it is essential to take the time necessary to truly learn about those cultures before even beginning to engage in the ethical analysis. It is not possible to gauge the ratio of happiness to unhappiness for a group of people if you do not know what makes them happy and unhappy. And you cannot respect a person's autonomy if you do not know what her projects are. Thus the first step in making an ethical decision is to learn as much as possible about the beliefs and desires of those people who are involved in the situation. It's very easy to act immorally toward those people whose beliefs and desires you do not understand.

COMPETING FACTUAL CLAIMS

Many ethical disagreements, both across and within cultures, are based not on a different understanding of ethics, but on a different factual claim. For example, the debate between the Callatians and the Greeks was not "Should we honor our ancestors?" The controversial premise dealt with *how to go about* honoring ancestors.

Think of a specific cultural disagreement. Now consider the argument on both sides. Be charitable, and try to construct a sound argument for each position. Write down these arguments. Then compare the premises. Can you identify where the disagreement rests?

Concluding Thoughts

At this point you should be able to:

- recognize and construct sound arguments
- identify inconsistent premises
- explore the similarities and differences underlying cultural practices
- recognize different definitions of the term "good"

You also should have a sense of your own views on ethics. Are you a Kantian? A Utilitarian? Or do you have a different definition of the "right" and/or the "good?" Maybe you like different aspects of both moral theories. Regardless of your response, you now have these tools at hand to help you analyze your own choices. You can also use them to help you formulate opinions on contemporary social issues. If this introduction to ethics has made you want to know more, here are a few books you might want to take a look at:

- For a more detailed introduction to ethics, and for more definitions of the term "good," you could read James Rachels's *The Elements of Moral Philosophy*[8] and Simon Blackburn's, *Being Good: A Short Introduction to Ethics*[9].
- If you are interested in ethical issues related to nonhuman animals, you should definitely read Peter Singer's classic article, "All Animals Are Equal"[10] (which is available online). For a longer discussion of ethics and animals, look at James Rachels's *Created from Animals: The Moral Implications of Darwinism.*[11]
- For more on cultural differences and similarities, you can read the first chapter of Rachels's *The Elements of Moral Philosophy.* Another interesting reading on this topic comes from an anthropologist. Marvin Harris's book, *Cows, Pigs, Wars and Witches*[12] attempts to explain the rationale behind different cultural practices, such as the Hindi prohibition of killing cows and the Kwakiutl potlach (a competition to give away or destroy the most goods).

Student Handout 2:
Marine Mammals and US National Security

In the summer of 2002, the US government granted the Navy permission to continue testing low-frequency active sonar (LFA). These tests had been criticized after scientists and environmentalists concluded that previous tests had caused death and injury to marine mammals.

The Navy wants to develop LFA in order to monitor the new super-quiet submarines being produced by countries such as Russia and China. The Navy claims that, without LFA, US national security is compromised.

The sonar can generate up to 215 decibels of sound, more than enough to severely injure human divers. Sound is very important to marine mammals, who use their vocalizations to communicate. Dolphins rely on echolocation, a kind of sonar, as their primary sensory modality. When dolphins become deaf, they lose their ability to navigate, identify companions, and find food.

There have been a number of incidents related to Navy LFA tests. During one test off the islands of the Bahamas, sixteen whales and dolphins beached themselves. When scientists examined the animals, they found hemorrhaging in the animals' brains and around the bones of their ears. Such injuries are caused by exposure to extremely loud sounds. A 1996 beaching incident that took place off the coast of Greece has been identified with similar testing by NATO.

According to critics, the Navy's Environmental Impact Statement does not say how long-term LFA testing will affect marine mammal communities, and other experts agree that we currently do not have enough information to know how safe or dangerous LFA testing will be for marine life.

As the Navy prepares for more testing, environmental groups are organizing protests and letter-writing campaigns.

Discussion Questions

1. Identify the cast of characters. Who is involved in this situation, and what moral status does each or should each character have?
2. Analyze the situation from a Utilitarian perspective. What are the likely consequences if the Navy tests LFA? If the Navy doesn't test LFA? Who will be hurt? Who will be helped? Which case will maximize the happiness overall? Is there an alternative that will maximize happiness? If yes, what is it?
3. Analyze the situation from a Kantian perspective. Whose rights and interests are being respected by the Navy? By the critics? Who is acting out of concern for others? Which action will protect individual autonomy?

4. Construct a sound argument in support of LFA testing from the perspective of the Navy. Which premise makes an ethical claim? What definition of good does this argument rely on?

5. Construct a sound argument against LFA testing from the perspective of the critics. Again, identify the ethical premise and the definition of good.

6. Can you identify the fundamental disagreement between the two parties? Is it based on an ethical premise, or are the facts under dispute? Do both parties agree about who counts?

7. What would you suggest the two parties do to resolve their disagreement?

8. Are we obligated to refrain from acting when we don't know what the consequences will be, but there is some evidence that the consequences will cause harm? Why or why not?

9. Suppose that the critics found that LFA testing was harmful to a human population (rather than to marine mammals). Do you think this would change the debate? Should it change the debate? Why or why not?

10. In a case where there is a conflict between human and nonhuman interests, can we place emphasis on the human interests? What reason can be given to justify privileging human interests?

11. During the 2003 war with Iraq, the US military used dolphins to help locate submerged mines around the port of Umm Qasr. Given that the US military relied on the help of dolphins to keep the troops supplied, is there a corresponding military responsibility to protect the interests of the dolphins? How might a Kantian or a Utilitarian answer this question?

Student Handout 3:
An Opinion Piece on Marine Mammals
and US National Security

An analysis of this case shows that the Navy testing of LFA cannot currently be justified. The nonhuman populations injured by these tests have interests that must be acknowledged. These animals feel pleasure and pain, and scientists believe that whales and dolphins are highly intelligent, social creatures who communicate with one another, show emotion, and demonstrate cultural differences.

To say that animals do not count because they are not human is much like the sexist and racist claims of the past. Those who believe that humans have a special status in the world must draw some clear distinction between humans and other animals. There is good reason to think that such a distinction cannot be found, given the theory of evolution and the continuity of the physical and mental across species. Any argument that bases the distinction between humans and animals on some property such as language use, problem solving, self-awareness, etc. would inevitably discriminate against some disabled humans. Thus none of these properties can be used to justify human superiority without allowing for mistreatment of any human that does not share that property. These considerations lead me to conclude that the whales and dolphins injured by the Navy sonar tests are being harmed.

However, we must also compare the harm that is caused by the tests with the harm that would result if there were no testing. So we also must consider the risk to US national security. Will the lives of humans be at risk if the Navy does not engage in these tests?

I suspect the answer to this question is no. The Russians and Chinese are not serious threats to US security. The United States currently has the strongest military in the world, and anyone who attacks the United States knows that retaliation will follow. Thus there is reason to believe that even with the advantage of super-quiet submarines, it is unlikely that other states would use them to initiate attacks against the United States

The argument against LFA testing may become clearer if we suppose that humans rather than animals are at risk. Imagine what would happen if the United States announced it would resume testing nuclear weapons at the Nevada Test Site. Though scientists suspect that the testing would be fatal for some number of the local human population, this is not proven; therefore, the military's official position is that the long-term health effects of these tests is unknown. People around the world would be horrified by this position, I suspect. Why then is there not more outrage at a similar disregard for marine mammal life? I conclude that this can only be due to the disregard most humans have for nonhuman life, which is based on mere prejudice.

If human lives were at stake, the Navy would devise some way of protecting the vulnerable, or it would find another, less damaging way of detecting submarines. There exist other options that must be explored. This is not a case of whales and dolphins vs. humans. The human population can most likely retain security without having to kill anyone in the process. The American military has proven itself quite good at developing new technologies, so there is reason to believe that different techniques for detecting the new submarines can be discovered.

Discussion Questions

1. What moral theory does the author assume in this opinion piece?
2. Reconstruct the author's main argument.
3. How might a Utilitarian criticize the author's argument?
4. How might a Kantian criticize the author's argument?
5. How could the author strengthen this argument?

Debriefing

After working through the different exercises, you may want to invite students to think about the role of ethics in international relations. For example, you might ask students what role ethics currently plays in international relations, and what role they think it should play. Are the ethical aspects of IR currently dominated by Kantian or Utilitarian thinking? Challenge students to think about how the world might be different if ethics was a larger part of international relations, or if different ethical theories were applied. You could ask students to apply one of the ethical theories to historical events. For example, if President George W. Bush were a Kantian (or a Utilitarian), how might the 2003 war with Iraq have been different? Would following Kantian or Utilitarian principles have led to different outcomes with regard to dropping the atom bombs in 1945, the failed humanitarian interventions in Kosovo in 1999 and in Goradze in 1994, etc.?

Toolkits 2 and 3 are designed to be used in conjunction with one another as introductions to the roles and sources of ethics in global politics. After students have read and discussed both, ask if they see a conflict between the two toolkits. Encourage them to look for similarities and differences, and to ask if the differences are based on underlying values that they share.

Selected Bibliography

In Print

Blackburn, Simon. *Being Good: A Short Introduction to Ethics*. Oxford: Oxford University Press, 2001.

Kant, Immanuel. *The Groundwork to the Metaphysic of Morals*. Cambridge: Cambridge University Press, 1998; also online at www.swan.ac.uk/poli/texts/kant/kantcon.htm

Mill, John Stuart. *On Liberty*. New York: Viking Press, 1982; also online at www. bartleby.com/130/

Mill, John Stuart. *Utilitarianism*. Indianapolis: Hackett Publishing Company, 2002; also online at www.utilitarianism.com/mill1.htm

Rachels, James. *The Elements of Moral Philosophy* (3rd edition). New York: McGraw Hill College Division, 2000.

Singer, Peter. *One World: The Ethics of Globalization*. New Haven: Yale University Press, 2002.

Related Web Sites

www.petersingerlinks.com/animals.htm Peter Singer's article, "All Animals are Equal."

www.epistemelinks.com An excellent guide to philosophy on the Web. Click on Topics to read about ethical theories, applied ethics topics (including environmental ethics, medical ethics, and business ethics), political philosophy, and other issues. You can also link to E-texts from this page.

www.religioustolerance.org/welcome.htm One of the best ethics sites on the Web. The goal of this Web site is to promote peace among states by helping us understand and be tolerant of ethical and religious differences. Controversial issues, such as abortion, use of landmines in war, female genital mutilation, and capital punishment, are examined from different ethical and religious perspectives.

http://home.earthlink.net/~lfdean/carroll/puzzles/index.html This is one of many pages on the Web where you can hone your logical reasoning skills by playing games.

www.cut-the-knot.org/LewisCarroll/index.html Another Lewis Carroll logic page that is a bit more mathematically oriented.

www.ditext.com/carroll/tortoise.html E-text of "What the Tortoise Said to Achilles," by Lewis Carroll. This is a dialogue on the importance of and the difficulty with logic.

Appendix

Answers, pages 44

Kathy's argument at the beginning of the dialogue:

1. A fetus is a human.
2. It is wrong to kill.
3. Abortion (the killing of a fetus) is wrong.

The premise at issue in this dialogue:

The controversial premise is (2). Both characters agreed that premise (1) is true.

The variations of this premise that are made throughout the dialogue:

2'.   It is wrong to kill humans.

2''. It is wrong to kill humans, except in self-defense against a guilty person.

2'''. It is wrong to kill humans, except in self-defense.

2''''. It is wrong to kill humans, except in self-defense, unless killing is necessary to stop a greater harm.

How Kathy could make her argument consistent with the morality of some wars and euthanasia:

Premise (2) could be modified to read: It is wrong to kill people against their will, unless killing is necessary to stop a greater harm.

Answers, page 61

1. Utilitarianism. The author is concerned with the consequences in both cases, and specifically refers to animals' ability to feel pleasure and pain.
2. Nonhumans have the same moral worth as humans. LFA testing will almost certainly hurt nonhumans. Refraining from LFA testing is not likely to hurt humans. We must act so as to minimize pain and maximize happiness. Therefore, we ought not to allow LFA testing.
3. A Utilitarian might disagree with the claim that refraining from LFA testing is not likely to hurt humans, for example.
4. A Kantian might criticize the idea that humans have the same moral worth as animals. She might say that, even if harm to animals is certain and benefit to humans is only possible, we can still engage in the testing because only humans matter.
5. The author could strengthen this argument by doing more research into LFA, detailing exactly how much harm may result (e.g., how many whales and dolphins are likely to die), compared to how much good might result from the testing.

Endnotes

1. Although some people make a distinction between ethics and morals, there is no consensus among analytic philosophers about what these terms mean. Many philosophers use them interchangeably, as I do in this toolkit.

2. See, for example, the Lewis Carroll Web sites cited in this toolkit's Selected Bibliography. Lewis Carroll, the author of *Alice in Wonderland*, created some very odd logical puzzles. Here's one:

1. Babies are illogical.
2. Nobody is despised who can manage a crocodile.
3. Illogical persons are despised.
4. All babies can manage crocodiles

Is this argument valid or invalid?

3. Kant places emphasis on rationality when he says that all intrinsically valuable creatures must be rational agents. This privileging of rationality is related to his formulations of the Categorical Imperative, which requires agents to have some ability to reason logically in order to determine what the moral truths are. Many contemporary Kantians reject Kant's emphasis on rationality, for they want to include infants and animals in the category of things that are intrinsically valuable. Kant, for example, thought that animals were not of intrinsic moral worth. Rather, they are only valuable insofar as they may be valuable to rational agents (namely us). This line of reasoning could also be used to support colonialism; Kant notoriously excluded the South Sea islanders from the class of moral agents. To avoid these results, you may want to argue that all humans (and perhaps some nonhuman animals) are rational agents, and thus are intrinsically valuable. This might require an extension of the notion of rationality to include things like social intelligence and emotion. Or you may want to reject the reliance on rationality altogether and substitute some other property. Taking this second option leads many people toward accepting some variety of Utilitarianism. Of course, it does not do any good to reject rationality as a criterion for moral standing without substituting some other property. If there is to be an important moral distinction between a ballpoint pen, a rock, and a human, there needs to be some suggestion of the salient differences between the members of these categories that make some worthy of moral concern and others not worthy.

In order to avoid the controversy around the term "rational agent" I will refer instead to "people." This term is also not without controversy; although it is often taken to refer only to humans, there are those who argue that the term ought to be expanded to include nonhuman animals. For more on this point, see section 3.

4. "Categorical" because the moral law applies to all rational agents at all times; it is universal. "Imperative" because the law commands you to act.

5. Immanuel Kant, *The Groundwork to the Metaphysic of Morals* (Cambridge: Cambridge University Press, 1998).

6. Donald Griffin, *Animal Minds: Beyond Cognition to Consciousness* (Chicago: University of Chicago Press, 2001).

7. James Rachels, "The Challenge of Cultural Relativism" from *The Elements of Moral Philosophy,* 3e (New York: McGraw Hill, 2000).

8. Rachels, *The Elements of Moral Philosophy.*

9. Simon Blackburn, *Being Good: A Short Introduction to Ethics* (Oxford, UK: Oxford University Press, 2001).

10. Peter Singer, "All Animals Are Equal" from *Animal Rights and Human Obligations* (Englewood Cliffs, NJ: Prentice Hall, 1989).

11. James Rachels, *Created from Animals: The Moral Implications of Darwinism* (Oxford, UK: Oxford University Press, 1998).

12. Marvin Harris, *Cows, Pigs, Wars and Witches* (New York: Vintage Books, 1974).

The United States Is Not the Globe

Helena Meyer-Knapp and Lucinda Joy Peach

About This Toolkit

This toolkit brings to the foreground concepts, central in many countries around the world, which are rarely, if ever, discussed in the higher echelons of US strategic thinking or in most contemporary global institutions where Western notions of logic, law, freedom, utility, and power prevail. The prominence of Western ideals is revealed in core documents, such as the UN Charter and UN Declaration of Human Rights that structure international institutions. Both UN documents contain large sections directly modeled on the documents, which frame the US constitutional system (see Student Handout 2 for specific examples).

This toolkit offers one small glimpse into some normative traditions that risk being ignored in the swirl of globalization. For example, prioritizing individual and private rights or giving preferences to community commitments is one arena in which ethical standards differ dramatically among the world's cultural traditions.

In the late 1990s, practical economic problems developed as a result of the international community's assumption that Western values about the private nature of property were universal. Global challenges to Western dominance in international institutions became public and sometimes violent, partly because the World Trade Organization defined legal procedures and free trade regimes that placed high value on individual liberty at the expense of other cultural and economic practices.

Analytical problems arise as well when scholars derive their theories exclusively from European and Western notions. As David Kang said in an article on the inaccurate predictions that result from applying Western models to Asia, "Eurocentric ideas have yielded several mistaken conclusions and predictions about conflict and alignment behavior in Asia . . . It is an open question whether Asia, with its very different political economy, history, culture, and demographics, will ever operate like the European state system. This is not to criticize European-derived theories purely because they are based on Western experience. . . .Rather these theories do a poor job as they are applied to Asia."[1] This toolkit awakens in students an appreciation of the specific variety of ethical norms that constitute global politics, so they can carry out accurate research and analysis in varied cultural contexts. It also prepares them to discern whether real-world plans for future international relationships and institutions are appropriate in a truly global environment.

Toward these ends, a further reading (Chapters 2 and 3 in Michelle LeBaron's *Bridging Cultural Conflicts: A New Approach for a Changing World*) makes a useful optional addition to the reading contained in Student Handout 2. The exercise we use in relation to the handout provides tangible evidence of the penetration into seemingly global documents of US constitutional norms. Chapter 2 in LeBaron's book explores some of the key features of the Western tradition and unpins claims for the universal applicability of the dominant tradition. Chapter 3 offers specific examples of communication strategies that enhance cultural fluency, thereby enabling students to consider the potential impact of policy options in a wide variety of cultural contexts.

Miniglossary

Realism An approach to the analysis of international relations which assumes that human nature is naturally competitive and aggressive. Realism achieved prominence during the Cold War era and remains the dominant approach practiced in the United States today. Scholars and strategists who espouse this perspective assume that human nature is naturally competitive and aggressive. Consequently, morality is considered to be marginal, if not irrelevant, inapplicable, and/or ineffective in relation to war.

Universal The view that because certain principles or concepts, such as views of ethics, are presumed to be rationally self-evident, they are or should be shared by everyone universally by virtue of the human capacity to reason. For example, European philosopher Immanuel Kant thought that the moral law derived from his categorical imperative was universal in that it applied to all rational agents at all times.

Global This toolkit gives particular weight to this term, which we associate with the ability to situate policy options and moral choices in appropriate cultural contexts, while viewing the larger framework and recognizing that ethics in international relations in an era of globalization must be built from a multitude of traditions.

High-context/Low-context negotiators High-context negotiators are typically relationship and situation-oriented. Social context and social harmony are paramount; negotiations are but one step along the path of any relationship.

Moreover, to those who hold this perspective, the world is too complicated and ambiguous a place to mold to one's wishes. The wise person adjusts to the environment and develops an adaptive personality in order to live comfortably within irresolvable differences. Communication in these cultures tends to emphasize politeness, tact, indirectness, and building strong interpersonal relationships.[2]

Low-context negotiators typically favor the Western emphasis on individualism and personal agency. These can-do types assume that people can effectively manipulate their environments in ways that maximize personal objectives. They are solution-oriented. Their negotiation strategies tend to focus on instrumental rationality, linear logic, competition, and dichotomous choices. In negotiations, they are described as believing that it is useful to clarify, to talk things out, and to address problems directly. Communication in these cultures is typically direct, without much use for allegories or formal rituals.[3]

Step-by-Step Directions

We believe that it is of primary importance for students to explore actively the ethical concepts presented in Student Handout 1. For that reason, this toolkit contains two in-class activities. One evening of outside reading and reflection prepares students for the first activity. If there is time for more work on these issues, a second set of readings—Student Handout 2 and the two chapters from LeBaron—provide the foundation for a second, optional exercise to be conducted in a subsequent class.

Preparation for Day One

1. Photocopy Student Handout 1: Similarities and Differences in Approaches to the Good Life and the Good Government, and distribute to students as assigned reading to be completed outside of class.

2. Point out the three focus questions at the end of the handout. Have students write one- or two-sentence answers to each of the sub-questions (for themselves) in the form of notes after they have completed the reading. Instruct them to bring these notes and the handout to the next class, as they may want to refer to them during the activity.

3. Prepare three one-paragraph descriptions of current, heated policy dilemmas in global politics. Photocopy these as well, but don't distribute them until the day of the exercise. Issues from late 2003 could have included:

   a. US dilemmas about whether and how to allow Islam to become the official religion of a post-war government in Iraq.

b. The US president's decision to forgo tariff protections for US steel jobs for the sake of freer global trade.

c. Given the hostile tone of relations with their well-armed neighbor, North Korea, Japanese political leaders considered whether to renounce their post-WWII constitutional commitment to nonmilitary solutions.

Day One: Applying a Variety of Ethical Values to Contemporary Problems

1. In class, distribute the three one-paragraph policy dilemmas. Students choose the dilemmas they want to work with. They then divide into small groups, each interested in the same policy dilemma (more than one group to an issue improves the effectiveness of the later discussion). *Based on the ethical positions they espoused in their earlier out-of-class responses to the focus questions,* groups formulate policy options to their chosen dilemmas. This normally requires about 30 minutes.

2. Groups present their suggestions in whole class format. Encourage the class to evaluate and discuss the recommendations. If different groups studying the same issue came to different conclusions, explore their differences as a whole. This requires about 15–30 minutes.

3. If possible, save 5–15 minutes to identify the activity's impact on students. The first debriefing section contains suggestions on how to do this.

Optional Extension: Day Two/Exercise Two Comparing US and UN Values Articulated in Core Documents

1. Photocopy Student Handout 2: Comparing Formal Instruments of the United States and United Nations, and distribute to students as assigned reading to be completed outside of class. Also assign Chapters 2 and 3 from LeBaron's *Bridging Cultural Conflicts.*

2. Point out the focus questions at the end Student Handout 2. Have students write one- or two-sentence answers in note form after they have completed the reading. Tell students to bring the handout and their notes to the next class, as they may want to refer to them.

3. Calculate the number of groups of four your class can be divided into. Bring to class a single copy of the UN Charter broken up into its key sections, so that each group receives one segment.
4. Each group searches their segment for language that conforms to one or more of the norms listed in focus question 2 of Student Handout 2. This requires about 30 minutes.
5. The whole class reconvenes to share findings, assess the degree to which these norms may be more congenial to high- or to low-context negotiators, and discuss the implications of this for ethical global politics. This takes about 30 minutes.
6. Save some time to debrief students. The second debriefing section suggests ways to do this.

Student Handout 1:
Similarities and Differences in Approaches
to the Good Life and the Good Government

This exercise neither claims to present all of the world's most important ethical ideals, nor offer a comprehensive survey of key texts from around the globe. Instead we identify several key notions for which US legal and policy standards, taken virtually as self-evident by Americans, are likely to seem inappropriate in other cultures. Many of the ethical stances presented here have their origins in major religious/ethical traditions, such as Buddhism, Confucianism, Islam, and Pan African traditional practices, all of which predate by centuries the moral philosophies of both Kant and Mill. In the United States, such ancient religious traditions are routinely described as "minority" viewpoints, though in other parts of the world they are predominant. We also present two additional stances, pacifism and feminism, which have particular bearing on international affairs and have Western adherents, although these, too, represent "minority" positions in the United States.

The topics selected for this survey fall into two conceptual categories. The first—The Good Life—encompasses life and death, liberty and community, the pursuit of happiness, and suffering. The second—The Good Government—addresses religion and the state, and nonviolence and war. In each, you will have a chance to consider several subtopics, presented in the form of a short quote from a key text and a brief commentary about the quote.

The Good Life

Three notions—the nature of existence after death, the relationship between individual and community, and the connection between happiness and suffering—exemplify wide divergences among cultures in their assumptions about how people live out a good life.

Life and Death

Under the US Constitution, the right to life is primary, in part because death is seen as final, an absolute loss. In this, American culture and law are congruent with Jewish, Christian, and Muslim traditions, all of which envision a single earthly life with heaven as the destination of the soul after death. Where Hindu and Buddhist traditions predominate (India, Sri Lanka, Southeast Asia, and traditional communities in China and Japan), reincarnation into a new life on earth is a given, and the death of the Self does not ultimately exist.[4] The contrast between the Western dualistic philosophy regarding life and death and the Asian philosophy regarding reincarnation is exemplified in three textual selections. The first is about heaven and hell, from the Qur'an (Muslim), and the next two are about reincarnation, from the Bhagavad Gita and the Upanishads (Hindu).

The Qur'an: On Heaven and Earth

> Every soul will know the taste of death. You will get your rec-
> ompense in full on the Day of Resurrection; and he who is
> spared the Fire and finds his way into Paradise will meet his
> desire. As for the life of this world, it is nothing but a merchan-
> dise of vanity.[5]

In Western and Middle Eastern religious traditions, each person has only
one life, at the end of which the soul goes either to heaven or hell. To
reach heaven both Islam and Christianity prescribe similar virtues during earthly existence: a promotion of community service (*zagat* in Islam)
and charity, a prohibition on adultery and murder, and a commitment to
systematic, public participation in spiritual rituals. The last line of the
quote above also speaks for both Christian and Muslim religious codes:
earthly existence is fundamentally unimportant in the context of what
the Muslims call "The Day of Resurrection," and Christians call "The
Day of Judgment." Instead, the most important purpose of human existence is preparation for death, and thus for life in another world after
death

By contrast, in Asian religious traditions, which hold a belief in reincarnation, each time a person's body dies, it is understood that his or her soul
will find a new home in a new body here on earth. The actual form of reincarnation is based on living virtuously in this life, so both Buddhists and
Hindus place a high value on today's good life. Indeed karma, the unfin-
ished difficulties and deficiencies we carry from life to life, may if neglected
lead to rebirth as a lesser animal, a fish, or even a flea. The critical distinction here with Western and Middle Eastern understandings is that the day-
to-day living energy we humans experience at home and at work cannot
die, but lives on forever here on earth.

The Upanishads: On Death and Rebirth

> The Supreme Teaching *Death:* When the human soul falls into
> weakness and into seeming unconsciousness, all the powers of
> life assemble around. The soul gathers these elements of life-fire
> and enters into the heart. And when the Spirit that lives in the
> eye has returned to his own sources, then the soul knows no
> more forms.
>
> Then a person's powers of life become one, and people say:
> "he is no more. . . . Even as a caterpillar, when coming to the
> end of a blade of grass, reaches out to another blade of grass,
> and draws itself over to it, in the same way, the Soul, leaving the
> body and unwisdom behind, reaches out to another body and
> draws itself over to it."[6]

According to modern dating, the Upanishads, the oldest religious text known to exist, was written in 900 BCE. In this text, death is a simple procedure, no more complicated than a caterpillar moving onto a new blade of grass. There are no great moments of accounting, no dramatic changes, no decision between heaven and hell. The old body is dead, but the spirit immediately enters into a new one.

Bhagavad Gita: On Death and Rebirth

Never was there a time when I did not exist, nor you, nor all these kings; nor in the future shall any of these cease to be.

As the embodied soul continuously passes, in this body from boyhood to youth to old age, the soul similarly passes into another body at the time of death. A sober person is not bewildered by such a change.

For the soul there is neither birth nor death at any time. He has not come into being, does not come into being, and will not come into being. He is unborn, eternal, ever-existing, and primeval. He is not slain when the body is slain.

As a person puts on new garments, giving up old and useless ones, the soul similarly accepts new material bodies, giving up old and useless ones.[7]

The Bhagavad Gita is a key Hindu text and part of the Indian classic epic Mahabharata, composed between 200 BCE and 200 CE, and also had a lasting impact on the development of Yoga and Buddhism. This text also assumes that each of us, as an individual, will live forever. But our eternal life is here on earth, not in heaven.

Still, in India as in the West, those who are left behind are obligated to help the dead make the transition to a new life through appropriate rituals. Hindu families hope to take their dead loved ones for cremation at Varanasi on the Ganges River, so as to scatter the ashes on a river they consider sacred, a source of life. The banks of the river are covered with mourners who then swim in the river too, to gather in the healing of these waters for their own lives. At cremation, they believe they are handling only a dead body, confident that the true person is already on the way to a new life. Since there is no ultimate day of judgment, there is less to fear when someone dies.

Liberty and Community

The US Constitution states in its very first clause, in the preamble that precedes the main body of the document, that it exists to "secure the blessings of liberty to ourselves and our posterity." The word "blessing" shows the almost sacred and certainly fundamental commitment Americans have to liberty. US courts have consistently protected individual freedom from unnecessary intrusions and constraints. Community supervision of private behaviors is strictly limited. After the age of 18, children are treated as completely independent beings. In other cultures, community obligations are as important as individual rights. In the following excerpts, Confucius spells out the responsibilities adults have towards their aging parents; South Africa's Archbishop Desmond Tutu describes the high value African tradition places on human interdependence; and Leslie Marmon Silko's story illustrates the bonds between a Native American community and its ancestral land.

Confucius: On Family Responsibilities

> The Master said: "In serving your mother and father, admonish them gently. If they understand, and yet choose not to follow your advice, deepen your reverence without losing faith. And however exhausting this may be, avoid resentment."
>
> The Master said: "While your mother and father are alive, never travel to far off places. Or if you must, always follow a definite plan."
>
> The Master said: "If you leave your father's Way unchanged for three years of mourning, you are indeed a worthy child."[8]

Confucius lived around 500 BCE, and the Chinese have written and rewritten his notions numerous times in the centuries since. In cultures where the Confucian tradition remains influential today—Japan, China, and Korea in particular—dependence on the older generation, senior staff, and people in authority is experienced both as protective and constructive, less a constraint than an asset. Japanese workers and students seek out a *senpai*, a guide/mentor. As students, they may first meet in a club, playing soccer or studying calligraphy, but the *senpai*, an upper-classman, knows that this is the beginning of a life-long relationship. The *senpai* will help his junior *kohai* get a job, help him with promotions, and be his ally in all walks of life. Though they are almost the same age, the dependent relationship will never really change—after all the *senpai* himself has a *senpai* who is also just a few years older, ready to help out whenever needed.

While a Confucian should be focused more explicitly on immediate family than on the community in general, the sense of community ascribed to many African cultures is more broadly focused, explains Desmond Tutu, a South African Archbishop.

Desmond Tutu: On Interdependence

> *Ubuntu* is very difficult to render into a Western language. It speaks of the very essence of being human. When we want to give high praise to someone we say, *"Yu u nobuntu;"* . . . Then you are generous, you are hospitable, you are friendly, caring and compassionate. You share what you have. It is to say, "My humanity is caught up, is inextricably bound up, in yours." We belong in a bundle of life. We say, "A person is a person through other persons." It is not, "I think therefore I am." It says rather: "I am human because I belong. I participate, I share."[9]

Desmond Tutu, writing about South Africa's post-apartheid Truth and Reconciliation Hearings in 1999, is describing an ancient African tradition that existed long before written culture came to the continent. Tutu claimed it was *ubuntu* which made possible the post-apartheid hearings that offered both the possibility of amnesty for the accused and reparations to their victims. Their deeper and explicit purpose was to ensure that black and white could live well side by side in the future—that the harmony of the community be restored.[10]

Leslie Marmon Silko: On Land, Community, and People

Chinese and African traditions take as a fundamental principle that all individual humans are interdependent with other human beings. Leslie Marmon Silko, a modern Native American writer, describes interdependence formed in ancient times between a Native American community and the land on which they lived.

> I understood then that this it what it means to be a people and to be a Yaqui village and not just another Tucson neighborhood. To be a people, to be part of a village, is the dimension of human identity that anthropology understands least, because this sense of home, of the people one comes from, is an intangible quality, not easily understood by American-born Europeans.
>
> The Yaquis may have had to leave behind their Sonoran mountain strongholds, but they did not leave behind their consciousness of identity as Yaquis, as a people, as a community. This is where their power as a culture lies: with this shared consciousness of being part of a living community that continues on and on, beyond the death of one or even of many, that continues on the riverbanks of the Santa Cruz after the mountains have been left behind.[11]

The Yaqui have in fact been moved from their ancient homelands, but have proved able to recreate, within the boundaries of a modern American city, the very same kind of society whose integral strength is based on land. The Sonoran mountains have, it seems, been transferred to a flat city neighborhood, and continue to shape the relationships among the people. Beyond a shared identity, Silko also claims for land and community the same capacity to endure beyond death and rebirth that we saw in Hindu texts.

Happiness and Suffering

Having examined life and liberty, we now move on to the question of whether life's purpose really is the "pursuit of happiness," that powerful image first enunciated in the Declaration of Independence in 1776. Although this phrase does not appear in the Constitution, the pursuit is as embedded in America's passion for shopping as in a parent's desire to have her children's lives be better than hers, or in the hope that more money will bring more happiness. This time the contrary sources are Buddhist, focusing on the Buddha's core insight that human suffering is inevitable, if only because every person inevitably becomes ill and all of us must die. From this devolves the Buddhist ethical stance that the highest human purpose is to respond to and to heal suffering. Furthermore, unnecessary suffering is brought on by inappropriate actions. The Law of Karma means that inappropriate acts will surely come back to haunt us, unless expunged by restorative action. Such notions are not confined to the Buddhist tradition; medieval Christian theologians, who were convinced that the central problem of existence was to grapple with original sin and salvation, would be astonished at the emphasis in our contemporary consumer culture on the pursuit of happiness. Indeed, in the history of Western ethics, it was secular thinkers who introduced happiness as moral good.

The Buddha: On Suffering and Release

Life is suffering; birth is suffering and so are old age, illness and death, because everything and everyone is impermanent and yet also interdependent...

Additional suffering is caused by the fact that we reject reality and instead we desire permanence and independence...and suffering can be eased acknowledging impermanence and interdependence, and letting go of our cravings...which is realized by following the eight-fold path

right views (on these facts of life)
right purpose/thinking (to do no harm)
right speech (no lies, meanness, vain talk, or harsh language)
right action/conduct (no drinking, harmful sex)

right livelihood (appropriate jobs)
right effort (to prevent more suffering)
right mindfulness/recollection (controlling anger, greed
  and delusion) and
right contemplation/meditation.[12]

The Buddha lived around 500 BCE. He gave his first public sermon after attaining enlightenment, listing the above principles commonly called the Four Noble Truths and the Noble Eightfold Path in the Deer Park at Varanasi. While he wrote none of these teachings down himself, the story of this first sermon is well documented in Buddhist literature. The Buddha's kingly father had tried to shield his child from any sight of suffering, but the issue became obsession once the Buddha, then known as Prince Siddhartha, reached manhood and discovered the existence of sickness, old age, and death. So Siddhartha abandoned home and family in a search for a cure for suffering. After years of wandering, he finally experienced enlightenment while meditating under a tree. He later propounded the Noble Eightfold Path—which he called "The Middle Way"—for living both wisely and compassionately, and thus alleviating suffering.

On Karma/The Law of Cause and Effect

The Dalai Lama points out,

> Your suffering is due to your own karma, and you will have to bear the pain of that karma anyway in this life or another, unless you can find some way of purifying it. In that case, it is considered to be better to experience the karma in this life of a human being when you have more abilities to bear it in a better way than, for example, an animal who is helpless and can suffer even more because of that.[13]

Buddhists and Hindus share the notion of karma, that each life is shaped by the heritage, both healthy and harmful, that we carry on from our previous lives and activities. Every one of our actions is a cause with its own karmic effects. Those of our actions, and there are many, which result in negative consequences, must be resolved—if not in this life, then in some future one. Karma governs life, death, and rebirth, which determines the nature of our next life to come. However, by responding judiciously to the unexpected events that life presents to us, people can successfully rebalance the karma that is following them.

The American tradition is focused on the individual. Thus far, this chapter too focused on the private life of individuals, looking at the nature of the good life and good death for each person. What we find is that our definition of an individual is open to challenge—by the fact that some see a single life as merely one of our many lives, and by the fact that others cannot imagine separating out a person from his family, his community and his land. It is time to turn now to our lives as citizens, to the relationship between government and religion, and to the distinctions between militarism and non-violence.

The Good Government

This section is divided into two broad categories: the relationship between religion and civil government and approaches to war and pacifism. Within each broader category, we provide a number of varied perspectives.

Religion and Civil Government

A division between religion and government is nowadays considered essential by many in the United States; such a position would be alien to those European nations that have state religions (England, Germany, and Sweden for example), and would not be desired at all in many non-Western countries.[14] Two kinds of states that are both overtly religious in purpose—Islamic and Buddhist—are discussed below.[15] While Buddhism is declining as a state religion, with considerably less power in governing affairs in most countries than it has had in the past, Islam is increasing its political sway considerably.

Islamic Perspectives on Church-State Relations

The Qur'an, understood by Muslims to be divine revelation received by Mohammed, and the *hadith*, prescriptions laid down by him on the basis of his own reflections, are sacred texts for Muslims. Muslims live in states as varied as Malaysia in Southeast Asia, which is capitalist and intertwined with the modern industrial economy; Yemen on the Arabian peninsula, a small desert country with a preindustrial economy; and the United States. There is no single way of living in an Islamic state, but every Muslim is enjoined to ensure that religion permeates all aspects of life, from government to business, from family to community. The illustrations of Islam and government are from Pakistan, Iran, and Iraq.

After independence in 1947, Pakistan became the first modern state to integrate Islamic law into the governing structures of a democratically ruled nation, and thus it became a germinal modern example of Mohammed's original vision of a coextensive state and religion. Pakistan maintained its religious underpinnings even in the constitutional amendments promulgated after a military coup in 1999. While all other aspects of the earlier constitution went into abeyance, Islam was reaffirmed:

♦ **Pakistan: Provisional Constitution Order No. 1 of 1999**
"(4) . . . [A]ll provisions of the Constitution of the Islamic Republic of Pakistan embodying Islamic injunctions...shall continue to be in force ..."

The insertion on July 15, 2000 of this clause into the October 1999 order was accompanied by the proviso that the amendment is necessary "for removal of doubts," and to ensure "the continuity and enforcement of the Islamic injunctions in the Constitution of the Islamic Republic of Pakistan."

Iran, which adopted an Islamic government in 1979, devoted many paragraphs of its constitution to defining specific religious obligations.

♦ **Constitution of the Iranian Republic (1) General Principles, Article 1**
"The form of government of Iran is that of an Islamic Republic, endorsed by the people of Iran on the basis of their longstanding belief in the sovereignty of truth and Qur'anic justice...through the affirmative vote of a majority of 98.2% of eligible voters, held after the victorious Islamic Revolution led by the eminent marji' al-taqlid, Ayatullah al-Uzma Imam Khumayni."

The Iranian Constitution also recognizes that the Islamic State came into being thanks to a revolution inspired by a powerful religious leader, Ayatullah Khumayni. This is entirely compatible with Islamic tradition, in which *ulama* (learned clergy) have always been close to the center of government.

♦ **Constitution of the Iranian Republic (1) General Principles, Article 2**
The Islamic Republic is a system based on belief in:

(1) the One God (as stated in the phrase "There is no god except Allah"), His exclusive sovereignty and the right to legislate, and the necessity of submission to His commands;

(2) Divine revelation and its fundamental role in setting forth the laws;

(3)...the return to God in the Hereafter, and the constructive role of this belief in the course of man's ascent towards God;

(4)...the justice of God in creation and legislation;

(5)...the exalted dignity and value of man, and his freedom coupled with responsibility before God; in which equity, justice, political, economic, social, and cultural independence, and national solidarity are secured by recourse to:

(i) continuous *jtihad* of the *fuqaha'* possessing necessary qualifications, exercised on the basis of the *Qur'an* and the *Sunnah* of the *Ma'sumun*, upon all of whom be peace;...

Seen from the Iranian perspective, the Islamic community exists to manifest Allah's sovereignty, although even here the dignity and freedom of Man are essential (see item 5 in Article 2). Freedom and dignity are achieved by a simultaneous commitment to the Qur'an, to modern science and arts, and to the ending of all forms of oppression.

By contrast, the Constitution of Iraq, which prior to the ouster of Saddam Hussein prioritized socialism over religion, provided no description at all of the religious duties or purpose of the state:

♦ **Constitution of The Republic of Iraq (1990)**
  "Chapter I: Article 4 [State Religion] Islam is the religion of the State."

Buddhist Perspectives on Church and State Relations

Buddhist cultures, like Islamic ones, traditionally have made no sharp distinction between Church and State, religion and politics. Two examples illustrate the Buddhist tradition, which holds the ideal ruler to be a *Cakravartin*, literally a "wheel turner," who rules in accordance with Dharma, the teachings of the Buddha. The first ruler is Asoka, Emperor of India over two thousand years ago. The second is modern-day Bhutan, one of the few states where rulers still follow Buddhist practices.

♦ **Asoka: A King Who Finds Peace**
  Dharma can be translated as law, duty, or righteousness, and as such it has many overtones in Indian religion. However he intended it, in his edicts, Asoka seems to have been obsessed with Dharma. The Asokan State was to be governed according to Dharma. The people were to follow Dharma. Wars of aggression were to be replaced by peaceful conquests of Dharma. Special royal ministers were charged with the propagation of Dharma. True delight in this world came only with delight in Dharma, and the old royal pleasure-tours and hunts were replaced by Dharma-pilgrimages.[16]

Asoka died in 232 BCE at the age of about 50. He had been an astonishing warrior who conquered so much territory that for the first time ever the whole Indian subcontinent, from Afghanistan eastward, was under the same political control. The story goes that he became a Buddhist in remorse for the desperate suffering that resulted from his last conquest, the victory in Kalinga in 261

BCE. He came to see that he must practice *ahimsa*, nonviolence, in governing from thence forward. In the last years of his life, Asoka devoted himself to spreading Buddhism widely in his own land and in neighboring countries, including northward into Tibet, Nepal, and the Kingdom of Bhutan.

> ◆ **Bhutan: Dual Leadership**
> The parity between political and religious institutions in Bhutan is symbolized by the roughly equal status given to the governmental leaders, the king, and the Buddhist spiritual leader, the *je khempo*, who is the only person beside the king allowed to wear the saffron scarf. A central organization of Buddhist monks nominates the *je khempo*, who must be approved by the king. The monks hold a variety of governmental positions at all levels. . . . the government, in turn, maintains the major Buddhist temples and shrines.[17]

Interestingly enough, although Buddhism originated in India, it weakened dramatically in that country, particularly after the arrival of Islamic invaders in the thirteenth century. These days Buddhism is a minority religion in India, which has become a truly heterodox (multi-faith) state. Japan and Thailand, where Buddhists are a majority of the community, have hardly any official Buddhist basis for their governing organization. Nonetheless, in Japan local temples maintain the community social registers, and the government of Thailand officially recognizes and supports the Buddhist Sangha (the community of ordained male monastics). Buddhism also remains powerful in Sri Lanka, where it has long held a considerable sway over the central government.

In most places Buddhism, in contrast to Islam, is remarkable for its commitment to nonviolence. However, for nearly 20 years in Sri Lanka, prominent Buddhist leaders urged the government to continue the war against their Tamil minority. In the north of the island, Hindu Tamils were seen to be challenging the supremacy of the Buddhist religion.

Pacifism: Traditional and Feminist

In the gender-structured society of the United States, realism has been the culturally dominant and presumptively correct view.[18] Realism argues that our competitive and aggressive human nature makes war inevitable and unavoidable. Some among those who hold the dominant, realist view even consider morality to be irrelevant, inapplicable, or ineffective in relation to war. The presumption in favor of war is evident in the work of otherwise liberal academics, such as Michael Walzer,[19] who intends his theory of just war based on the protection of human rights to provide an alternative to realism, but who fails to give more than cursory and pessimistic consideration to alternatives to war.

In contrast to the United States' reliance on realism, and thus on using war to resolve international conflicts, the codes mandating nonviolence also date back centuries. Even Christianity took a comprehensively pacifist approach until the development of the just war theory in medieval Europe. Just war theory continues to be developed, and contemporary international law proposes a set of criteria designed to determine when, and to what extent, limited participation in armed conflict may be moral. Just war theorists generally share with pacifists a basic presumption that aggressive and excessively violent war is morally wrong. However, whereas pacifists share a firm belief that war is never a moral means to achieve just goals, those subscribing to just war theory are open to being persuaded that war may be morally justified in certain circumstances.

Building on their own ancient, religious traditions, twentieth-century Asian pacifist leaders challenged the realists and just war theorists about the necessity of the use of militaries and armed force. Modern feminist philosophers, concerned about the exclusion of women's knowledge and ways of knowing from the debates about war and nonviolence, also provide a critique of conventional militarist ethics. The following selections illustrate both of these alternative approaches to conflict resolution.

Traditional Pacifism

Traditional pacifism is illustrated by the writings of Mohandas K. Gandhi and His Holiness the Dalai Lama, each of whom argued that the violent way is less practical and "realistic" than an approach based in nonviolence.

Gandhi coined the term *Satyagraha*—truth force—for his method of resisting violence with a campaign of nonviolent resistance, to distinguish it from the European term "passive resistance." He applied this truth force to change the mind and heart of the opponent to compel attention and to set an example not by his violence, but by his unobtrusive humility. While his strategies often entailed risk and danger to both leader and followers, they remained steadfast in their refusal to endanger their opponents.

♦ **Gandhi, the Mahatma (Great Soul): Pacifism Is Victorious**
 Nonviolence is therefore in its active form good will towards all life. It is pure Love. I read it in the Hindu scriptures, in the Bible, in the Koran [sic].

 Nonviolence is a perfect state. It is a goal towards which all mankind moves naturally though unconsciously. In our present state, we are partly men and partly beasts and in our ignorance

and even arrogance say that we truly fulfill the purpose of our
species when we deliver blow for blow and develop the measure
of anger required for the purpose. We pretend to believe that
retaliation is the law of our being, whereas in every scripture we
find that retaliation is nowhere obligatory. Retaliation is indul-
gence requiring elaborate regulating. Restraint is the law of our
being. For highest perfection is unattainable without highest
restraint.[20]

Mohandas Gandhi was born in 1869 and trained as a lawyer when young.
Gandhi's life-long, deep trust in nonviolence was fully vindicated by the
final triumph of the Indian Independence movement in 1947. His methods
of nonviolent resistance have spread widely since his lifetime, including
their adoption by Martin Luther King Jr. in his struggles to secure the civil
rights of African Americans in the United States in the 1950s and 1960s.
When millions gathered in Washington, DC to challenge the government's
policy of racial segregation, they were resting both on the US constitutional
protection of free speech and on Gandhi's insight that ordinary people
walking together can make change.

Where Gandhi found support for his principles in the Bible and the
Qur'an, as well as in his own Hindu beliefs, His Holiness the Dalai Lama
has rooted his argument for peace on the core Buddhist imperative to
reduce suffering.

♦ **The Dalai Lama: Pacifism Is Practical**
Chairman Mao once said that political power comes from the
barrel of a gun. Of course it is true that violence can achieve certain short-term objectives, but it cannot obtain long-lasting
ends. If we look at history, we find that in time, humanity's love
of peace, justice and freedom always triumphs over cruelty and
oppression. This is why I am such a fervent believer in nonviolence. Violence begets violence. And violence means only one
thing: suffering.

Some people will say that while the Dalai Lama's devotion to
nonviolence is praiseworthy, it is not really practical. Actually, it
is far more naïve to suppose that the human-created problems
which lead to violence can ever be solved through conflict. . . .[21]

The Dalai Lama is the leading religious authority to Tibetan Buddhists and
was, until his forced exile in 1959, also the head of the Tibetan government.
In the aftermath of the 1959 Chinese conquest of Tibet, the Dalai Lama has
advocated the use of nonviolent strategies in the struggle for the survival of
Tibetan culture and its Buddhist tradition. He makes his arguments for

nonviolence from an explicitly global perspective. He is interested in ending the resort to war, but does not advocate a retreat from engagement in world affairs. Indeed, all the great practitioners of nonviolence—including Martin Luther King Jr., Nelson Mandela in South Africa, Ang San Suu Khi in Burma, and Maha Ghosananda in Cambodia—have relied to a significant degree on a worldwide approbation for their courage to achieve success when confronted by a violent opposition.

Feminist Pacifism

Feminist analyses reveal how abstraction in the application of just war theory has resulted in: 1.) a neglect of the horrors of war and its effects on individual bodies; 2.) a perception of the enemy as "Other"; and 3.) a fixation on principles of justice and rights, rather than the needs and interests of specific persons in particular conflicts. Feminists reject an emphasis on rights and justice as relying on male-derived and biased conceptions that fail to accord with the way human beings, committed to love and caring, are actually constituted. Realism's tendency to privilege the state over the individual allows too many innocents to die for the "social good."[22] In this section, we feature two modern philosophers working in the United States today: Cynthia Enloe and Sara Ruddick.

♦ **Cynthia Enloe: On War and Human Nature**
Resorting to militarism as the primary means of conflict resolution has a myriad of negative effects on women's lives.

[I]t is easy to slip into imagining that militarization is always accompanied by government-directed overt violence, by war. Yet what the exploration of the lives of military wives and of women working as military prostitutes reveals for us is that militarization creeps into ordinary daily routines; it threads its way amid memos, laundry, lovemaking, and the clinking of frosted beer glasses. Militarization is such a pervasive process, and thus so hard to uproot, precisely because in its everyday forms it scarcely looks life threatening . . .

But the persistence of the presumption that women's militarization is simply the outcome of nature or custom is one of the things that grants gendered militarization its stubborn longevity.[23]

The author of this piece is Cynthia Enloe, an American feminist philosopher who argues that assuming that war is "human nature" makes it too easy to avoid recognizing that US Army bases and military social hierarchies compel behaviors by both men and women that confirm the assumption. Enloe's contemporary, philosopher Sara Ruddick, proposes "maternal thinking" as an ethical practice engaged in by those who "mother," which contains resources for creating nonviolent alternatives to war.

♦ **Sara Ruddick: On War and Maternal Thinking**
Nonviolent action, like maternal practice at its best, requires resilient cheerfulness, a grasping of truth that is caring, and a tolerance of ambiguity and ambivalence.... Peace itself can be conceived for both activists and mothers as depending on a connective "love" that still struggles "toward definition, grow[s] out of confusion, knowledge, misery and necessity." None of these makes most mothers peaceful.

In sum, a feminist mother becomes increasingly clear-sighted about the violences she has suffered or inflicted and increasingly able to resist them.[24]

The ethical claim Ruddick makes is that, since many women must learn how to think like a mother, simultaneously offering protective liberation and social guidance to their children, they develop specific analytical strategies which make them ideal participants in a politics focused on peace rather than war. As Ruddick says, a feminist ethic of peace depends on "peacemakers [who] create a communal suspicion of violence, a climate in which peace is desired, a way of living in which it is possible to learn and to practice nonviolent resistance and strategies of reconciliation."[25]

Realism and just war remain the dominant and preferred strategies of American government officials. Yet thinkers and traditions as widely separated in time and space as South Asian Buddhists in antiquity and American feminist philosophers in the twenty-first century show us that, even if war is "natural," it is ethical diversity in response to war—not a uniform, predictable response—that is characteristic of human nature.

Conclusion

If the authors of this essay have been successful, you will have acquired some tools with which to approach international events using perspectives that are usually not articulated within Western scholarship or in US government public policy making. The selections presented demonstrate that many customs present a healthy challenge and an alternative set of paradigms for thinking about ethical issues. As you encounter conflicts in global politics—inside or outside of class—you should now be able to consider each from different ethical perspectives and examine consciously the assumptions you hold about the good life and good government.

Focus Questions

1. What's your reaction to the argument this handout makes: that many of these values are not typically considered in US government decision-making circles? Should they be? Why or why not?

2. This reading argues that many of these attributes and values are expressed by voices in danger of being lost in the swirl of globalization (which some argue is led by the West). Are all of these voices being lost or are some very audible in international discourses of normative issues? If some voices and their values are not represented in international conversations regarding normative issues, what might the costs of this be and to whom? What would be necessary to rectify such a situation? How do you imagine citizens of other countries or value systems may react to the dominance of Western values in international political discourse?

3. Francis Fukuyama wrote a classic post–Cold War political science book, in which he proclaimed that with the demise of the Soviet Union, the West, capitalism, and democracy had won.[26] Without the ideological rivalry of the Cold War and without significant competitors looming on the horizon, we had arrived at the "end of history." Samuel Huntington, on the other hand, saw no such coming cultural convergence by virtue of victory.[27] Instead, he predicted a coming "clash of civilizations" between the West, East Asia, and Islam, because of irreconcilable differences in their mindsets. Moreover, Huntington argued that this clash would be exacerbated by the West's belief that Western culture is universal. Do you support either of these competing predictions about the future of global politics? Why or why not? Do you see the future of global politics as a competition between value systems? If so, which ones?

Student Handout 2:
Comparing Formal Instruments
of the United States and United Nations

In the three sections below, we present articles from critical documents that control UN policy development and clearly echo directly US standards and values set down 200 years before the UN was created at the founding of the United States. When you have read the excerpts, turn to the Web and look quickly through the entire UN Charter. Consider these statements and the Charter as you read Chapters 2 and 3 of LeBaron's *Bridging Cultural Conflicts* in preparation for class. Also consider how well the UN documents demonstrate cultural fluency.

Life and Liberty

The Universal Declaration of Human Rights was formally adopted by the UN General Assembly in 1948. Some features of the document are a virtual echo of US constitutional documents. While this declaration was crafted by people from many countries, the document nonetheless explicitly mimics US political and social values. The first of numerous US/UN parallels is evident in the use of the word "Declaration." Comparing the 1776 American Declaration of Independence and the United Nations Declaration of Human Rights reveals still more.

DECLARATION OF INDEPENDENCE	UNIVERSAL DECLARATION OF HUMAN RIGHTS
We hold these truths to be self-evident, that *all men are created equal*, that they are *endowed* by their Creator with certain inalienable *Rights*, that among these are *Life, Liberty* and the Pursuit of Happiness.	Article 1: *All human beings are born free and equal* in dignity and *rights*. They are *endowed* with reason and conscience and should act towards one another in a spirit of *brotherhood*. Article 3: Everyone has the right to *life, liberty* and security of person.

The UN Declaration describes people as "human beings" rather than "men," but both documents are equally universalist in their claim that "all" "are endowed" with "rights." According to both declarations everyone is entitled to "life" and "liberty." According to the UN, we are also endowed with "reason" and "conscience," qualities of mind highly valued in European and American philosophical traditions. The UN Declaration leaves the question of responsibilities to the community—as opposed to rights—to the very end and makes no more than a very general statement about the issue. Article 29 (1) specifies that "Everyone has duties to the community in which alone the free and full development of his personality is possible," while part (2) of Article 29 states that everyone is subject to limitations on their freedom, solely for the purpose of securing recognition and respect for the rights and freedoms of others.

Church and State

The United States Supreme Court has argued that the purpose of what are called the "religion clauses" in the First Amendment to the US Constitution was "to erect a wall of separation between Church and State." The wall itself has been viewed in numerous ways. For some, it is primarily to protect the Free Exercise rights of citizens. A more conservative view holds that these clauses were to prohibit only the official establishment of a federal-government-sponsored church or government preferences among religious sects and denominations.[28] For still others, the point of Church-State separation is to maintain the secular character of government, or to prevent the corruption of religion with worldly concerns. It is well established, however, that the principle of Church-State separation precludes the US government from declaring an official church or religious denomination.[29] The religion clauses explicitly state that separation is the proper relationship of religion and government. Once again, although the UN Declaration is more detailed than the US Constitution, an echo of this fundamental separatist vision is to be found in the Universal Declaration of Human Rights.

US CONSTITUTION	UNIVERSAL DECLARATION OF HUMAN RIGHTS
Congress shall make no law respecting an establishment of religion, or prohibiting the free exercise thereof.	Article 18: Everyone has the right to freedom of thought, conscience and religion; the right includes freedom to change religion or belief. [And free exercise of religion means the] freedom, either alone or in community with others and in public or private, to manifest his religion or belief in teaching, practice, worship and observance.

Just War Justified

Much Western thinking on international relations and politics accepts the dominant ethical assumption that the use of armed force is necessary to achieve and to maintain peace around the world. The framers of the US Constitution clearly considered war to be a normal part of the business of the state. They spelled out that the power to declare war lies with Congress. They assumed that the citizen must be able to bear arms so as to be an effective member of a militia. The Constitution declares that the President, while serving as the civilian executive, also serves as the Commander in Chief of US military forces. The UN Universal Declaration of Human Rights, the international text we have been focusing on, is silent on war and nonviolence. Still, the UN's founding Charter asserts that even the UN has the right to go to war.

US CONSTITUTION	UNITED NATIONS CHARTER
A well regulated militia being necessary to the security of a free State, the right of the people to keep and bear arms shall not be infringed.	Chapter VII, Article 42: Should the Security Council consider that measures [not involving armed force] provided for in Article 41 would be inadequate or have proved to be inadequate [to maintain or restore international security], it may take such action by air, sea, or land forces as may be necessary to maintain or restore international peace and security. Such action may include demonstrations, blockade, and other operations by air, sea, or land forces of the United Nations.

These two documents are congruent with an ethical perspective technically known as "realism," the dominant US policy since the end of World War II.

Focus Questions

1. Are these provisions better suited to high- or low-context actors? Why? What are the practical implications of your conclusion?
2. Many policy makers today assume that all but "rogue" states share a common list of goods: the preservation of the society of states, state sovereignty, anti-imperialism, the balance of power, patriotism, protecting the interests of one's country, nonintervention, self-determination, international law, collective security, economic sanctions under specific circumstances, the diplomatic system, modernization, economic cooperation, democratic institutions within states, and human rights.[30] Which of these values are expressed in the UN Charter? What are the implications of this? Do these "settled" international norms reflect your values?

Debriefing

Day One/Activity One
Return to the focus questions contained in Student Handout 1. Have students' views changed as a result of the exercise? If so, how?

Day Two/Activity Two
Review students' responses to the focus questions in Handout 2. Discuss: What is your reaction to the argument this handout makes? Should official UN documents be amended to take better account of norms from traditions beyond the Western ones which predominate today?

Selected Bibliography

In Print

Curtin, Deanne. "A State of Mind like Water: Ecosophy and the Buddhist Traditions." From *Chinnagounder's Challenge: The Question of Ecological Citizenship*, 116–135. Bloomington, IN: Indiana University Press, 1999.

Doi, Takeo. "The First Idea of Amae." From *The Anatomy of Dependence*, Translated. John Bester, 11–27. Tokyo: Kodansha International, 1973.

Feldman, Jan. Note: Pages 951–55. From "The Establishment Clause and Religious Influences on Legislation." *NorthWestern University School of Law,* no. 75 (1980): 944–76.

Midgley, Mary. "On Trying Out One's New Sword." From *Heart and Mind: The Varieties of Moral Experience*, 69–75. New York: St. Martin's Press, 1981.

Noddings, Nel. "War." From *Women and Evil*, 178–93. Berkeley, CA: University of California Press, 1989.

Wilson Ross, Nancy. *Buddhism, a Way of Life and Thought*, 58–62. New York, NY: Vintage Books, 1981.

Related Web Sites

www.udhr.org/index.htm *Franklin and Eleanor Roosevelt Institute Web Site*. This site, originally a fiftieth anniversary commemorative site, is now designed as a resource for all those who want to join in the ongoing struggle for human rights.

http://meadev.nic.in/Gandhi1/nonviolence.htm Gandhi's reply to Lajpat
Rai's critical article on his concept of nonviolence in the *Modern Review*
of July 1916.

www.archives.gov/national_archives_experience/declaration.html The
Declaration of Independence and the Constitution as presented by the
US government archives office.

http://etext.lib.virginia.edu/toc/modeng/public/HolKora.html *The Holy Qur'an*,
Electronic Text Center, University of Virginia Library. This university
maintains an online text center with materials from ancient to modern
cultures and all parts of the globe.

www.buddhistnews.tv/ Buddhist News Network. Includes current news
items regarding Buddhism's interaction with government, politics, and
society around the world.

Endnotes

1. David Kang, "Getting Asia Wrong: The Need for New Analytical
Frameworks," *International Security* 27, no. 4 (2003), 57–85 at 58.

2. Raymond Cohen, *Negotiating Across Cultures: International Communication in an Interdependent World,* revised ed. (Washington, DC:
United States Institute of Peace, 1997): 36–37.

3. Cohen, 36–37.

4. In the Buddhist tradition, the Self is thought to be ultimately non-
existent. See Steven Collins, *Selfless Persons: Imagery and Thought in
Theravada Buddhism* (Cambridge, UK: Cambridge University Press,
1982).

5. Ahmed Ali, prepared by, *The Qur'an, 3: 18* (Princeton, NJ: Princeton
University Press, 2001), 70.

6. Juan Mascaro, transl., *The Upanishads* (London: Penguin Classics,
1961), 138–9.

7. Swami C. Bhaktivedanta Prabhupada, transl., *A Bhagavad Gita* (Los
Angeles, CA: The Bhaktivedanta Book Trust, 1983), Section 2.12–13.

8. David Hinton, transl., Confucius, "Villages and Humanity," from *The
Analects* (Washington, DC: Counterpoint Press, 1999), 27.

9. The word Tutu refers to is *ubuntu* from the Nguni group of languages,
and *botho* from the Sotho group of languages. Desmond Tutu, *No Future
Without Forgiveness* (New York: Doubleday, 1999), 31.

10. See Module 8: Truth Commissions.

11. Leslie Marmon Silko, "The People and The Land are Inseparable," from *Yellow Woman and a Beauty of the Spirit, Essays on Native American Life Today* (New York: Simon and Schuster, 1996), 85–91 at 90.

12. F. L. Woodward, ed., *Digha Nikaya (Some Sayings of the Buddha)*, ii. 312 (Oxford, UK: Oxford University Press, World Classics, 1945), 11–13 (with additional language supplied by Robert Aitken Roshi).

13. Sogyal Rinpoche, *The Tibetan Book of Living and Dying* (San Francisco: Harper Collins, 1992), 375.

14. In Germany the state tax system collects, from everyone, a contribution toward the upkeep of the Lutheran Church. The Anglican Church in England and Wales and the Church of Scotland are both parts of the government of the United Kingdom.

15. As the discussion suggests, there is something normative to Islam about having an Islamic state, which is not true of Buddhism. Thus, whereas Islamic states represent the ideal, Buddhist ones are more the result of contingency or coincidence than the outcomes of a prescription or promotion of religious states in Buddhism.

16. John Strong, *The Legend of King Asoka* (Princeton, NJ: Princeton University Press, 1983), 3–4.

17. Mark Jurgensmeyer, "Bhutan," from Stuart Mews, ed., *Religion in Politics: a World Guide* (Chicago, IL: St. James Press, 1989), 23.

18. Duane Cady, *From Warism to Pacifism: A Moral Continuum* (Philadelphia, PA: Temple University Press, 1989), xi–xii.

19. The editors, "On Just Wars: An Interview with Michael Walzer." *Tikkun* 6, no. 1 (1991), 40–42.

20. Mahatma Gandhi, "The Practice of Satyagraha," from Ronald Duncan, ed., *Gandhi: Selected Writings* (New York: Harper & Row, 1971), 73–78.

21. His Holiness the Dalai Lama, *Ethics for the New Millennium* (New York: Riverhead Books, 1999), 201–7.

22. These paragraphs have been taken from Lucinda Peach, "An Alternative to Pacifism? Feminism and Just-War Theory." *Hypatia* 9, no. 2 (1994), 152–72.

23. Cynthia Enloe, *Manuevers: the International Politics of Militarizing Women's Lives* (Berkeley, CA: University of California Press, 1999), 1–2, 32–33.

24. Sarah Ruddick, *Maternal Thinking: Towards a Politics of Peace* (Boston, MA: Beacon Press, 1989), 220–21, 238–239.

25. Ruddick, 244.

26. Francis Fukuyama, *The End of History and the Last Man* (New York: Free Press, 1992).

27. Samuel Huntington, *The Clash of Civilizations and the Remaking of the World Order* (New York: Simon and Schuster, 1996).

28. *Everson v. Board of Education,* 330 US 1, 15–16 (1947); 435 US 618, 637 (1991) (Brennan, J., concurring).

29. Scholarly evidence suggests that there are multiple traditions represented in the Constitution rather than a single one, with widely differing interpretations of what the framer's aspirations were for the religion clauses of the First Amendment. The intentions of the Constitution's framers have been used to support narrow as well as liberal interpretations of the scope of the religion clauses. The history of the debates over the Bill of Rights indicates that some of the framers were concerned about the religious tyranny that could result from religious institutions having access to the reins of government.

30. This particular list is more fully developed in Mervyn Frost, *Ethics in International Relations: A Constitutive Theory* (Cambridge, UK: Cambridge University Press, 1996); see Chapter 4.

PART TWO

PROBLEM-SOLVING IN ETHICS AND GLOBAL POLITICS

THE USE OF
ARMED FORCE
IN CONFLICT

What's So Unique About the Nuclear Era?

April Morgan

About This Module

A former department head tells the story of a graduate student who focused so much on the contemporary significance of Thucydides in a comprehensive exam that during the follow-up oral exam, the professor asked the student if *anything* had changed in international relations since Thucydides' time (471–400 BC). The student responded, "No." The professor gave him a second chance by probing, "Nothing at all?" The student reflected a moment, but stuck to his guns. "No, not really." The professor pounced, "Wrong!" and proceeded to cite a litany of changes in intercultural relations since 400 BC. Nuclear weapons were at the top of his list, because of their incredible destructive power.

One of the key purposes of this exercise is to encourage students to grapple with the drama and significance of nuclear weapons in view of *their* personal values. As Antwone Fisher says near the end of his autobiography, "A person's natural language...is the electricity of his or her soul, and to disconnect it is to shut them down."[1] With this in mind, this activity requires students to identify and articulate their own values in their "natural languages," in the hopes that this will encourage them to connect with the issue.

When students have completed this module, they should be able to answer these questions:

1. Was the use of atomic weapons in 1945 consistent with *your personal values*? Why or why not?
2. Do you think *your* goals and values *should* guide such policy decisions? Why or why not?
3. What is the legacy of this action for the *future*?

Miniglossary

Rationality Rationality as a term of art in international relations comes from economic definitions of "rational" as "efficient." According to economist Anthony Downs,

> whenever economists refer to a "rational man" they are not designating a man whose thought processes consist exclusively of logical propositions or a man without prejudices, or a man whose emotions are inoperative. In normal usage, all of these could be considered rational men. But the economic definition refers solely to a man who moves toward his goals in a way, which, to the best of his knowledge, *uses the least possible input of scarce resources per unit of valued output*...Rationality thus defined refers to processes of action, not to their ends or even to their success at reaching desired ends.[2]

Nuclear weapons The nuclear age had begun in 1945 when the United States detonated two atomic bombs over Hiroshima and Nagasaki, Japan to bring about the end of World War II. While nuclear weapons have evolved in design and power over the ensuing sixty years, their explosive energy continues to be derived from chain reactions within the atom's nucleus (typically a combination of fusion and fission). These weapons represent more than a technological advance in military might, because in a worst-case scenario involving all-out global nuclear war, their unparalleled destructive power threatens human survival.

Step-by-Step Directions

On the first day of class, I have students fill out an index card with name, e-mail address, year in school, and major. (I use this information to learn their names.) On the back of this card, I ask them to list and rank the seven values or principles by which they live their everyday lives. The utility of this is threefold:

1. No one's values are left out, because they insert whatever values they choose into the equation (rather than being directed to utilize a given set of values).
2. It gives them an immediate stake in the activity, because it's all about them.
3. It helps them create or recognize a philosophy of life, and thus achieve a common goal many students declare they want to fulfill through college.

Whatever their frameworks (or mixes thereof), I emphasize that they must be as specific as possible in presenting these principles. Simply saying "faith" is not sufficient; they have to explain how they define these concepts in daily practice in a couple of sentences that enable me to understand what these words mean to them.

These values run the gamut; they range from religious to antireligious, from politics to the movies. Some students have said, "Violence is unacceptable, except in self-defense." "Show me the money!" "Stick to your commitments." "There is no one concrete truth." "Individual property rights." They then write a sentence on how they have applied these principles in the real world. I keep these cards for the semester and we refer back to them from time to time.

As we go through the first third of the term, I present the major philosophical frameworks in international relations and explain rational choice theory's cost/benefit analysis in detail, so that students can walk through its essential steps in any decision-making situation. We practice this methodology by recalling the primary values they listed on the index cards and by analyzing the rationality of specific policy and personal choices in pursuit of these goals. Are their actions cost-effective means to fulfill stated goals? Does their behavior suggest that they're really actualizing different goals from those stated, ends other than what they said they were going after? Are they rational or irrational actors? Then we apply the technique to state behavior.

In the second third of the term, we cover conflict and discuss nuclear weapons. At the end of this section, a written assignment is due in which students evaluate the rationality of dropping atomic bombs on Japan in 1945, given *their* stated goals as ranked on the index cards (or modified as they see fit by this time; there is no reason to hold them to their original statements). Although students initially list seven primary values to jump-start their thinking on this subject, the paper portion works best when students focus on only one or two of them, which they must explicitly identify. This exercise is *not* a rehash of Truman's decision; rather, it is an opportunity for them to decide what they would have done and why.

I direct them to the most comprehensive Web site I have found that presents original documents detailing everything we think we know about President Truman's decision to drop these bombs. There, students scan firsthand accounts of nuclear tests, read passages from Truman's diary, and evaluate casualty estimates of other alternatives. Then, instead of critiquing Truman's decision, they analyze the cost-effectiveness of the use of nuclear weapons to achieve *their* goals in global politics, and come to a conclusion as to whether or not this would have been rational *for them*. They write this assignment as a three- to five-page paper. Although they protest, I find that shorter papers make for better products in this case. Otherwise, they drift toward descriptive, historical narratives that do not satisfy the assignment's criteria. The page limit also provides excellent practice in editing one's own work.

In the process, students practice a simplified version of rational choice methodology, confront the reality of one type of weapon of mass destruction, and evaluate the appropriateness of inserting individual goals into national security decision-making processes. Above all, this activity tries *not* to tell students what to think of this watershed event and to create a space for them to reach their own conclusions. When students claim that the Web site I have chosen is biased, I challenge them to find (or create) better ones, and discuss the importance of evaluating the legitimacy of Web sites for research.

Student Handout: Atomic Bomb Paper

Go to this *required reading* Web site:
    www.dannen.com/decision/index.html
Optional Web site:
    www.cia.gov/csi/monograph/4253605299/csi9810001.html
These Web sites house many of the publicly available documents related
to the decision to use atomic bombs on Hiroshima and Nagasaki, Japan. By
reading what is presented on these sites, you can:

- Scan eyewitness accounts of the Trinity Test.
- Read what people who were responsible for deciding to bomb and for
  dropping the bombs had to say.
- See the official order, and listen to an excerpt of President
  Truman's radio speech announcing the decision to drop the bomb.
- Evaluate casualty estimates of possible alternative scenarios.

Ponder and critically evaluate this information thoroughly. Then write a
three- to five-page paper in which you *analyze this event based on your personal values.* The purposes of this exercise are for you to learn the empirical facts about this unique occurrence and to reach your own opinion about
*whether or not this action helped the United States achieve your personal
goals.*
    This paper conforms to a specific format. *Follow these steps:*

1. State seven principles or goals that guide your life choices. Be specific.
   Name each. Explain what it means to you.
2. Rank them from 1 to 7, in which 1 is your highest priority/most
   important goal and 7 is your lowest priority/least important goal.
3. Based on your interpretation of the ability of these bombings to
   achieve your stated goals, answer these three questions:

   - Was dropping these bombs "rational," *given your primary (top
     one or two) stated goals?* Did it promote or demote the achieve-
     ment of your goals?
   - Should the United States have dropped these bombs? Why or
     why not?
   - If not, what should the United States have done differently?
     How would this alternative path have achieved your goals?
     Why is it preferable to the bombings?

Some questions you may find useful to ask yourself in order to develop your
thinking and follow it through to its logical conclusions may include:

- Do you think your goals and values should *guide* such policy decisions? Why or why not?
- What is the legacy of this action for the *future?* If you arrive at a conclusion, hypothesis, lesson, or the creation of a new school of thought about world affairs, articulate it here.
- Did the United States know—at any level—about the long-term implications of this use of nuclear weapons?
- Was Truman honest and accurate in describing Hiroshima as a military base?
- Was *unconditional* surrender necessary?
- Was the second bomb necessary?
- Why was there no demonstration or warning of the use of nuclear weapons?
- Why were civilians targeted?
- Can there be any justifiable reason to abandon your seven values in the global arena?
- How do you justify the selection of the standards you use to determine an outcome here?
- Under what circumstances would you condone this action in the future?
- What is the legacy of this act for international relations? Was it a change for the better?
- How does your position intersect with the schools of thought we have studied thus far in international relations?
- Do you see evidence of a denial psychosis in your thinking and/or research?
- Why don't companion Web sites on the Japanese decision-making process exist?
- What does your conclusion tell you about this question: Do you really live your life by the values you say you do?

Be careful *not* to write a historical narrative of why Truman reached his decision. Rather, the focus here is on what *you* would have decided (given your values and goals) and why. Be sure to look forward as well as backward in your paper. Analysis of your values, goals, and philosophy is essential.

Your paper must include all appropriate footnotes. Remember that footnotes are necessary for direct quotations from others, paraphrasing of others, and any information (facts, lines of argument, analysis, etc.) that is not common knowledge or the result of your own experience or thought. Any paper that does not contain adequate indication of source material (footnotes) will be considered incomplete. The maximum grade such a paper can receive is a C, and an F may be given.

Debriefing

Instead of using prescripted discussion questions, I have students read aloud passages I select (and highlight) from their papers to the rest of the class after they have been graded. (I first ask for permission; some students prefer not to read their own works, but don't mind if I do.) Some of these papers are poignant. One young woman interviewed her grandmother about her grandfather's capture by the Japanese during WWII. She learned how handicapped her entire family was by his absence while he was held as a prisoner of war in inhumane conditions. Her paper explained that, since her primary goal would have been to bring her grandfather home alive as soon as possible, she would have dropped the bombs without a second thought. It was personal for her rather than a hypothetical historical question. National security was not her top concern; getting her grandfather home as soon as possible was.

One key to success in this stage is to emphasize to students that this phase of the activity is about listening, not criticizing. It's about paying attention to how someone with different values and/or goals may reach what is technically a perfectly rational decision, even if the decision seems absurd to others. This stage is key to international relations, because it has the power to demonstrate that those who behave in ways that may initially appear crazy or evil to us may actually be quite sane. Thus, what begins as a lesson in self-knowledge can become a lesson in otherness/difference without descending into demonization.

Moreover, once students see the way their peers have applied different values to the same process, they can apply values explained in Toolkits 2 and 3 by asking, "How might someone who prioritizes *these* values perceive the outcome differently?" These variations on a theme can be conducted as class discussions or as 5-minute reaction papers at the end of class, in which everyone writes for 5 minutes on a given topic. These extensions give them all a chance to have their say. They might also engage in online discussion with Japanese students. Once such pluralism is introduced, students may move toward development of a global theory of mind.

Selected Bibliography

In Print

Beckman, Peter, Paul Crumlish, Michael Dobkowski, Steven Lee, eds., *The Nuclear Predicament: Nuclear Weapons in the Twenty-first Century,* 3rd ed. (New York: Council on Foreign Relations, 2000).

Bundy, William, *The Nuclear Controversy* (New York: Council on Foreign Relations, 1981).

Fisher, Antwone. *Finding Fish* (New York: Perennial/HarperCollins Publishers, 2001).

Related Web Sites

www.nukefix.org Detailed, award-winning game that prompts students to solve the nuclear dilemma in an updated threat environment. Free to download and play. Appropriate for advanced students with some prior knowledge of global politics and weapons of mass destruction, as well as analytical skill. Time required to complete the game is equivalent to that of a research paper (at least several weeks).

www.thebulletin.org Home of *The Bulletin of Atomic Scientists*. View the Doomsday Clock.

www.ceip.org/files/nonprolif/map/default.asp The Carnegie Endowment for International Peace maintains an interactive nuclear status map.

Endnotes

1. Antwone Fisher, *Finding Fish* (New York: Perennial/HarperCollins Publishers, 2000), 291.

2. Anthony Downs, *An Economic Theory of Democracy* (New York: Harper & Row, 1957), 5–6. Italics mine.

Just War Theory and the 2003 War Against Iraq

Gabriel Palmer-Fernandez

About This Module

It is my firm conviction that teaching the ethics of war is essential for responsible democratic citizenship for at least two reasons. First, unlike other kinds of political regimes, in a democratic republic the business of war cannot be left to the military. For us, war is or ought to be a common undertaking and a shared responsibility. That responsibility is discharged when citizens are informed of the justice of a particular war waged by the government or when they become soldiers fighting in a just war. Second, when at war, the goal of victory is so crucially important that we can easily lose sight of how we gain it. The military can and does engage in excesses of power that sometimes corrupt the justice of a war. The massacre at My Lai in the Vietnam War and the killing of some five thousand retreating Iraqi troops on the road to Basra in the 1991 Persian Gulf War are two prominent examples.[1] Public debate informed by just war theory (JWT) on when we may wage war and how we win is a significant obligation of democratic citizenship.

This module aims to introduce students to the principles of JWT and enable application of those principles to the 2003 Iraq War. It also contains module options, which allow students to apply JWT to the War on Terror and to the 1991 Persian Gulf War. When utilized in its most complete form with these options, this module takes approximately four to five class days and time outside class to complete a short reflection paper.

Upon completion of this module in either the short or long form, students should be able to:

1. identify, articulate, and evaluate the basic moral principles of JWT.
2. explain how those principles apply to the war against Iraq.
3. defend their judgments on the justice of that war.

In effect, students will be able to respond to two questions: What are the basic principles of JWT? Was the 2003 war in Iraq justified by those principles?

The module is designed for any level of undergraduate instruction. It assumes no prior knowledge of JWT, ethics, or military history. Nor is the relevance of the module restricted to courses in ethics, whether in philosophy or religious studies, global politics, or political science. It is, I believe, of practical use in a wide range of courses, including twentieth-century history, critical thinking, English composition, and current events, among others.

Miniglossary

Jus ad bellum A Latin phrase meaning justice in going to (or resorting to) war. A set of moral principles establishing *when* it is permissible or obligatory to wage war. It includes: just cause, right intention, legitimate authority, formal declaration, reasonable hope of success, last resort, and proportionality (different from *jus in bello* proportionality, in that it considers the balance of good over evil consequences that will result from the political objective sought by going to war).

Jus in bello A Latin phrase meaning justice in war. A set of moral principles establishing *how* war should be fought. It includes proportionality (determining that the amount of destruction permissible must be proportionate to the value of the military objective sought) and noncombatant immunity.

Terrorism Threat or act of violence against a civilian population in pursuit of a political objective. Thus defined, terrorism can take a variety of forms: state or enforcement terrorism (to repress domestic opposition to the established political regime); revolutionary terrorism (to change the established political regime); war terrorism (to compel the civilian population to oppose its government participation in a war); and, more recently, religious terrorism (partly or wholly motivated by religious beliefs).

Step-by-Step Directions

Reading to be Completed Outside of Class Prior to Day One

Before introducing JWT, it is important to present, even if only briefly, two perspectives that frequently compete with it: realism (see Toolkits 1 and 3 and the article "Political Realism" in the *Internet Encyclopedia of Philosophy* [*IEP*] at www.iep.utm.edu/p/polreal.htm) and pacifism (see Toolkit 3 and the article "Pacifism" in the IEP at www.iep.utm.edu/p/pacifism.htm). The view known as the just war theory lies between the extremes of realism and pacifism. It takes the position that in some cases war is necessary to protect important moral goods. In my experience, some students endorse variations of both realism and pacifism. Awareness of these intellectual predispositions enables students to more fully appreciate why they take the positions they do on JWT.

Day One: Film

As many students will have no direct experience of war, a good film can illustrate some of war's realities and provide a common framework for reflection and discussion. I have used fictional and documentary films. Of the former, these range from the surreal to the historical: *Apocalypse Now* and *All Quiet on the Western Front* respectively. I prefer the latter type. The PBS Frontline documentary, *Remember My Lai* is powerful and very conducive to our purposes. It describes events leading to the massacre at My Lai and shows interviews with Vietnamese survivors and American soldiers, including some who on grounds of conscience refused to engage in the atrocities.

My experience with using films in class is that students are rarely ready to comment on the film immediately after viewing it. Some time to digest it seems necessary. View the film prior to class and make notes on issues you wish to raise.

Day Two: Students Generate Moral Principles of War

On this day, students generate their own moral principles of war. Begin with a moral language they already know, the language of rights. Just as people have certain basic rights—for example, to life, liberty, and self-defense—so, too, states have similar rights—for example, to territorial integrity and political sovereignty. To defend those rights, states have a right to war. Michael Walzer's classic text, *Just and Unjust Wars,* takes this language of rights as its point of departure. But the exercise of the right to war must be justified; that is, it requires strong, compelling reasons.

First, have students think about and discuss those reasons that, *according to them*, might be sufficiently strong and compelling to justify war. Students are to respond to the question, What, if any, conditions justify waging war? They can work either in one large group or several small ones. I prefer the latter, as it puts more responsibility on them and frequently aids in getting discussion started. Either way, I write on the board students' responses, and have them explain what they mean by them. No proposal is excluded. Then their suggestions are tested and pruned. What reasons support a particular principle? What might be the consequences of adopting each principle on a global basis? Should all states conduct themselves in wartime in accordance to it? In responding to these questions, students articulate and defend in their own manners what the theory has referred to as *jus ad bellum* since its most formative period in the Middle Ages. My experience is that most students come up with ideas that are functionally equivalent to the principles of the theory.

Next, move to how we ought to fight wars. Here, having viewed a film, particularly a historical one and especially a documentary like *Remember My Lai*, is of great value. If this or some other suitable film is not available, you and students can access the companion Web site for the PBS/WGBH series, *Vietnam: A Television History* at www.pbs.org/wgbh/amex/vietnam/index.html. What was it about My Lai that made it a massacre and not an act of war? What made the killing of several hundred women, children, and old men a crime and not an act of war? The discussion now has to move to more general questions. Are there in war legitimate and illegitimate acts of killing? How do we distinguish between them? Or is all killing in war of one and the same kind? By engaging students in a discussion of how we ought to fight wars, they begin to think about and discover the moral principles of the theory specified under the heading *jus in bello*.

Day Three: Just War Theory and Iraq 2003

Any Web search for just war theory will provide the student with a wealth of information on the theory (my last search brought up over sixteen thousand sites). But not all of the information on the Web is of equal quality. I strongly recommend that students access the article on JWT in the *IEP* at www.utm.edu/research/icp/j/justwar.htm (an alternative and equally useful article on just war theory is found in *Stanford Encyclopedia of Philosophy* at http://plato.stanford.edu/entries/war/#2 or the brief outline provided by the Pew Foundation at http://pewforum.org/issues). Prior to the third day of this module, students read at least two articles outside of class: 1.) *IEP*'s online definition of JWT and 2.) "Just War Theory and Iraq: A Symposium" at http://pewforum.org/events.

In Student Handout 1 I summarize JWT's principles according to the standard division of *jus ad bellum* and *jus in bello*. Photocopy Handout 1 prior to class and distribute this recap at the beginning of Day Three. Then, on a sheet of paper, students develop for each of the principles a two-column list of Permissions and Prohibitions; that is, what is permitted and what is prohibited by each of those principles. For example, under the *jus ad bellum* principle of Just Cause, the column under Permission obviously includes self-defense and the column under Prohibition likely lists colonial expansion. Ideally, there will be significant overlap between some of the principles of the theory and some of the student's own reflections articulated during the prior class discussion. Discussion and comparison of the students' and theory's principles is encouraged.

Next, students apply the principles of JWT to the 2003 war against Iraq by drawing on the symposium material.[2] Begin by asking which speakers they agree with and why. Look for reasons that support the students' opinions, which are grounded on principles of JWT (i.e., help them translate their opinions into the JWT framework). Finally, the assumptions accepted by the four panelists should be questioned. At the time of this writing there is no evidence to support the panelists' assumptions. No chemical or biological weapons have been found in Iraq. No direct connection with al-Qaeda has been established. If, then, Iraq posed no imminent threat to the United States or its allies, is that war unjustified according to JWT? Why or why not?

OPTIONAL ADDITIONAL ACTIVITY: APPLYING JUST WAR THEORY TO THE 1991 PERSIAN GULF WAR

You may want to introduce an additional activity here. The conditions leading to the 1991 Persian Gulf War against Iraq were quite different. Iraq had invaded Kuwait, the Security Council of the United Nations authorized military action against Iraq, and there was a broad international coalition against Iraqi aggression. The value of introducing the 1991 war is that the conditions leading to the war appear compatible with just war principles. Nonetheless, some argued that in spite of the clear just cause this was not a just war, as not all diplomatic means of resolving the conflict had been exhausted. In the Selected Bibliography I provide three Web sites that are useful for this purpose.

Day Four: Extending the Analysis to Terrorism and the War on Terror

One of the primary reasons initially given in support of the war against Iraq was its alleged connection with terrorism in general and al-Qaeda in particular. While that connection is now largely regarded as false, we should nonetheless explore terrorism and its (im)morality.

The first task to undertake is definitional. At the end of the third class, challenge students to reflect on these questions: 1.) What is terrorism? and 2.) How does it differ from war? They may access material from the Web outside of class to prompt their thinking.[3] Alternatively or additionally, you may choose to photocopy and distribute Student Handout 2 to provide some background. Then on day four, students compare the differences, if any, between terrorism and war. They may compare, for example, the kind of social organizations that engage in terrorism and those that engage in war, their respective tactics, the targets they select, whether the way they conduct their hostilities is in accordance with *jus in bello* principles, and whether terrorists should be considered combatants or something else.

Next, students apply just war principles to determine whether terrorism is a kind of political violence that can be morally justified by those principles. A straight application of the principles will yield a negative answer, as terrorism intentionally targets noncombatants. Here you may wish to push the theory and inquire whether there are any circumstances in which noncombatants may intentionally be killed. One possible justification Michael Walzer presents is the doctrine of supreme emergency. If the obliteration (also called "terror") bombing of German cities during the early years of World War II was justified, might terrorism be justified under similar circumstances? Why or why not?

This four-class module is capped by the completion of a short reflection paper that allows students to synthesize the material presented over these four days. Students write a five-page paper that either critically evaluates one or more of the theory's principles or applies some principle(s) of the theory to the war against Iraq or terrorism. Student Handout 3 can be photocopied and distributed at the end of day four to lay down the guidelines of this assignment, *or* you may include these directions directly in the class syllabus (under course requirements, for example).

Student Handout 1

Moral Principles of Just War Theory

The requirements of just war theory divide into two sections: the *jus ad bellum* (when it is just to resort to war) and the *jus in bello* (how just wars may be fought). All of the specific moral principles contained in these two categories must be satisfied to establish that a particular war is just.

Jus Ad Bellum

Just Cause War may be waged only to correct a prior injury, to protect sovereign territory or political integrity, or to defeat an imminent threat, that is, for self-defense or to prevent humanitarian abuses. But just cause—while necessary—is not alone sufficient to justify war, unless the remaining principles are met.

Legitimate Authority Gives authority to wage war to the sovereign of a properly constituted government. Private individuals or others who are not legitimate representatives of a community never have this authority. This principle does allow for revolutionary insurrection, where a government has lost its legitimacy, giving the authority to wage war to extragovernmental bodies such as a revolutionary council.

Reasonable Hope of Success Even when there is a just cause for war, there must be relative confidence of achieving the legitimate goals of war. A small and militarily weak nation is unlikely to have any success against a militarily powerful state. The deaths and other evils unleashed by a war lacking this principle will then prove futile in bringing about justice.

Right Intention While just cause refers to an injury or wrong committed by one state against another, right intention refers to the legitimate motives for war. Accordingly, one may wage war with the intention to defend the territorial integrity of one's state, having suffered unjust aggression. But one may not wage war with the intention to dominate or annihilate the enemy state, or out of vengeance, lust of power or violence, or racial or religious animosity.

Formal Declaration A public and formal declaration of war allows the offending nation an opportunity to redress the injury it caused or the wrong it committed. It also specifies the reasons that justify war and assures that it is not being waged by private initiative.

Proportionality As war will unleash many evils (for example, death of soldiers and civilians, destruction of property, possible further instability in international affairs), it is necessary to weigh them against the value of justice. For example, a minor violation against the territorial integrity of one nation will hardly justify a major defensive war. But the evils that such a war will unleash might be justified when the violation is an invasion of one's territory.

Last Resort Meeting the above principles is not sufficient to declare a particular war just. Prior to waging war all nonviolent diplomatic mechanisms of resolving conflict must be exhausted. Those mechanisms include bilateral or multilateral negotiations, as well as regional or international bodies, for example, the Organization of American States or the United Nations respectively.

Jus In Bello

Noncombatant Immunity Noncombatants are civilians, that is, persons who are not involved in waging war; for example, educators, students, bakers, nurses, lawyers, children, the elderly, and the infirm. As they are not soldiers involved in waging war, intentionally killing them is prohibited and, some argue, morally equivalent to murder. This principle limits the extent of permissible destruction and prohibits total war, that is, war without the distinction between soldiers and civilians.

Proportionality Similar to *jus ad bellum* proportionality requiring a weighing or balancing of values. But here proportionality applies to battlefield tactics, limiting the permissible level of destruction to what is strictly necessary to meet a legitimate military objective. It weighs the harm or evils caused by a particular military tactic against its expected military advantage.

Student Handout 2:
On Terrorism

The term "terrorism" is notoriously difficult to define, and nearly every author who has written about it goes to some length to define it. Alex Schmid, in his excellent survey, *Political Terrorism: A Research Guide*,[4] devoted over one hundred pages to examining more than a hundred definitions of terrorism. Official US government definitions do not wholly agree with each other. For example, the State Department defines terrorism in accordance with Title 22 of the United States Code, Section 2656f(d): "premeditated, politically motivated violence perpetrated against noncombatant targets by subnational groups or clandestine agents, usually intended to influence an audience." The FBI, on the other hand, defines terrorism as "the unlawful use of force or violence against persons or property to intimidate or coerce a Government, the civilian population, or any segment thereof, in furtherance of political or social objectives." The US Department of Defense defines terrorism as "the unlawful use of—or threatened use of—force or violence against individuals or property to coerce or intimidate governments or societies, often to achieve political, religious, or ideological objectives." The USA Patriot Act, passed by Congress in October 2001, gives yet a different definition.

The history of the term itself is hardly useful in providing an explanatory definition. It was first coined in the 1790s among the Jacobins. In 1798 the supplement to the *Dictionnaire* of the Académie Francaise defined terrorism as a "system of terror," referring to the period in the French Revolution between March 1793 and July 1794. The first English-language use of the word dates from 1795, and was used to describe a mode of governing or type of action by the state to suppress political dissent. There is further historical evidence of the use of this word to describe actions by states that include arbitrary arrest, torture, and execution of their own citizens. This meaning is retained in *Webster's New International Dictionary* (2nd edition), where terrorism is defined as "a state of intense fear by the systematic use of violent means by a party or faction, as bloodshed, imprisonment, and confiscation to maintain itself in power."

By the late nineteenth century, the meaning of the word had undergone significant change. Anarchist movements in Russia, France, Spain, Italy, and the United States employed violence as a means to effect domestic political change. Here, terrorism is a way of fighting rather than governing, and its use seems to have been restricted to the assassination of highly placed political figures. There was during this period hardly a trace of indiscriminate violence against civilian populations. On the contrary, an important feature of terrorism during this period was the attempt to arouse the spirit of revolt among a people. This understanding of terrorism continued well into the twentieth century. In Hardman's 1934 entry in the *Encyclopedia of the Social Sciences,* indiscriminate violence was not yet a feature of terrorism: "Terrorist acts are directed against persons who as individuals, agents, or representatives of authority interfere with the consummation of the objectives of a [revolutionary] group."[5]

It was during the Second World War, perhaps as early as 1940, that terrorism emerged in its present form as a way of fighting by acts of indiscriminate violence, with the aim of intimidating, creating fear, and undermining the morale of a population. The paradigm case is the intentional indiscriminate bombing of German cities, where it was thought that subjecting large segments of the population to the terror of aerial bombardment would produce domestic unrest and widespread opposition to the war. The use of terror by revolutionary groups in the past few decades differs from indiscriminate aerial bombardment only in degree, not in kind. They both aim for the same goal: to undermine civilian morale and arouse political opposition by random killing and other acts of indiscriminate violence.[6]

In spite of the lack of agreement on the meaning of terrorism, it is possible to identify several features of this kind of violence that may contribute to an explanatory definition. First, terrorism always targets civilian populations (or their property). Second, it seeks to have an effect on a group much larger than its victims. And third, the effect it seeks to have is political.

In view of just war theory, terrorism presents at least two important moral problems. The more prominent is the intentional use of indiscriminate violence, that is, willfully targeting civilian populations. The principle of noncombatant immunity explicitly condemns the practice. A strict application of the principle will judge terrorism as murder. Some will argue, however, that such is the nature of modern war and cite as examples the bombing of German cities, the fire bombing of Tokyo, and nuclear bombing of Hiroshima and Nagasaki. If a powerful state is justified in using indiscriminate violence against civilians in wartime, so too may groups use that kind of violence to defend themselves or to overthrow an unjust regime.

The second problem is the requirement of legitimate authority. Just war theory distinguishes war from private violence by requiring the declaration of war by the sovereign of the state. Since most, if not all, terrorism groups (for example, the Basque ETA, Irish IRA, Palestinian Hamas, and al-Qaeda) are subnational, they lack a sovereign and so fail to meet this requirement. Indeed, any violence by groups other than states is, by this account, immoral. But why should it be so? Is violence by states of an entirely different moral quality from violence by nonstate groups? Surely, some will argue, if violence is, under specific conditions, justified between states, then it is hard, under similar conditions, to extend the justification to other types of groups.

Student Handout 3:
The Capstone Paper

Write a five-page paper that either (i) critically evaluates one or more of the theory's principles or (ii) applies some principle(s) of the theory to the war against Iraq or to terrorism. Reflecting upon some of the questions below may assist you in developing your thoughts for this assignment.

Just Cause

- Is the threat of aggression by another state a just cause for war?
- What are the necessary conditions of a threat? How imminent must the threat be?
- Does the right of self-defense (clearly a just cause) allow for preemptive war?
- Did the United States have a just cause for war against Iraq?
- May a state wage war in order to secure resources (for example, oil, gas) necessary to its way of life?

Legitimate Authority

- Is United Nations approval necessary to wage war for collective security?
- If such approval is not secured and a state wages war against another, shall that war be considered a war of aggression?
- Does that war of aggression give the victim state the right of self-defense?

Last Resort

- How extensive must diplomatic and other nonviolent means of conflict resolution be explored before reaching the point of last resort?
- By your account, was the point of last resort reached prior to waging war against Iraq?
- Must the enemy's armies be at our borders before the point of last resort is reached?

Discrimination

- Is the deliberate killing of civilians in war always prohibited by this principle?
- How should we draw the difference between soldiers (who are legitimate targets of death) and civilians (who are not)? Is a cook in an army unit a legitimate target, while the farmer who raises the food he cooks is not?

- May infrastructure and other so-called "dual-use" targets (electric power plants, sewage treatment facilities, water purification plants, bridges) be directly targeted, or are they prohibited civilian objects protected by this principle?[7]

Proportionality

- Suppose you reasonably expect that more civilians than soldiers will be killed in a war. Would that war be judged unjust by this principle?
- The principle of double-effect allows for unintended, sometimes also called collateral, civilians deaths. Are those civilian deaths still allowable when one foresees that very large numbers of such deaths are inevitable in modern war?
- Where is the point at which civilian deaths become disproportionate?

Debriefing

My experience is that careful reflection can sometimes alter and at other times strengthen one's original position on a particular issue. This has happened to me personally, and I have observed it in many of my students. Moral reflection is, I believe, an exciting and frequently threatening process. We discover new ways of thinking that may require us to abandon deeply held views. This process is all the more acute when we commit our thoughts to writing.

After I have graded students' papers, I use a follow-up discussion to create further learning opportunities. I ask, for example, if students' original positions on the paper's topic changed. If so, I ask them to describe some of those changes and explain what may have caused them. If not, I ask why not? Did the application of just war theory confirm their original opinion of the war? How did they arrive at that original opinion? Perhaps a student's original opinion of the war was neither altered nor confirmed, because that student finds the theory in some way irrelevant or meaningless. If this or something similar is the case, that student's view is explored.

There are other questions which can be pursued here. The application of just war principles will not necessarily motivate the same conclusion. There is likely to be disagreement among those who employ the same theory. How does this happen? And, when there is disagreement, how might it be resolved? Can we achieve agreement on moral issues?

Selected Bibliography

In Print

Coady, Tony and Michael O'Keefe. *Terrorism and Justice.* Melbourne: Melbourne University Press, 2001.

Johnson, James T., *Just War Tradition and the Restraint of War.* Princeton: Princeton University Press, 1981.

Kelsay, John. *Islam and War: A Study in Comparative Ethics.* Louisville, KY: Westminster/John Knox Press, 1993.

McKeogh, Colm. *Innocent Civilians: The Morality of Killing in War.* New York: Palgrave, 2002.

Miller, Richard B., *Interpretations of Conflict: Ethics, Pacifism, and the Just-War Tradition.* Chicago: University of Chicago Press, 1991.

Palmer-Fernandez, Gabriel, ed., *Encyclopedia of Religion and War.* New York: Routledge, 2003.

Related Web Sites

www.pbs.org/wgbh/pages/frontline/gulf On 1991 Persian Gulf War.

www.pbs.org/wgbh/pages/frontline/shows/iraq On 2003 war against Iraq.

www.pbs.org/wgbh/pages/frontline/shows/longroad On 1991 and 2003 wars against Iraq.

Endnotes

1. While the massacre at My Lai has received significant debate, the attack on the retreating convoy on the road to Basra has not. On the morality of that attack, see Martin L. Cook and Phillip A. Harmann, "The Road to Basra: A Case Study in Military Ethics," *Annual of the Society of Christian Ethics* (1994) and my "White Flags on the Road to Basra," *Journal of Social Philosophy* 32:2 (Summer 2001): 143–156.

2. The best companion site I have found for this purpose is from the Pew Foundation site entitled "Just War Theory and Iraq: A Symposium," at www.pewforum.org/events. It contains the transcript of remarks made by four prominent scholars: Gerard Bradley, William Galston, John Kelsay, and Michael Walzer. All of them endorse some version of the just war theory. The symposium was held on September 30, 2002, prior to the war against Iraq. It assumes, for the sake of discussion, that Iraq did possess chemical and biological weapons and, given its history of aggression, that it might use them in the future or make them available to terrorists.

3. To address the first question, I recommend www.askasia.org/teachers/Instructional_Resources/FEATURES/AmericasCrisis/BG1/whatisterrorism.htm. It outlines some of the problems with defining terrorism, and provides a few definitions. A useful, though controversial definition is Brian Jenkins's found atwww.csmonitor.com/specials/terrorism/expert_text. html.

4. Alex P. Schmid, *Political Terrorism: A Research Guide* (New Brunswick, NJ: Transaction Books, 1984).

5. Quoted in Walter Laqueur, *Terrorism* (Boston: Little, Brown and Company, 1977), 135.

6. The paragraphs on the history of terrorism are abridged from my "Justifying Political Assassination: Michael Collins and the Cairo Gang," *Journal of Social Philosophy*, 31:2 (Summer 2000): 160–176.

7. According to one study conducted by the Harvard University School of Public Health, some one hundred seventy thousand children under the age of five were predicted to die in Iraq within one year of the 1991 Persian Gulf War from the delayed effects of bombing infrastructure targets. "Harvard Study Team: Public Health in Iraq After the Gulf War," May 1991, unpublished ms.

The Drama of International Relations

Helena Meyer-Knapp

About This Module

International relations courses traditionally immerse students in the structural elements of theory and include a judicious mixture of case examples to demonstrate the accuracy of the theoretical models. As a result, students can identify and characterize state actors, and many also learn a good deal about dramatic turning points in history (see, for example, Module 1: What's So Unique about the Nuclear Era?). These words, "actor," "characterize," and "dramatic" reflect the nature of the active learning described in this module. My courses center around war and conflict in the broadest sense: War Stories compares three archetypal engagements—the Trojan War, the Crusades, and World War I; The Future of International Conflict takes a global view of very near-term local conflicts; and The Cold War examines the violence and the economic and political hostilities over a 40-year time span. In courses like these, as an alternative to traditional case study methods, I use informal, in-class, staged readings of plays to embody and relate to course themes: war and peace, negotiation, and the heritage of colonization among others.

These staged readings enable my students to engage international events as participants, by speaking others' words and moving among the people and cultural frameworks in which international relationships unfold.[1] Entering into international relations this closely increases student respect for the complexity of those relationships, and it deepens their commitment to understanding foreign affairs, even for those whose major field of study is elsewhere. These play-readings are part of a regular course, a complement to the more distant view of the world that comes from listening to lectures and asking questions while seated quietly in a classroom.

During the readings, students experience historical/international events from all sides, developing empathy for people almost none of them would normally see face-to-face. They develop their own capacities to speak ideas articulately and to convey their passions expressively. Finally, as the production team develops the performance, the members experience in microcosm the intricacies of multiparty negotiation and decision-making. This active learning project usually takes an entire semester to complete, requiring a small part of the class time over some weeks and a large part just before performance.

Staged readings get the students up in front of an audience, confronting them both as speaker and as audience with the full range of physical, interactive, and spoken elements that make up an effective presentation. Much more deeply, though, staged readings of plays get students to set aside the youthful arrogance with which they so often judge past or present leaders, replacing their detached mistrust with real empathy. Making and mending relationships across cultures in the midst of conflict is really difficult, and play readings make vivid the nature of the real challenges in international relationships.

I have never found a quicker or deeper mechanism than these play readings by which to take my rather "local" students (adult and place-bound) out into the "global" community. They take risks when they act. As a teacher with little drama training, I took a risk in designing this kind of learning. The rewards are worth the risk for all concerned. The integration of play reading into courses came about as an adaptation of the case-study method of teaching international relations. Case studies routinely require students to carry out role-playing exercises to probe the case and its possible outcomes. All too often, however, the roles and interactions the students construct are stereotyped and superficial. Hence, I resort to professionally written plays, because 1.) the scripts are much richer than extemporaneous skits, and 2.) the dramatist has worked long and hard to distill the conflicts and relationships to their critical essence. Thus the results are similar to, but much richer than, role-playing in a case study. I provide a week-by-week schedule in the Step-by-Step Directions.

The play reading is easy to integrate into assessment tools such as final exams. Students will know the text well, and can be expected to engage in sophisticated analysis of the relationship between the "actors" on the international stage and the action they have been following in class. Also, for those students whose major or graduation requirements demand public presentation skills, this work can serve to fulfill that expectation. The particular questions they can answer will depend on the plays selected, but students should be:

1. showing more skill in crafting appropriately complex descriptions of a multiparty international interaction.
2. able to characterize their own strategies as a participant in a small-scale multiparty project.
3. able to reflect more honestly about their own strengths and limitations as citizens in the global system.

Miniglossary

The fields of international relations and drama each have systems of technical terminology that give the same terms very different meanings. In addition to this Miniglossary, I suggest that students also brainstorm a list and come up with additional contrasting definitions (see Homework 1).

TERM	THEATRICAL DEFINITION	INTERNATIONAL RELATIONS DEFINITION
Theater	A place for viewing plays and dramatic spectacles. In ancient times it was always open air.	In military discourse, the setting in which an operation—a campaign, and exercise—is carried out.
Actor	A performer on a stage.	A person who is the agent of decisions in international affairs.
Scenario	A sketch or outline of the plot of a play giving the scenes, characters, and outcomes.	A possible policy option, with its details and consequences spelled out.

Step-by-Step Directions

These instructions come in two groups. First, I give general advice about selecting the play and integrating it into the classroom. Then I provide a week-by-week schedule for preparing the production.

Selecting the Play

I select a play or a series of scenes from a play to illustrate key topics in the course. I make no attempt to select a text to serve as a synthesis of the entire subject matter. Over the years I have discovered that the learning is intense and rather unexpected no matter what the play, and that close linkages between the theme of the play and the course as a whole are less important than one might think. Still, the library of useful and wonderful plays is large, and fit is always possible.

Berthold Brecht's *Mother Courage* illuminates the plight of civilians, women in particular, in war. Peter Shaffer's *Royal Hunt of the Sun* makes vivid the drama of colonization. Lee Blessing's *A Walk in the Woods* offers an intimate evocation of the intricacy of diplomatic negotiation and a partial synthesis of later issues in the Cold War. Vaclav Havel's *The Memorandum* also evokes the Cold War, and manages at the same time to bring home the burdens of bureaucratic procedure on workers everywhere. *Antigone*, in both the classical Greek and Anouilh versions, gives students a chance to observe the powerful conflicts that arise between state interests and individual convictions. At the end of this module I have included an annotated bibliography of plays I have used or have considered; these represent only a small fraction of the available sources.

General Integration of Text and Class

The final product requires devoting one or two class sessions to a full, though informal "staged reading" of the play (or scenes), allowing enough time also for feedback and discussion. The week-by-week schedule spells the details out more fully, and it is evident the time commitment is noticeable. Although active learning components need occupy only a fraction of the available classes each week, it still takes weeks rather than hours for amateurs to construct the performance. I have never done it in less than 6 weeks, and for a newcomer to such teaching I would advise a full semester or quarter.

The students should not memorize their parts, although at the performance they should move in relation to each other within a schematic set using minimal props. While many students have done drama in high school or studied public speaking, some class time must be devoted to teaching very basic performance technique: how to follow-on the cues, move while speaking, face the audience, and stay in character, etc. They should perform only once. The intensity of this one-time experience brings remarkable polish and prowess out of the rankest novice. The learning of international relations would be undermined by any greater efforts to perfect dramatic skills.

I have always taught and performed in ordinary classrooms, moving aside tables and chairs, allowing only a small stage area. While most production groups choose to dress with care for the performance, they often do no more than come in a uniform color, say blue tops and black pants or skirts. Sometimes they costume a little more. The basic set needs—tables, chairs, drapes, lamps, plates, boxes, swords, or whatever—are constructed from classroom and lobby furnishings, with small portable items that students bring from home. It is our job as teachers to read the text carefully in advance to identify and help arrange any furnishings that are essential. Often, however, as the students do their work, they begin to decide on their own what is essential.

The class should be divided, with each group taking responsibility for only a portion of the action. There are two reasons for this: 1.) Students think more deeply about the action when they get a chance to see how others interpret the play, and 2.) each group serves as the audience when others are on stage. My classes almost never allow outsiders to attend, although sometimes students decide among themselves to allow exceptions to this rule. We also never make recordings of any kind, although someone usually takes a group photo. In this exercise, as in real diplomacy, the chance to speak one's mind is gone forever once the designated time passes.

Week-by-Week Schedule

Week 1: Introductions. Explain the project the very first week of class, anticipating that at first you will need to reassure students that they can do the work, and that play-reading, like a case study, will illuminate important concepts effectively.

Homework 1 (see Student Handout 1, Definitions of Terms): Crafting contrasting definitions of the same terms in theater and international relations after the brainstorm exercise helps students see the link between the two worlds.

Week 2: Picking Parts. Reading the play, or their own portion of it, is the next assignment. Students read so as to decide which part to take. Casting will likely demand crossing race, age, nationality, sex, and other types, which the students ultimately find has a positive effect. In a small class, students may have to double up parts, so you must prepare ahead to ascertain which characters can be paired; these are characters that never appear in the same scene, and can thus be assigned to the same person. If the class is large, simply divide the play into small segments, so that all students get a chance to act; this kind of learning only works well if all students have to speak or at least appear on stage.

Homework 2 (see Student Handout 1, Character Autobiography): Once parts are assigned, crafting an autobiographical sketch of their characters helps students develop the empathy that is essential to transforming their understanding of the issues.

Weeks 3–7: Practice. In this period, the class schedule must offer time for reading the play aloud with each other, and some additional time for learning basic "acting" techniques. It will probably take about 1½–2 hours over 3 weeks for the reading process. The task is to hear and speak the text out loud, just once. In addition, allot about 20–30 minutes in each of four to six classes to teach the following skills: picking up on cues, voice projection, stage movement, and minimalist staging. Midway through the process I also ask the students to schedule and carry out a single, out-of-class, extended rehearsal to do a full read-through with some movement.

Homework 3 (see Student Handout 2): The readings from Anna Deveare Smith and David Mamet (see Sources on the handout) orient students to the ways in which dramatic performance links to real life.

Weeks 8–10: Group Dynamics Review. This is the time in the semester when the students become aware that they are in the midst of a microcosm of multiparty negotiations. Some of their peers may well be doing less than the required amount of work: they may have missed a rehearsal or they keep messing up on the reading; they may fail to bring the set pieces and props they have offered. As the teacher, you must avoid being heavy handed with the recalcitrant students, although you must be ultimately prepared to reassign the roles to ensure that the performance itself is protected. At this time the groups practice the hardest scenes in class, and resolve their conflicts. Since most plays and stage directions make explicit directives about the action, if the conflicts continue, I become the arbiter and use the text as a guide for my decisions.

Homework 4 (see Student Handout 3): Background research for the project, including a brief sketch of the playwright, play, and historical period/ issues under discussion, ensures that students come away with a well-grounded, conceptual understanding of the topics addressed in the play.

Weeks 11–12: Dress Rehearsal. This will occupy at least one entire class period. All the groups complete a run-through of their segment. Each group gets use of the stage for part of the period to ensure that the set works and they know their way around; but for the rest of the rehearsal process they also will have to find other nearby spaces to finish the final run-through. (If the class meets for short periods—less than 1½ hours—the best option is to schedule extended sessions. Or you can use two regular sessions).

Weeks 13–14: Final Performances. It is likely that the two halves of the performance may have to occur on different days unless, like me, you are lucky enough to meet in 3-hour blocks. If the time allows, and if the course has anything like a budget, a short version of each of the Homework 4 essays can be collated, along with a cast list and production credits, into a "program" for the performance. Since two or more groups are performing different parts of the same play, students also learn from the distinctions between the respective "programs."

However long the sessions, it is important for the students to arrive early and set up quickly, so they can start the performance as close to the start of class as possible. Likewise, the "audience" needs to gather promptly. I always remind my students that, in French, an audience does not merely *attendre* a performance, it is actually asked to *assister.*

* * *

Each of handouts that follow may be made more specific depending on the play/plays you choose. It is also possible to simply use each one in the more general terms offered here.

Student Handout 1:
Definitions of Terms and
Character Autobiography

Definitions of Terms

With the other actors in your group, construct a list of terms that have a technical meaning in theater and a second, quite different meaning in international trade, conflict, or globalization. Using dictionaries and encyclopedias, provide formal definitions of at least three terms. Remember to cite your sources carefully.

Character Autobiography

You have selected one or more characters from this play. Based on the information in the text and questions you find yourself wanting to ask the character(s), write a short "autobiography" of each. You can base the writing on the major life stages by describing where each character was born, the parents, her or his upbringing, etc. Include details about each character's work and adult life to death. Alternatively, you can build the autobiography around pressing issues that set the major turning points of each person's life in motion, thereby illuminating their goals and purpose in life.

Keep these points in mind as you construct each autobiography:

1. Your choice of details must be congruent with the character as portrayed in the text.
2. You will have to imagine and invent "facts" or "attitudes," and explain how each character came to be as he or she is.
3. You must write in the first person; for example, "I was born in Atlanta, Georgia, in dangerous times."

Your essay should be at least two pages long.

Student Handout 2:
Drama and Public Life,
and Sources

Drama and Public Life

Read the assigned pages from the books by Anna Deveare Smith and David Mamet. Anna Deveare Smith is an African American writer and performer. She develops her scripts from live interviews. David Mamet is of European descent and writes plays and films. His scripts are imaginative fiction. Each writer has considerable experience with the theater, but in these essays they are writing about different settings. Anna Deveare Smith is concerned about public decision-making and David Mamet is concerned about drama as a part of daily life.

Contrast these essays; explain their relationship to the theatrical performances you are planning by answering the following questions:

1. Can the performances for this class be considered theater or politics or both? Is there a difference?
2. How do you know?

Sources

Anna Deveare Smith, "Prologue, Wild Waves and Bonfires," *Talk to Me, Travels in Media and Politics* (New York: Anchor, 2000), 3–12. On the nature of truth and acting.

David Mamet, "Part 1 The Wind Chill Factor," *Three Uses of the Knife, on the Nature and Purpose of Drama* (New York: Vintage Books, 2000), 3–12. On the nature of dramatization in everyday life.

Student Handout 3:
Background for
the Performance

Among the actors in your play section, assign the following research questions. Each actor should prepare a short written report, to be sent via e-mail to all other members of the performance group.

Students must also respond directly to each submission received, either with a follow-up question or with a comment about ways to integrate the insights on the day of the performance, if that is possible.

Write one of the following:

1. A brief biographical sketch of the playwright
2. A description of the setting and people involved in the first performances
3. Summaries of reviews of productions of the play
4. A brief sketch of facts related to the historical period under discussion
5. A minimally annotated bibliography—five to ten sources to illuminate other features of this author's work
6. A minimally annotated bibliography—five to ten sources to illuminate this period or set of events
7. A description of other ways the events described in the play have been presented; for example, make a list of the novels, plays, paintings, and other sources that address the play's events.

Debriefing

Immediately after each performance segment the audience and actors debrief, discussing the excitement of the performance risks and the immediate insights that came to them about relationships and the dynamics of the interactions. This session is best left quite unstructured, since the performance itself will so powerfully affect their insights.

At the class meeting after the performances, the entire community of students discusses the material from the performances in relation to the conceptual class. You will have selected the play to illuminate a particular conceptual notion or a particular system of relationships. In preparation for this second debriefing session, you may want to ask for a reflective essay on a particular key concept. Another possible assignment is to return to the dictionary brainstorm, asking students to craft definitions of the terms from within the structure of the play. Each course allows students to consider the following issues in international relations:

1. Does the play mimic international relations theories you are learning or current international events?
2. In what way are statesmen and women truly like actors as they carry out their official duties?
3. Have new words come into the students' international relations vocabulary as a result of this exercise?

After 10–15 weeks of planning a performance, the students will have become a true learning community, a collaborative group integrating their shared strengths for the greater good. And that, if we are lucky, is the very same outcome that we can expect from successful international relations.

Selected Bibliography

Plays and Their Possibilities

The following annotated list of plays provides publication information; a summary of the number of parts; a general statement about length; a one-line plot summary (**PS**); and one or two conceptual frames (most often with Learning Outcomes [**LO**]) available in each play. The plays are listed by title, since these are likely to be more familiar than the names of playwrights.

Accidental Death of an Anarchist, Dario Fo (adapted by Gavin Richards from a translation by Gillian Hanna; Introduction by Stuart Hood)

(London, UK: Methuen Drama, 1990). Six parts, all quite large; medium length; **PS:** The police engage in an over-the-top comedy about false arrest with unexpected consequences; **LO:** Under Homeland Security, police powers over political figures have a new meaning.

Antigone: Sophocles (Introduction by Eugene H. Falk; translation by Michael Townsend) (New York, NY: Harper Collins, 1962). Ten parts: three large, plus spoken group chorus; very short; **PS:** Against the wishes of the king, the princess wants to have a ritual burial for her brother, who was killed in an attempted revolution; **LO:** Intersections of ethics, both personal and collective, with policy decisions; the role of public opinion in policy.

Antigone, Jean Anouilh (adapted by Lewis Galanteire) (New York, NY: Samuel French, 1973). Twelve parts, no group chorus; rather longer than Sophocles's *Antigone*; **PS:** Princess wants to give a ritual burial for her brother, killed in an attempted revolution, against the wishes of the king; **LO:** Best done in contrast to the classical version, to compare ancient and modern characterizations of events.

Asian Plays, David Hare (London, UK: Faber and Faber, 1986). Three Plays:

- *Fanshen:* Nine parts; two acts, twelve sections; **PS:** An entirely Chinese cast dealing with relations between leaders and the led in Chairman Mao Tse-tung's time.
- *Saigon, Year of the Cat:* Twelve parts; three acts (teleplay); **PS:** The aftermath of the Vietnam War told through Vietnamese lives and struggles.
- *A Map of the World:* Fifteen parts; two acts; **PS:** Decline and colonization in the Third World today.

LO: Any Asian-focused course must consider these plays, since there is so little drama about public and political events in that region of the world. Students performing *Fanshen* must create a world with no white characters at all.

A Walk in the Woods, Lee Blessing (New York, NY: Plume Book, New American Library, 1986). Two parts; two acts; **PS:** An old Soviet diplomat and a young American diplomat try and nearly succeed in ending the stalemates of the Cold War through surprisingly frank, but secret talk; **LO:** Differences between trust and power; the importance of secrecy.

Copenhagen, Michael Frayn (London, UK: Methuen, 1998). Three parts; three acts; **PS:** Two scientists and the wife of one of them face choices about science, the bomb, and the Nazis; **LO:** Connections between science and international affairs; events that look different from each person's perspective.

Cyrano de Bergerac, Edmond Rostand (translated by Lowell Blair) (London, UK: Penguin, 1972). Forty-five parts, about ten large; very long, but can be cut to include only Act 1 about honor and Act 4 about combat; **PS:** Headstrong and brilliant soldier is frustrated by his own unconventional and yet honorable behavior; **LO:** The relationship between honor and conflict; combat as seen from a soldier's-eye view.

Indian Ink, Tom Stoppard (London, UK: Faber and Faber, 1995). Fifteen main parts, plus extras; two acts; **PS:** An English woman returns to the Indian setting in which her family's life and that of a brilliant local painter intersected; **LO:** The modern legacy of colonization; gender in the practices of colonization.

Journey to Utopia, Tom Stoppard (London, UK: Faber and Faber, 2002). Three plays: *Voyage, Shipwreck,* and *Salvage*; each play has about six main parts and about ten smaller ones; **PS:** The revolutionary philosophers of the late nineteenth century who focus on Russia meet to try to make the world a better place; **LO:** Intersections of philosophical thinking and social change; also the intersections of social change and personal experience.

Master Harold and the Boys, Athol Fugard (London, UK: Penguin Books 1982). Three parts; one act, short; **PS:** Rich white children and black staff children grow apart as adults; **LO:** Racism, oppression, and apartheid from inside; discerning the value of theater as a vehicle for present-day political change.

Mother Courage and Her Children: A Chronicle of the Thirty Years War, Bertholt Brecht (English version Eric Bentley) (New York, NY: Grove Press, 1966). Thirteen parts, all significant, two to three very large; twelve scenes, long; **PS:** A traveling saleswoman follows the war, switching sides when expedient, but still losing her children to the war, one by one; **LO:** Theater that explicitly avoids the magical; war, gender, and family life.

Royal Hunt of the Sun, Peter Shaeffer Harmondsworth (UK: Penguin Plays, 1986). Six to eight main parts, plus any number of smaller ones; two acts; **PS:** The Conquistadors' arrival in Peru, and the competition between Inca and Christian worldviews; **LO:** Church as state actor; conflicts caused by cultural distance.

Stalin, Two Plays, David Pinner (London, UK: Oberon Books, 2000).

- *The Teddy Bear's Picnic:* Fourteen parts; two acts, quite long; **PS:** Stalin and his "mafia" are obsessed with the minutia of their lives, while their policies are turning the USSR into a labor camp.

- *The Potsdam Quartet:* Five parts; two acts, much shorter; **PS:** A quartet of musicians is struggling with their commitments to each other, echoing the Big Four Powers whose leaders are also breaking apart in the aftermath of World War II.

LO: Subsidiary and peripheral events illuminate the bigger picture; large complex negotiations.

The Deputy, Rolf Hochhuth (translated by Richard and Clara Winston; Preface by Albert Schweitzer) (New York, NY: Grove Press, 1964). Forty-two or more parts; three acts, very long; **PS:** A priest realizes the Holocaust has begun, that the Church as institution refuses to try to prevent it, and that he must still decide as an individual whether and how to act; **LO:** The role of individual dissent and conscience; the Church as a state actor.

The Memorandum, Vaclav Havel (translated by Vera Blackwell) (New York, NY: Grove Press, 1993). Fifteen parts; twelve scenes, cannot be cut; **PS:** A mysterious order arrives in the office, requiring all documents to be written in a language no one can speak. How and whether to obey or resist the order occupies everyone, from manager to secretary; **LO:** The importance of language; bureaucratic and institutional inertia.

Ubu and the Truth Commission, Jane Taylor (Cape Town, South Africa: University of Cape Town Press, 1998). **LO:** Challenges the official line that the recent work of the South African Truth and Reconciliation Commission contributed positively to peace.

Via Dolorosa, David Hare (London, UK: Faber and Faber, 1998). One part (monologue); one act; **PS:** the playwright's reflections on the war in Israel/Palestine; **LO:** Deep and searching reflection about a troubled place does not necessarily help bring peace.

Background Materials on Theater and "Rough" Theater, in Particular

I first learned about these notions from a faculty colleague in theater, and I recommend that teachers planning this kind of course consult with members of the drama department and with local theater directors. For those who prefer to begin by reading, the Grotowsky and Brecht essays make a good starting point. To hear actual people discussing theater, politics, and the real world, one can do no better than the movie, *My Dinner with André.*

Grotowski, Jerzy, *Towards a Poor Theater* (New York, NY: Touchstone Books, 1968), 13–60. Chapters on the reasons for doing this kind of work, and two interviews with Grotowski.

Brecht, Bertholt, "Alienation Effects in Chinese Acting," "Two Essays on Unprofessional Acting," and "The Folk Play," from *Brecht on Theater* (translated by John Willet; Boston, MA: Hill and Wang Reissue, 1994), 91–100, 148–57.

My Dinner With André, a film directed by Louis Malle, 1981 (Los Angeles: Fox Lorber DVD, 2001). The film portrays a discussion between André Gregory and Wallace Shawn about work, art, and politics.

Endnote

1. This is not a drama course in any sense. Nonetheless, theatrical theorists shape the staging process suggested. Bertholt Brecht advocated "alienation," which entailed reminding audiences repeatedly that they were in the "real" world and not in a magical or mysterious environment. One of his successors, Jerzy Grotowski, took this still further, advocating "rough" theater performances in which setting and costuming were minimal. See references above for additional advice about learning to use drama in an IR course.

German, Polish and Czech Support for the 1999 NATO Intervention in Kosovo: "How Does the Power of Norms Interact with the Norms of the Powerful?"[1]

Meredith A. Heiser-Durón

About This Module

This module focuses on the norms, ethics, and supranational aspects of military intervention. Defense and foreign policy specialists generally ignore these three areas, because military actions are often characterized by competition, not cooperation. One state's increased security is frequently gained at the cost of another state's security. Realist scholars in particular tend to regard the state as the most important unit of analysis in conflict situations, and ignore individual leaders or international organizations, not to mention public sentiment.[2]

This module goes beyond the assumptions of realist theory. By simulating the Kosovo crisis, students examine the policies of three very different European states and their leaders' difficult decisions to support North Atlantic Treaty Organization's (NATO's) 78-day intervention in Kosovo in 1999. (NATO is an organization pledged to the *collective defense* of its members that was founded in 1949 in response to the threat of Russian and communist expansionism in Europe.[3]) The positions of these countries are then compared and contrasted with those of the most powerful states on the United Nations Security Council (UNSC).[4] In this manner, students learn not only about security, but also about the effect of different values and political cultures and the effect of multilateralism and elite/public opinion on security. Students consider whether NATO, not the UNSC, should and can appropriately decide which norm prevails in this crisis situation.

While many realists expected NATO to collapse at the end of the Cold War, Kosovo shows how new humanitarian missions have extended NATO's "lease on life."[5] However, Kosovo raises a number of difficult questions. First, as NATO expands further as an organization that promotes common values of democracy in both members and nonmembers, how can it appropriately deal with the difficult questions it faces about why, when, and how to use force? A second issue raised by the Kosovo crisis is whether humanitarian intervenor is an appropriate role for NATO to play. In Kosovo, NATO intervened outside the area of its traditional mandate. The Kosovo crisis did not involve a security threat in the narrowest sense, but instead a question of norms: sovereignty for Serbians versus the minority rights of Kosovars.[6]

A third difficult question raised by Kosovo is whether the newly configured NATO represents an equitable distribution of power among states. NATO is a simple confederation of states, "an association of sovereign states which, through an appropriate treaty, reach an agreement on given issues,"[7] and it gives smaller states a voice on security, which is greater than their relative power capabilities. However, as NATO decides to extend its mission to defend common global values, other countries may believe their sovereignty or their values are threatened—even large powers—as we observe in the Russian and Chinese reaction to the NATO intervention in Kosovo. This simulation, therefore, clarifies moral and strategic dilemmas for small powers, medium powers, and larger powers in humanitarian intervention.

A fourth difficult issue raised by the case is whether an expanded NATO mandate places impossible demands on the individual leaders of NATO member countries, especially the newest members from Central European states. Ironically, the three new Central European members (Hungary, Poland, and the Czech Republic) joined the alliance in 1999 to gain military strength, and NATO's intervention in Kosovo began twelve days later.[8] They joined largely because of NATO's emphasis on collective defense in Article V, under which all members pledge to defend one another against an attack by an outside power. However, as F. Stephen Larrabee has noted, "Kosovo had little to do with collective defense—no member of NATO was attacked or threatened with attack."[9]

The module asks students to think theoretically about domestic and institutional factors, as well as international reasons for intervention in a sovereign country. By considering the worldviews of specific actors, and not just states or international organizations, this module also provides students with the opportunity to measure their own behavior in the light of moral standards, rather than simply being critical of the behavior of political leaders. In the words of Joel Rosenthal, International Politics scholar and President of the Carnegie Council on Ethics and International Affairs, "what we are looking for is a sustained, analytical discussion of the principles that guide our actions."[10]

Thus it is also worth considering whether Kosovo has restructured our thinking about international relations. By "reshaping relations between regional security organizations and the United Nations, between major powers East and West, between friends and allies in those camps, between force and diplomacy," and by touching on humanitarian principles and state sovereignty, does Kosovo reveal new patterns in the post-Cold War world?[11]

At the end of this exercise, students should be able to answer the following questions:

1. When is it justifiable to use military force for the preservation of certain norms—in this case, for humanitarian purposes and to stop ethnic cleansing? How does one define "humanitarian"? How many civilians can justifiably lose their lives if an intervention is to succeed in being humanitarian?

2. How do Poland, the Czech Republic, and Germany come to agreement on intervention and the norms involved in Kosovo? Was each state motivated to act more from self-interest or from more global, moral considerations that transcend self-interest?[12] Was Czech President Vaclav Havel correct when he said, "This is probably the first war that has not been waged in the name of 'national interests,' but rather in the name of principles and values?"[13]

3. In humanitarian crises, is there a moral compulsion to act which transcends the demands of international law?[14]

4. What role does leadership play in intervention as leaders balance shifting domestic interests and international demands?[15]

5. What is the character of NATO as an institution in the Kosovo crisis, and how does its identity change? Is this change an atypical departure from NATO's traditional mandate or representative of a more lasting shift in orientation?

Miniglossary

Humanitarian intervention "consists of efforts by outside parties to ensure the delivery of emergency aid, and may include efforts to protect the rights of local peoples without the consent of local political authorities."[16] The term can be traced back to Grotius.

Liberal Institutionalism "is the school of thought among international relations theorists that recognizes that states are indeed the most important actors in international relations, but also claims that cooperation among them is achievable through involvement in transnational institutions, where common interests merge, transparency of others' actions is revealed, and transaction costs are reduced."[17]

Multilateralism in a quantitative sense means coordination of national policies in three or more states. However, John Ruggie argues that it should have a stronger qualitative meaning, where the kind of relationship is emphasized, not just the number of parties involved.[18]

Security community implies a shared identity of formally sovereign states, which could assure the "resolution of social problems without recourse to force."[19] This would be a step beyond collective security.

Supranationalism "is the development of authoritative institutions of governance and networks of policy-making activity above the nation-state."[20] This stands in contrast to the concept of *intergovernmentalism,* which treats states as the primary actors. Intergovernmentalism can, however, be distinguished from *realist theory*, because it also emphasizes the importance of institutions and domestic politics.

Step-by-Step Directions

This whole exercise takes five class periods or approximately 300 minutes. Prior to the actual simulation, use several hours to introduce students to basic theories of international relations and models of leadership to prepare students for their roles.[21] If this is a comparative politics course, you should also introduce students to the different parties that were in power in each state in 1999. Students learn about different political cultures in the simulation itself, and review what they have learned in the debriefing.

The module includes roles for fourteen students. There are two political leaders of each country (six students); one public citizen of each country, who is generally more critical of NATO intervention (three students); three students are UN Security Council representatives (one from Russia, one from China, and one from the United States); one who plays the role of Kofi Annan, Secretary General of the United Nations; and one who plays the role of NATO General Secretary Javier Solana. If there are more than fourteen students in the class, additional teams should be formed so there is, for example, a Germany A and a Germany B group. The module gains greater liveliness if the instructor plays the NATO Secretary General or the American Security Council Representative.

Assign students who have a preference for realist theory to roles as UN members or members of the public. Students who have a preference for liberal institutionalism should play national leaders. Although guided by the same institutional and political constraints as the characters they are playing, students should also be encouraged to rethink their established views and possibly come to different decisions on these issues than the people/organizations they are representing.

After theories, concepts, and basic information on each country have been introduced, each student receives a description of his/her role, as well as that of the whole country or UN/NATO team. Several days prior to the simulation, hand out the Selected Bibliography; endnotes; specific and general background paragraphs; the map; and five questions to be answered after the simulation. Students need time outside of class to research their countries and roles. Each student then writes an initial position paper on his/her character's view of NATO intervention and the use of force in this situation. The paper should be dated March 24, 1999.

One day prior to the simulation (or during the simulation if time is lacking), students briefly introduce themselves in character to the class, carrying maps or other props and wearing appropriate clothes whenever possible. On that same day, students meet in groups with national teams and a UN/NATO team (consisting of the secretaries general and the three UNSC permanent representatives). Students read parts of their papers to their groups or the whole class.

At least one full class (two if possible)—the equivalent of 120 minutes—is devoted to playing the game. Photocopy the timeline (in Student Handout 2) on a transparency, so that it can be shared with the class on an overhead projector. Shifting circumstances challenge students and enhance the dynamism of the module. For example, did a lack of willingness to take casualties in the beginning of the Kosovo crisis extend the length of the war, as Charles Krauthammer has argued?[22] Do enemy civilian casualties become unacceptable at some point? If so, when?

If the game extends over two 1-hour class periods, students have 2 minutes to digest each event in the timeline. (I have found adequate student comprehension of the timeline requires 2 minutes per item.) During the game, country teams periodically send off one national member to try to convince NATO/UN officials of a certain position and vice versa. Citizens are excluded from these NATO/UN meetings, but can meet with one another and form an international NGO, which can consult with NATO or the UN.

Prior to a final class debriefing discussion (see Debriefing section), students write a two-page paper answering the five questions above and analyzing the differences between their initial positions and the positions they reached at the end of the 78 days. In these papers, they are to deal with how the "reality" of the political situation complicated their theoretical views. A 60-minute debriefing session follows.

Photocopy and cut out each role in the handouts. Distribute to students playing the roles.

A Note about Student Handouts 2–5: For roles and background information, I researched numerous sources, including the archives at www.tol.cz; Jean Blondel and Ferdinand Mueller-Rommel, eds., *Cabinets in Eastern Europe* (New York: Palgrave, 2001); and Thomas S. Szayna, *NATO Enlargement 2001–2015* (Santa Monica, CA: RAND, 2001).

Student Handout 1:
Background

General Background to the 1999 Intervention in Kosovo

In 1999, Poland, the Czech Republic, and Germany all had leftist leaders, which did not bode well for NATO intervention, given that European parties of the left generally tend to be more antimilitarist. While all three countries were somewhat reluctant to forcefully intervene in a non-NATO country, they had different levels of resistance and different reasons for resisting intervention. Moreover, Czechs and Poles had both been members of the Soviet bloc Warsaw Pact and, as a result, had important ties with the former Yugoslavia and Russia.

In Poland, President Aleksander Kwasniewski came from the reformed communist movement, and his party, the Democratic Left Alliance (SLD), was split on intervention. Still, Kwasniewski was supportive and represented the majority of Polish public opinion in adopting this position. In the Czech Republic, President Vaclav Havel was allied with social-democratic forces, yet he was the only Czech politician to indicate strong support for intervention.

Germany, mostly due to its "collective memory" of WWII, viewed itself as a "civilian power" and an advocate for the new Central European members of NATO. Germany's leaders and its public preferred multilateralism to unilateralism and diplomacy over force, especially given the collective memory of how the German Nazi regime victimized Yugoslavia in particular during WWII. German unification in 1990 increased this sense of Germany as a civilian power, as East Germans, who were part of a militarily aggressive Soviet bloc, were even more attracted to an ideology of pacifism.[23]

Specific Background

In October 1998, NATO concluded a cease-fire between the Kosovo Liberation Army (KLA) and the Serbs. This cease-fire was to be enforced by the threat of NATO air strikes as well as by the Organization for Security and Cooperation in Europe (OSCE)[24] Verification Mission. As part of the agreement, Yugoslav President Slobodan Milosevic was allowed to keep twenty thousand military, paramilitary, and police troops in Kosovo. However, this OSCE mission had only three thousand staff and a small budget. It ultimately withdrew in March 2003, because of the escalating violence.

Serb and KLA fighting renewed in December 1998 after the massacre of ethnic Albanians in Racak. On January 28, 1999, Kofi Annan met with NATO members and urged them to learn from Bosnia, saying "bloody wars of the last decade have left us with no illusions about the difficulty of halting internal conflicts—by reason or by force . . . nor have they left us with any illusions about the need to use force, when all other means have failed."[25] The peace conference in February 1999 in Rambouillet, France resulted in failure.

On 19 March, the United Nations High Commissioner for Refugees (UNHCR) estimated that two hundred forty thousand ethnic Albanians had been forced from their homes, including sixty thousand since the end of the first round of peace talks in February. Talks between US envoy Richard C. Holbrooke and Milosevic, held March 22–23, yielded no results. On March 23, the US Senate passed a resolution supporting US participation in NATO air strikes. Those senators who opposed this resolution cited two reasons: concern about attacking a sovereign country and concern about putting US troops at risk.

In addition to becoming familiar with the facts in this handout, be sure to examine the map of the region at www.lib.utexas.edu/maps/europe/yugoslav.jpg

Student Handout 2:
The Czech Team

Vaclav Havel

You were born in Prague in 1936 and you were first elected to the Czech presidency in 1993. You are now serving your second and final term as president after having been reelected in 1998. Although your popularity has declined since your initial election, you still stand up strongly for your moral principles.

You were once a dissident and somewhat of a pacifist. Now you are a strong supporter of NATO membership for your country; however, you have not lost your idealism. You view NATO as key to the guarantee of human rights. You generally trust civil society more than states. You also want to prove Czech credibility as a new NATO ally, although the Czech Republic is a small state with a small military, which is making further cuts in defense spending. However, your government and your own party, Czech Social Democrats (CSSD), do not support your position on Kosovo. Although you were originally a member of the Civic Forum (OF), the party split into a left wing and a right wing. You are allied with the former, while former Prime Minister Vaclav Klaus is part of the latter.

Vaclav Klaus

You were born in 1941 in Prague. You are the former prime minister of the Czech Republic—you were forced to resign in 1997, but you remain very influential. The present social democratic government is a minority government, which relies on your party, the Civic Democratic Party (ODS) to stay in power. You serve as the parliamentary speaker.

Although you were instrumental in your country's NATO membership, you are now more critical of NATO membership and European Union (EU) membership, because you believe that the costs may outweigh the benefits for your small state.[26] The present social democratic prime minister, Milos Zeman, and the Communist Party join you in skepticism concerning the obligations of NATO membership. When serving as prime minister (1993–1997), you thought that links with Slovakia and Poland would hurt your country's goal to be first to join the EU and NATO. You also never saw any particular responsibility to assist your neighbors to integrate into these institutions. Similarly, you now feel no moral obligation to go the assistance of the Kosovars.

Czech Citizen

You were born in the countryside in 1930. You are still struggling to run your family's farm, and you are quite disappointed in your country's new democratic government. You became a member of the Communist Party in the 1950s, as you saw it as key to economic growth and social justice for farmers. You have remained a member of the party, because you do not trust the other new parties.

The Czech Republic, in your opinion, should be more focused on domestic and immediate regional problems. You feel strongly that NATO and the EU are taking advantage of you and your countrymen. You do not support membership in an organization run by the former enemy, NATO. You are especially angry about NATO's invasion of a former ally, Yugoslavia, and you want no part in it.

Student Handout 3:
The Polish Team

Aleksander Kwasniewski

You were born in Bialogard, Poland in 1954. You were elected president in 1995, replacing Lech Walesa. You are fluent in Russian, and served as a former communist party official. You are now a member of the Democratic Left Alliance (SLD), although you have declared yourself above party politics as president. Your party has taken two different positions on NATO and Kosovo. One wing of the party has strongly objected to the war, because NATO acted as an aggressor and was really motivated by anti-Russian sentiment. You, however, belong to the mainstream of the SLD, which strongly supports the NATO campaign.

Moreover, your country is geographically removed from the former Yugoslavia, so the invasion is not such a sensitive topic. Your role as a former communist developing defense policy can be compared to that of Nixon developing American détente—no one could really accuse Nixon of being soft on communism, just as no one can accuse you of being a war hawk. Throughout 1998, you have also been active in improving relations with Russia, in spite of NATO enlargement.

Jerzy Buzek

You were born in 1940 in Smilowice. You became prime minister in 1997. You were chosen in part because your background was in chemical engineering, making you a technician, not a politician. (In post-communist countries, leaders frequently have technical training, because those with political training, or those who acted as politicians in communist regimes, have been disqualified or tainted by their pasts.) You represent a coalition between Solidarity Election Action (AWS), a group of right-wing parties and social groups headed by the Solidarity labor union, and the Freedom Union (UW), which is a reform-oriented centrist party. You are a member of the former. While both parties are socially conservative, your coalition partner (UW) is especially anxious that NATO's campaign in Kosovo not fail. The UW is very liberal on economic policy, and is a proponent of globalization, as well as European Union and NATO membership. You represent a good bridge to the UW, because you coauthored the AWS-UW economic program.

Polish Citizen

You were born in the Polish countryside in 1950. You moved to the suburbs of Warsaw in the 1990s, where you work as a laborer. As a member of the Catholic Church, you have always been a strong believer in Christianity and nationalism. Because you believe in Polish nationalism, you believe in the right of all nations to sovereignty.

In your view, the global liberals, who advocate intervention in Kosovo, are your greatest enemy. By considering intervention, NATO is violating a fundamental principle. As an active member of the Christian National Union (ZChN), a populist party, which supports moral positions more strongly than more elite parties, you are not defending Milosevic or ethnic cleansing but you are defending sovereignty.[27]

Student Handout 4:
The German Team

Gerhard Schroeder

You were born in 1944 in the state of Lower Saxony, where you served as minister-president (governor) prior to your election as chancellor of Germany (prime minister) in 1998. You had been in office for 4 months when you had to give your fellow Germans news of the NATO decision to bomb Kosovo. You are a member of the Social Democratic Party (SPD), and represent the 1968 generation in Germany, which rebelled against its parents who wanted to forget Germany's role in WWII. You and your party initially objected to Chancellor Kohl's position on Germany's military intervention in Bosnia. However, due to the failure of the United Nations in Srebrenica in 1995, [28] you are rapidly readjusting your view, and more so since the Social Democratic-Green coalition was elected in 1998.[29] Your coalition is open to an intervention that is multilateral and in the defense of human rights. Still, there are some differences between the Social Democratic Party and the Greens, whose members are more resistant to the idea of military action.

The SPD and Greens hold only a slim majority in parliament, so your policies are under attack by both the Christian Democratic Union (CDU) and the reformed Communist Party (PDS). The CDU says your party is opportunistic in foreign policy and unwilling to spend enough to back up your policies. The PDS is attacking your position on principle, arguing that only the United Nations should decide when force is to be used. You would prefer that the United Nations approve such actions, but you do not insist upon it.

Joschka Fischer

You are also considered a member of the 1968 generation. You were born in 1948 in the state of Baden-Würtemberg. You worked a lot of odd jobs before becoming one of the founding members of the Green Party and a member of the German parliament in 1983. However, it is rumored that you once actively participated in the Red Army Faction. You admit to an association, but nothing more. You became foreign minister of Germany, because the SPD-Green coalition wanted a Green party member in this position.

Your view on Kosovo has changed even more radically than that of your chancellor. You have gone from being a strong dissident and pacifist to advocating a new trend in foreign policy. You have urged your party to shift from its pacifist position to that of a NATO supporter, especially in the field of peacekeeping and peacemaking. You take strong moral positions, but you are also known for your sense of humor.

Although you feel strongly about UN approval of NATO actions, you view Kosovo as an exception because of the genocidal nature of the threat to the Kosovars. You represent the more realistic leadership of your party, but you face a very idealistic membership. You are very opposed to the PDS, not viewing it as a true party of the left, but as a very conservative party that is still connected to its communist past.

German Citizen

You were born in 1970 in West Berlin, but you now work at Humboldt University, which is in the former East. You initially voted green, but you feel the Green Party has deserted its pacifist position. While many think the PDS is only a party of old people and malcontents, as a university employee, you now vote PDS because it strongly advocates the role of the UN in *all* international decisions concerning the use of force. Once in power, the Greens deserted their principled position. As the PDS has almost no chance to be in power at the federal level, you think it will maintain a principled position opposed to all use of force without UN approval.

You are glad that the PDS supports German membership in NATO, but you want a NATO that is not involved in out-of-area disputes. If that is its purpose, what is the United Nations for? You would also prefer that German soldiers not participate in any kind of NATO combat, but only in peacekeeping activities.

Student Handout 5:
The UN/NATO Team

United Nations Secretary General Kofi Annan

You were born in Ghana in 1938. You went to college in the United States and France. In your previous position as undersecretary general (1993–1996), you presided over unprecedented growth in the United Nation's peacekeeping operations. As you report on your UN Web page, seventy thousand peacekeepers were deployed in 77 countries in 1995.[30]

You are the seventh secretary general of the United Nations, and you were elected for a four-year term in this office in 1997. You were the first secretary general to come from the ranks of the UN staff and are very effective in this position, but you have not lost your idealistic enthusiasm. Prior to the particular case of Kosovo, you insinuated that you support the use of force in exceptional circumstance to bring about human rights. You have support from developing and developed states, and you are also known for working very closely with nonstate actors, including the private sector and nongovernmental organizations, as well as state actors.

Russian Ambassador to the United Nations Sergei Lavrov[31]

As the Russian Permanent Representative on the United Nations Security Council (UNSC), you are very critical of NATO bombing in Kosovo. Russians are ethnically related to Serbs, and you are very worried about the territorial integrity of your own country. NATO might use the principles of Kosovo as a reason to attack Russian troops in Chechnya. Moreover, Russia's intervention in Chechnya suggests that air strikes are not the most effective means to deal with political conflicts concerning ethnic problems.

NATO has just added three new members from the former Warsaw Pact, which greatly expands NATO's room for maneuver, and this is something that your state cannot just dispassionately accept. Furthermore, other leaders from the Commonwealth of Independent States (CIS)[32] may see this as a model for resolving their conflicts with your country and may look to NATO for assistance in this regard.

Your country has three main questions:

1. What is the role of international law and the United Nations in this crisis?
2. Is Russia to be an important part of the new order or left out entirely?
3. What is a justifiable use of force internationally?

While your state has a wide domestic definition for justified use of force, your country is greatly alarmed by NATO's new use of force out-of-area without UN approval. Whether you are able to serve as a mediator between NATO and former Yugoslavia depends on how NATO and its new members respond to your country's diplomatic and military overtures.[33]

Chinese Ambassador to the United Nations Quin Huasin

As China's Permanent Representative to the UNSC, you cannot believe that NATO would wage war on a sovereign state that is not a member of NATO and has made no threat to NATO. You worry that the United States will establish a new alliance in Asia, so it can attack China based on some trumped up charge of abusing minority rights or humanitarianism. Furthermore, you wonder what adventuristic overtures might the United States make to Taiwan?

Your country expected peace and cooperation at the end of the Cold War, not more violent confrontation on hard ideological lines and American hegemony. NATO argues for a new type of interventionism based on a new justice, but who decides when to intervene and how? Clearly, in your view, the answer is the United Nations and the UNSC.

Maybe the United States wants to launch a new Cold War against communist/socialist countries. You emphasize that there must be mutual respect for sovereignty and territorial integrity, as well as for nonaggression and noninterference in other countries' internal affairs. In your view, NATO, an organ of the Cold War, should consider disbanding as the Warsaw Pact did.[34]

US Acting Representative to the United Nations
Peter Burleigh

You are a career diplomat and an expert on Asia and the Middle East. Although Richard C. Holbrooke has been nominated as the American Permanent Representative to the UNSC, you have been serving as the acting representative after the departure of Bill Richardson in 1998, and you remain acting permanent representative until Holbrooke is confirmed by the US Senate.[35]

While this position is normally awarded to a political appointee, you think it is an advantage to be a career diplomat, as the British, French, Russian, and Chinese permanent representatives all come from this background. You would prefer UN approval for NATO action, but you know that UN Security Council approval of NATO intervention is unrealistic because of the Chinese and Russian veto power. The United States cannot idly sit by and witness this violation of human rights, so NATO intervention is justified without specific UNSC approval.

NATO Secretary General Javier Solana[36]

You were born in Spain in 1942. It is ironic that you, a former member of the Spanish Socialist Workers Party (PSOE), are now the Secretary General of NATO. You think that your country's evolution, and your own personal evolution, can set an example for the new Central European members of NATO. Of course, until Franco died in 1975, you did not want Spain to be affiliated with NATO. You saw NATO as part of a larger military dictatorship. However, after Franco's death, you could see how NATO (along with the European Union) could help Spain become more of a democracy. You lobbied for Spain's entry into NATO, and became the ninth Secretary General of NATO in 1995. You see the Kosovo action as a proving ground for the new members of NATO.

You are trusted by the Americans and the other eighteen NATO members. You promoted NATO expansion, but also worked very hard to get Russian approval for this step. You are key in holding together the coalition on Kosovo. However, your personal vision of NATO is that the Europeans should be militarily stronger and more independent of the United States.

Student Handout 6:
Time Line[37]

March 24, 1999: NATO launches air strikes against the Federal Republic of Yugoslavia (FRY). American and British ships, along with American bombers, launch over fifty cruise missiles. More than sixty NATO warplanes attack from NATO's bases in Italy. Thirteen of NATO's nineteen members participate. Neither the Czechs, Hungarians, nor Poles are among those members, but Germany is among them.

President Clinton makes the following statement in the evening: "Ending this tragedy is a moral imperative. . . I am convinced that the dangers of acting are far outweighed by the dangers of not acting—dangerous to defenseless people and our national interest."

The EU issues a statement of support without specifically endorsing the NATO assault.

Russian President Yeltsin denounces the air strikes as "open aggression" and a "blow to the whole community." He announces the suspension of cooperation with NATO's Partnership for Peace, which was created in part to allow dialogue with Russia.

March 25: The United Nations High Commissioner for Refugees (UNHCR) has stockpiled humanitarian resources in Belgrade for one hundred thousand refugees.

March 26: Russia sponsors a UN resolution in the Security Council, which calls for an immediate end to the bombing and a peaceful solution in Yugoslavia. It is defeated 12–3, with Russia, China, and Namibia voting for it.

President Havel announces that the Czech Republic will fulfill its obligations as a NATO member.

March 27: Serbs announce they have shot down the first NATO plane, but the plane's pilot is rescued.

Parliamentary Speaker Vaclav Klaus, speaking on behalf of the Civic Democratic Party (ODS), accuses politicians in favor of air strikes of being "warmongers." Prime Minister Zeman calls them "troglodytes." Klaus says 50% of Czechs do not support air strikes.

NATO authorizes expanding the attack to targets in downtown Belgrade.

March 30: Russian Prime Minister Primakov travels to Belgrade to meet with Milosevic. Milosevic says he is willing to return to the negotiating table. Russian President Yeltsin announces that Russia will not be drawn into this conflict.

March 31: The United States pledges fifty million dollars to the attack, and Germany pledges forty million dollars.

NATO maintains it will not send in ground troops, while President Clinton says on *60 Minutes II* that he would be concerned about getting the troops out of FRY.

April 1: The UNHCR reports that more than one hundred sixty thousand Albanians have fled Kosovo since air strikes began on March 24, and two hundred sixty thousand more have been displaced from their homes.

April 2: NATO expands attack to include bridges.

April 3: A special session of the Czech parliament approves the use of airbases for NATO planes. The Czech Communist Party is unable to pass a motion questioning the cabinet's ability to make such a decision.

April 4: NATO member states pledge an airlift to take as many as one hundred ten thousand refugees from Kosovo. Four hundred thousand have already fled Kosovo. Turkey pledges to take twenty thousand of these refugees. Germany pledges to take forty thousand, but later in the day revises this downward to ten thousand.

April 5: NATO bombs hit two residential areas. Twelve civilians may have been killed and fifty injured.

United States agrees to send 2–8,000 more troops to operate and maintain twenty-four Apache helicopters.

Sixty-five percent of Germans think that air strikes should be halted to pursue a diplomatic strategy.

April 6: The Czech government agrees to open its air space and airfields to the NATO campaign. In a cabinet of nineteen members, two members abstain from voting and one votes against.

Milosevic pledges that he will begin a unilateral cease-fire, saying that he reached an agreement with Ibrahim Rugova, a political leader of ethnic Albanians. Rugova is reportedly under arrest and has not willingly come to speak with Milosevic.

NATO insists that Milosevic must fulfill two conditions: He must withdraw all Serb troops from Kosovo and must allow an international security presence to enter.

April 8: Milosevic declares peace has been restored to Kosovo.

April 12: NATO foreign ministers from all nineteen countries meet for the first time since bombing began and pledge to continue the campaign. They want to get Russia back into the process. *(Each national team should send one member to meet with NATO Secretary-General Solana to reenact this.)*

Polls in Poland show that 60% of Poles favor the Kosovo mission. In the Czech Republic, polls show that 35% of the Czechs favor the mission.

German Foreign Minister Fischer presents to the EU a peace plan that offers a political solution on Kosovo.

April 12: Russian Foreign Minister Ivanov meets with American Secretary of State Madeleine Albright. They agree that Milosovic must withdraw his forces. They disagree on the nature of an international peacekeeping presence.

Bombing in FRY escalates as better weather returns.

A Russian convoy arrives in Yugoslavia after Hungary persuades Russia to leave behind five armored vehicles and four fuel tankers. Hungary believes these could have military purposes.

April 14: German Foreign Minister Fischer presents his peace plan to NATO and the Russians.

Milosevic says he will accept international peacekeepers, but only if they are unarmed.

April 18: Serbs herd refugees to the borders, but prevent their crossing.

NATO admits it mistakenly bombed two convoys of refugees on April 14.

Clinton requests that Congress approve six billion dollars in emergency funds for NATO's FRY mission.

April 19: Czech Defense Minister Vetchy announces Czechs are now ready for allies to use their airfields.

Milosevic meets with a Western journalist, saying he would consider a return to diplomacy if the bombing ends, while NATO announces that Serbian military troops have increased by at least three thousand to more than forty thousand troops.

Clinton urges Russia to seek a greater role in the diplomatic resolution of the crisis.

April 21: Britain and France support the use of ground troops. NATO is reviewing this suggestion.

Vice President Al Gore says the United States will take twenty thousand Albanian refugees to be temporarily housed in the United States, and thereby abandons a plan to house these refugees at military base in Guantanamo Bay, Cuba.

April 22: In the Czech Republic, 5 hours of stormy debate concerning NATO's use of airfields is followed by an anti-NATO rally in front of parliament. Prime Minister Zeman and Foreign Minister Kavan declare that the Czech Republic does not support a ground offensive in FRY. Parliament, however, approves the stationing of NATO troops in the Czech Republic.

NATO bombs a Belgrade residence of Milosevic, and Milosevic meets with Russia's special envoy, Viktor Chernomyrdin.

April 23: After a 3-hour closed door meeting, NATO decides to support an intensified air attack, including railroads and overland pipelines as targets.

April 23–25: NATO celebrates its fiftieth birthday.

April 24: NATO begins to escalate strikes to include Milosevic's mass media.

Hungarian Prime Minister Orban opens three military bases for NATO after NATO officials remind Orban that he is obliged to make these available as a NATO member.

April 26: French President Chirac urges Russia to play a greater role in negotiations.

April 27: Chernomyrdin meets with US Deputy Secretary of State Talbott and NATO Secretary General Solana, which suggests that Russia will play a key role in modifying US and NATO positions.

Zeman states that only Russia can get Milosovic to accept an international military force, describing his own and his government's position on a NATO invasion of Kosovo as "unambiguously negative."

April 28: Clinton approves an order for thirty-three thousand American reservists to join active duty troops.

Chernomyrdin meets with German Defense Minister Sharping in Moscow.

NATO admits a laser-guided bomb hit civilians by mistake and killed up to twenty people, including eleven children.

Clinton says the bombing campaign may last several months. Meanwhile, a resolution to support the air attack is narrowly defeated in the US Congress. Congress is concerned about whether American ground troops will be required.

April 29: US Speaker of the House Dennis Hastert says, "I would hope the President would take this diverse debate as a signal that he better explain the goals, the costs, and the long-term strategy of why we are here."

Chernomyrdin meets with German Chancellor Schroeder, who later meets with UN Secretary-General Kofi Annan in Moscow *(students in these roles should meet)*. Schroeder advocates a Security Council Resolution to authorize the use of force in Kosovo. He also suggests a 24-hour halt in the bombing, if Milosevic begins to withdraw his forces.

April 29–30: More bombing runs are made in this 24-hour period than at any other time during the Kosovo campaign. Thus begins a strong military escalation.

April 30: Milosevic offers his own peace plan to withdraw Yugoslav and Serb forces and allow the return of refugees, if there is no armed international force. He would only accept European troops from non-NATO countries.

Fifty-five percent of Poles support the NATO air campaign.

May 1: After civil rights activist Jesse Jackson makes an appeal, Milosovic releases three US soldiers who have been held captive for 1 month. Jackson says this shows Milosovic's willingness to negotiate.

May 3: Clinton has a meeting with Jackson, at which Jackson delivers a letter from Milosovic. Jackson supports a halt to the bombing. Clinton also visits the three soldiers and Kosovar refugees in Germany.

May 5: Macedonia closes its borders, saying it will only take as many refugees as are air lifted out.

May 6: The Group of Eight (G-8) (composed of the United States, Britain, Canada, France, Germany, Italy, Japan, and Russia) agrees on principles for a diplomatic solution.

The US House of Representatives approves double the amount Clinton requested to fight in Kosovo: thirteen billion dollars.

May 7: Three Chinese civilians are killed when NATO mistakenly bombs the Chinese Embassy in Belgrade. Twenty are wounded. The United States blames this on faulty CIA information, but the Chinese are skeptical.

May 8: Yeltsin denounces this bombing, calling it "yet another flagrant violation of international law."

May 10: Milosevic announces the Kosovo Liberation Army (KLA) has been defeated, and his forces began troop withdrawal on May 9. NATO reports there is no evidence of this.

Chernomyrdin travels to China in an effort to gain support for the G-8 peace plan in the UN Security Council. The Chinese Foreign Ministry announces it is suspending discussions with the United States in two areas: human rights and certain military contacts. Foreign Minister Jiaxuan tells the US ambassador he must issue a full apology and punish those responsible.

Schroeder calls for a full investigation of the Chinese Embassy bombing.

May 8–11: Thousands of people protest in front of the US embassy in Beijing.

May 13: At a party conference, the German Green Party calls for a limited halt to NATO's bombing.

May 15: The United Nations Security Council (UNSC) issues a statement, which is a compromise between the United States and China, expressing "distress and concern" about the NATO bombing of the FRY.

May 16: After draftees' bodies are returned to several Serbian villages, there are twenty antiwar/antigovernment protests.

May 18: Kosovar leader Rugova visits NATO.

May 21–25: NATO attacks the electrical infrastructure of the FRY. This represents further escalation of the military campaign.

May 21: A bomb hits a hospital and prison by mistake, killing more than twenty people.

May 24: The UN War Crimes Tribunal indicts Milosevic on the grounds of "crimes against humanity." He is accused of forcibly deporting over seven hundred forty thousand ethnic Albanians. The United Nations requests that countries freeze his assets.

May 25: NATO agrees to expand original plans for the peacekeeping force by twenty thousand to forty-eight thousand. This force will consist of NATO and non-NATO forces, thereby guaranteeing Russia a role.

Serbs fire more than thirty missiles at NATO planes.

May 26: A Czech-Greek peace initiative is launched, calling for an end to the bombing and for Yugoslavia to comply with G-8 and NATO demands, which are incorporated in the Fischer peace plan.

May 27: Russia denounces the UN indictment of Milosevic as "politically motivated."

May 30: A poll shows that 30% of Germans favor the use of ground troops.

An anti-NATO demonstration of one hundred protesters, which attempts to block Czech Army headquarters in Prague, turns violent.

June 2: Chernomyrdin and the European Union emissary, Finnish President Ahtisaari, meet with Milosevic. In the past, Russia and NATO have differed on the composition, command, and number of troops in the peacekeeping operation. Now Russia and NATO agree, so Milosevic is isolated.

June 3: The Serbian parliament accepts a peace accord to end the 10-week bombing campaign. It is basically the ten-point agreement, which was written by the G-8. NATO agrees to restrict troops to Kosovo. There is a vague role for the United Nations and the G-8.

June 5: Talks are "constructive," but the Yugoslav delegation does not sign the document.

Serbian forces shell a border town holding refugees in northern Albania.

June 6: NATO resumes the bombing campaign.

June 7: There is disagreement at the peace talks concerning the lack of a specific role for the United Nations, which irks Russia and Serbia. Finally, it is suggested that the civilian leader in Kosovo should be a special representative of the UN Secretary-General and chosen by him.

June 9: NATO agrees to extend the Serb withdrawal from 1 week to 11 days, and to cut the size of the demilitarized zone from 25 to 5 kilometers. Then the FRY and NATO officially sign the peace agreement.

June 10: Solana announces the suspension of the 78-day bombing campaign.

The UNSC passes Resolution 1244 on a UN Mission in Kosovo (UNMIK), which creates the following: a UN civilian administration, a UNHCR organization, an EU reconstruction bureau, and an OSCE institutional body. By a 14−0 vote (China abstains), the UNSC authorizes a NATO peacekeeping force in Kosovo (KFOR). China, however, adds an amendment that emphasizes the primary responsibility of the Security Council for maintaining peace and security. China maintains that any further use of force should get the authorization of the UNSC.

NATO authorizes the use of NATO forces in Kosovo for a period of 12 months. Their status can be renewed.[38] Bombing can resume if Yugoslavia does not fully comply with NATO terms.

Immediate post-peace treaty developments are as follows:

June 16: Yugoslav forces entirely withdraw from Kosovo.

June 17: It is determined that five hundred to one thousand civilians died during the NATO campaign.

June 27: While on an official visit to Albania, Havel is the first NATO head of state to visit Kosovo.

Debriefing

Throughout the game and debriefing, students should look for convergences between theories and leadership models, and not automatically prefer one over the other before assessing how well they work in application. Issues to consider during the debriefing session include whether national leaders conducted this discourse in a way that assisted in identification with "global values"[39] and international organizations, goals that liberal institutionalists and constructivists would advocate. Or, alternatively, did the nationalist leaders conduct this discourse based on a need to remain popular, emphasizing primarily the population's concern for its own welfare, in accordance with realist expectations? There will probably be an overlap in students' identification with the nation, regional organizations, and international organizations. As Stephen M. Walt argues, "Most realists recognize that nationalism, militarism, ethnicity, and other domestic factors are important; liberals acknowledge that power is central to international behavior; and some constructivists admit that ideas will have greater impact when backed by powerful states and reinforced by enduring material forces."[40]

Harnisch and Maull describe this same approach as an "enlightened constructivist analysis." In their view, "actors neither pursue single-mindedly fixed material interests (as in rational choice theories) induced by system forces, nor do we expect them to hold to fixed normative preferences which they acquire in the past and which will determine their behavior in the future."[41] In other words, leaders are affected by their national material interest, but they also have changing norms. The challenge in the debriefing is to determine how and why they change their norms, in spite of general continuity in material interests.

During the debriefing, you might ask students to evaluate Andrew Michta's assessment about the new NATO members involvement in Kosovo: "Poland passed the test with flying colors, Hungary received only a satisfactory grade, and the Czech Republic had problems passing at all and needed 'extensive tutoring' from Brussels and Washington even to make it."[42] Moreover, students should reach conclusions pertaining to the role of the United Nations versus NATO as legitimate institutions to use force. Was Kosovo an "exceptional deviation" from international law? Was it an action consistent with the UN charter and international law?[43] Or was it an attempt to reinterpret the Charter and shift international law, so that (in humanitarian crises) the protection of people is more important than the sovereignty of states? Students who agree with the latter proposition should also consider the question, "How far should NATO go to secure democracy?" If its new mission is based on a concept of values rather than territory, one could assume that it might go very far indeed in further missions.[44] Finally, how did leadership style affect these leaders' ability to carry out decisions and convince their public that these decisions were correct?

This module enables students to experience these moral dilemmas as well as overlapping identities and institutional pressures first hand. It assists them in understanding a variety of diverse political cultures and values. Finally, it provides them with a solid understanding of the conflicting demands of collective security versus collective defense, of ethics versus international law, and of sovereignty and humanitarianism.

Selected Bibliography

In Print

Haftendorn, Helga, Robert O. Keohane, and Celeste A. Wallendar, eds. *Imperfect Unions: Security Institutions Over Time and Space* (New York: Oxford University Press, 1999).

Harnisch, Sebastian and Hans Maul, eds. *Germany as a Civilian Power?* (Manchester, UK: Manchester University Press, 2001).

Hermann, Margaret C. and Joe D. Hagan. "International Decision-Making: Leadership Matters." *Foreign Policy* (Spring 1998): 124–137.

Mearsheimer, John J. "The False Promise of International Institutions," *International Security* 19, no. 3 (Winter 1994/1995): 39–51.

Ruggie, John G. "The False Premise of Realism." *International Security* 20, no. 1 (Summer 1995): 62–70.

Schnabel, Albrecht and Ramesh Thakur, eds. *Kosovo and the Challenge of Humanitarian Intervention* (New York: United Nations University Press, 2000).

Related Web Sites

www.tol.cz The online successor to Radio Free Europe and Radio Liberty; has information on Central and Eastern Europe.

www.foothill.fhda.edu/divisions/unification A Web site created by myself and a colleague in German literature for interdisciplinary classes on post-WWII Germany. Contains information on German history and politics and the materials necessary to do a simulation concerning German unification.

www.nato.int/kfor/ Explains the past and current activities of NATO's peacekeeping force in Kosovo. The home site contains lots of information on NATO as well as Solana's speeches.

http://csis.org/ Georgetown University's Center for Strategic and International Studies. Has papers on Kosovo in the present and past, as well as articles on NATO expansion and reports on criteria for successful humanitarian intervention.

http://wwics.si.edu/index.cfm?topic_id=1422&fuseaction=topics.home/ The Woodrow Wilson International Center for Scholars. The section on the Program on Eastern Europe contains occasional papers and meeting reports on East European countries and NATO expansion. See especially wwics.si.edu/ees/special/2000/larrab.pdf.

www.carnegiecouncil.org/armedconflict.php The Carnegie Council on Ethics and International Affairs. This organization has ongoing debates concerning armed conflict and humanitarian intervention.

Endnotes

1. Hans-Martin Jaeger, *"Konstruktionsfehler des Konstruktivismus in den Internationalen Bezeihungen,"* Zeitschrift fuer Internationale Beziehungen 3, no. 2 (Fall 1996): 326–7.

2. For a nuanced, balanced interpretation of realist theory and its rewards and limitations, see Stephen M. Walt, "International Relations: One World, Many Theories," *Foreign Policy* (Spring 1998): 29–46 and Stephen M. Walt, "NATO's Future" in Pierre Martin and Mark R. Brawley, eds., *Alliance Politics, Kosovo, and NATO's War: Allied Force or Forced Allies* (New York: Palgrave, 2000). See also Toolkit 1.

3. NATO originally had 12 members. In 2003, it had 19 members and in 2004 has 26 members.

4. The United Nations is the successor of the League of Nations and was created in 1945 "to promote international cooperation and to achieve peace and security." www.un.org/aboutun/history.htm.

5. For more on this debate, see Stephen M. Walt, "Why Alliances Endure or Collapse," *Survival* 39, no. 1 (Spring 1997): 156–179. Some realists argue that this new "lease on life," as well as fear of Kosovar and Albanian immigration, was the real reason for intervention in Kosovo.

6. I define minority in political terms as less power or control over outcome. In Kosovo, Serbs had actually dwindled to the numerical minority by 1999, although they had been about equal with the Kosovars after WWII. This was one reason for Serb insecurity.

7. See Daniele Archibugi, "Principles of Cosmopolitan Democracy," in Daniele Archibugi, David Held, and Martin Koehler, eds., *Re-imagining*

Political Community: Studies in Cosmopolitan Democracy (Cambridge, UK: Polity Press, 1998), 212.

8. While Hungary, the third new NATO member, also shared this value, I am not including Hungary in this case study, since there were three hundred thousand Hungarians in the Vojvodina, the other autonomous republic in rump-Yugoslavia, which changed the weight of its national interest.

9. F. Stephen Larrabee, "The Kosovo Conflict and the Central European Members of NATO: Lessons and Implications" *NATO and Europe in the 21st Century: New Roles for a Changing Partnership* (July 2000 publication of the Woodrow Wilson Institute, which can be accessed at www.wilsoncenter.org.

10. He explicitly contrasts this more practical, hands-on approach with foundational issues discussed by meta-ethicists. See Joel Rosenthal, "An Ethical Approach to International Affairs" in *Perspectives on Ethics and International Affairs* 15, no. 4 (Spring 2001): 4.

11. Albrecht Schnabel and Ramesh Thakur, "Kosovo, the changing contours of world politics, and the challenge of world order," in Albrecht Schnabel and Ramesh Thakur, eds., *Kosovo and the Challenge of Humanitarian Intervention* (New York: United Nations University Press, 2000), 1. One might argue that Kosovo is irrelevant to the future of humanitarian intervention as a worst-case scenario, which exacerbates the differences between small, medium, and large states. However, one might also argue that Kosovo is very relevant, and that further NATO interventions will resemble this case study in extending beyond NATO's traditional mandate into out-of-area defenses of human rights, including actions to stop ethnic cleansing that potentially involve the use of force. If we look at recent NATO actions, such as in Macedonia, we see that similar humanitarian issues concerning minority rights have arisen. Even in the case of Afghanistan, which initially involved out-of-area defense, there is now a focus on creating a human rights regime, which guarantees the rights of all ethnic groups. Of course, this is also the case in Iraq, although it is not (yet) a NATO operation as of October 2003.

12. Finnemore and Sikkink argue the importance of going beyond institutional norms and finding a critical mass of actors who believe in certain norms, and are willing to persuade others. See Martha Finnemore and Kathryn Sikkink, "International Norm Dynamics and Political Change," in *International Organization* 52, no. 4 (Autumn 1998): 887–917.

13. Vaclav Havel, "Kosovo and the End of the Nation-State," *New York Review of Books* (10 June 1999), 4 and 6 (address to Canadian Parliament, 29 April 1999).

14. Andrew Linklater suggests, under emergency conditions, it may be necessary to go beyond the usual requirements of international law, but these decisions are more legitimate if they are taken multilaterally. See Andrew Linklater, "The Good International Citizen" in Albrecht Schnabel and Ramesh Thakur, eds., *Kosovo and the Challenge of Humanitarian Intervention* (Tokyo and New York: United Nations University Press, 2000), 482–495.

15. Cultural theorists, who often support the idea of continuity in security ideologies, may be surprised to see that changes in national security priorities can and do occur. While preferences may be fixed for crusading leaders, they may be fluid for more strategic or pragmatic leaders. Also, changing international conditions will probably affect all leaders' range of choices. For a criticism of cultural theorists, see in particular Brian Rathburn's criticisms of John Duffield in Brian Rathburn, "Cracked, Colored and Tinted Lenses: Red-Green Position and Policies on Humanitarian Intervention and the Use of Force in Germany" (unpublished manuscript presented at the German Studies Association [GSA] conference in Washington, D.C., Oct. 3–5, 2001). Also see John Duffield, "Political Culture and State Behavior: Why Germany Confounds Neorealism," *International Organization* 53, no. 3 (Autumn 1999): 765–803.

16. Weiss and Collins, *Humanitarian Intervention*, 205.

17. Weiss and Collins, *Humanitarian Intervention*, 206.

18. John Gerard Ruggie, ed., *Multilateralism Matters* (New York: Columbia University Press, 1993), 6.

19. Karl W. Deutsch, et al., *Political Community in the North Atlantic Area: International Organization in Light of Historical Experience* (Princeton: Princeton University Press, 1957), 5.

20. Ben Rosamond, *Theories of European Integration* (New York: Palgrave, 2000), 204.

21. For material on political theories and leadership models, as well as role-playing and information on Central Europe, see this Web site: www.bss.foothill.fhda.edu/heiser.meredith/

22. He argues that escalation was not achieved until the forty-first day (over halfway through the conflict), and that this is typical of humanitarian wars. See Charles Krauthammer, "The Short Unhappy Life of Humanitarian War," *The National Interest* (Fall 1999): 5–8.

23. East Germany became a NATO member automatically when it united with Germany in 1990. Although West Germany has belonged to NATO since 1955, the government always refused to participate in NATO's military responsibilities due to international agreements limiting its military to national self-defense. For more information on German history/politics, see this Web site: www.foothill.fhda.edu/divisions/unification

24. OSCE was founded originally as the Conference on Security and Cooperation in Europe in 1973. It grew out of the Helsinki talks between the United States and the Soviet Union. It is presently the largest regional security organization in the world, with fifty-five members from Europe, Central Asia, and North America. "It is active in early warning, conflict prevention, crisis management, and post conflict rehabilitation." See OSCE Web site, www.osce.org/general/.

25. Quoted in Ivo H. Daalder and Michael E. O'Hanlon, *Winning Ugly: NATO's War to Save Kosovo* (Washington, DC: Brookings Institution Press, 2000), 75.

26. For a general introduction to the benefits and costs of NATO for the new Central European members, see Stephen R. Burant, "After NATO Enlargement: Poland, the Czech Republic, and Hungary, and the Problem of Further European Integration," *Problems of Post-Communism* 48, no. 2 (March/April 2001): 25–41.

27. Ironically, it is the more populist parties which generally argue more forcefully for "moral" positions. See Cas Mudde, "The Peasantry, the People, and the Proletariat," *East European Politics and Society* 14, no. 2 (Fall 2000): 47.

28. Serbs murdered thousands of Bosnian Muslims when a UN safe area in Srebrenica was overrun. The red-green coalition in Germany viewed Srebrenica as a failure of moral courage, where Europe could not agree to take effective action. When it finally did take action, too few peacekeepers were sent too late and terms of a cease-fire were unclear.

29. In addition, the accusation that Germany was "free-riding" (gaining security at no cost) in the Gulf War in 1991 motivated the German public to support military participation. Although many Germans thought the German constitution forbade intervention, this issue was resolved by the German Constitutional Court, which decided in 1994 that intervention could take place as long as it was supported by a parliamentary vote. The new German leaders were asked on October 12 (before they were sworn in) whether they agreed in principle with NATO deployment on Kosovo. See Vladimir Handl and Charlie Jeffery, "Germany and Europe After Kohl: Between Social Democracy and Normalization?" *German Studies Review* 24, no. 1 (Feb. 2001): 70.

30. www.un.org/News/ossg/sg/pages/sg_biography.html. Also see Kofi Annan, "Peacekeeping, Military Intervention, and National Sovereignty in Internal Armed Conflict" in Jonathan Moore, ed., *Hard Choices: Moral Dilemmas in Humanitarian Intervention* (New York: Rowman & Littlefield Publishers, Inc., 1998), 55–69.

31. For more information on these permanent representatives, call their respective UN missions at (212) 861-4900 (Russia), (212) 634-7626 (China), and (212) 415-4000 (the United States).

32. CIS was created after the demise of the Soviet Union to encourage economic and military relations between all of the former republics with the exception of the Baltic nations (Latvia, Lithuania, Estonia).

33. This is adopted largely from Vladimir Baranovsky, "Russia: Reassessing national interests" in Schnabel and Thakur, eds., *Humanitarian Intervention*, 101–116.

34. This is adopted largely from the argument of Zhang Yunling, "China: Whither the world order after Kosovo?" in Schnabel and Thakur, eds., *Humanitarian Intervention*, 117–127.

35. Holbrooke was confirmed in August 1999. This happened in part because of his role in negotiations with Milosevic.

36. To consult Solana's speeches, go to www.nato.int and conduct a search using his name.

37. The timeline incorporates research of numerous sources, including *Facts on File World News Digest* 59 (March 25–June 24, 1999), 197–445; the *New York Times* (March 25–June 24, 1999); and Schnabel and Thakur, eds., *Humanitarian Intervention*.

38. As of October 2003, this force is still in Kosovo, although European militaries have largely replaced the American military.

39. It has been argued that humanitarian intervention is unique to the West. However, China cited this as the reason to invade Tibet in 1951, and Vietnam cited it in its intervention of Cambodia in 1979.

40. Walt, *Foreign Policy* (Spring 1998): 42–43. For further reflection on the overlap of theories, see Thomas Berger, "Beyond the Demonology of Power: the Study of German Foreign Policy After the Cold War," *German Politics and Society* 19, no. 1 (Spring 2001): 80–95.

41. Harnisch and Maull, *Civilian Power*, 129.

42. See Andrew A. Michta, "Poland: A Linchpin of Regional Security" in Andrew A. Michta, ed., *America's New Allies: Poland, Hungary and the Czech Republic in NATO* (Seattle: University of Washington Press, 1999), 196. It seems that Michta's otherwise cogent analysis is US-centric, as it entirely ignores the domestic challenges that leaders confronted.

43. This interpretation might be made if one thinks that UN resolutions or qualified majority voting in the General Assembly are sufficient to justify action when the Security Council is deadlocked. See Ove Bring, "Should NATO take the lead in formulating a doctrine on humanitarian intervention?" *NATO Review* 47: 3 (Autumn 1999): 24–27.

44. Sean Kay, "NATO Enlargement: Policy, Process, and Implications," from Michta, ed., *New Allies*, 179.

Flies in the Ointment: International Terrorists and Global Civil Society

Craig Warkentin

About This Module

In the range of international and comparative politics classes I teach regularly, one of my primary goals is to help students (better) define their political selves—that is, to help them develop clear positions on contentious political issues and explicitly connect their positions to their personal values. Toward this end, my aim is to encourage students to remain conscious of their own values, be willing to tackle new ideas and alternative perspectives, and discover for themselves that there is no (single) right answer for most global problems. With these goals in mind, this module engages students in a role-playing exercise to ethically address the problem of international terrorism from various vantage points.

For the module to be most effective, students should have a working familiarity with three key concepts: global civil society, terrorism, and constructivism. Global civil society and terrorism are explicit foci of this module, and students are required to complete assigned reading on these issues. I often simply present the constructivist framework in the classroom or use it implicitly to guide discussion and role-playing activities.[1]

Beyond these essentials, this module can be employed quite flexibly in any introductory course that addresses global politics. In basic form, with students doing some assigned reading beforehand, it can be completed in a single class session. The module can also be expanded over two or more class sessions by including additional reading (or online browsing) materials, video presentations (such as *PBS Frontline* documentaries),[2] and/or more extensive, formal writing assignments. For example, one productive and relatively simple way to expand the exercise and facilitate personal connections to the subject issues is to have terrorists speak for themselves through their writings or training manuals. (See this module's companion Web site cited in the endnotes for supplementary resources.)

Upon completing the module, students should be able to answer the following questions:

1. Is the notion of global civil society a useful tool for understanding contemporary international problems such as terrorism? How so, or why not?
2. Are states the only, or necessarily the most well-suited, actors to address the problem of international terrorism? Why or why not?
3. In which ways, and to what extent, can you (personally) reshape world politics to better address global problems such as terrorism?

Miniglossary

Global civil society In its most basic sense, global civil society is a socially constructed and transnationally defined network of relationships that provides ideologically variable channels of opportunity for political involvement. Through their ongoing interactions with each other, transnational actors (such as NGOs) create and maintain global civil society's constitutive network of relationships. These relationships in turn give rise to channels of opportunity that are employed by many different actors, working from various points on the political spectrum and often toward divergent ends.[3] Thus, global civil society both shapes and is shaped by the exigencies of IR; it exists "alongside other social institutions and political structures within the broader realm of world politics, while (at the same time) interacting with them."[4]

Nongovernmental organization (NGO) An NGO is a private, voluntary, nonprofit association whose membership and organizational activities cross national (state) borders.[5] Examples include Greenpeace, Human Rights Watch, and the International Olympic Committee. (Technically speaking, terrorist networks such as al-Qaeda are not NGOs, but they increasingly function as such and are treated by many scholars in much the same manner.) NGOs perform a variety of important roles in the context of international relations and global civil society, but most share a common primary objective: to change the social or political status quo in some way or another. In this regard, many organizations work toward progressive goals, while others seek more conservative ends.

Constructivism Sometimes called social constructivism, this "main theoretical challenger to established perspectives within the discipline of [international relations]" characterizes world politics as an ongoing cycle in which actors shape their social context and vice versa.[6] "What actors do and how they interact determines the nature of the social context. In turn, this social context shapes who actors are, what they want, and how they behave." Given its assumption of "constant dynamism and change," constructivism is more complex than most theories of international relations.[7] But by focusing on social interaction and change, this framework can address contemporary issues overlooked by conventional IR perspectives and offer new insights into old problems.

State As defined under international law, a state is an entity with a permanent population, a defined territory, a government, and the capacity to engage in relations with other states.[8] Examples include India, the United States, and Saudi Arabia. Each state encompasses a large web of interconnected actors and influences, yet the term state is usually used to denote only (the decisions and activities of) a national government. States have functioned as the building blocks of the modern international system and, given their sovereignty and available resources, tend to wield greater influence over the dynamics and processes of world politics than do other international actors.

Terrorism Definitions of terrorism abound, with none universally accepted. The US Department of State defines terrorism as "premeditated, politically motivated violence perpetrated against noncombatant targets by subnational groups or clandestine agents, usually intended to influence an audience."[9] This and other accepted definitions are problematic, since most scholars who study terrorism point out that states—particularly those ruled by authoritarian governments—also engage in terrorism. Yet subnational terrorists (individuals and groups) generally receive more attention than terrorist states, as has been the case in the wake of 9/11. One concise definition of terrorism, which avoids common shortcomings and can be used for this module, is "political violence that targets civilians deliberately and indiscriminately."[10]

Step-by-Step Directions

Out-of-Class Preparation

To begin, have students read Chapter 1 of *Reshaping World Politics* and browse the *Terrorism Questions & Answers* Web site. Optionally, if time and course context allow, students may also read the Introduction to *Reshaping World Politics*, additional material on terrorism, and/or a reading on constructivism. For each assignment, highlight specific portions of the reading, direct students toward particular Web pages, and/or introduce them to key terms (see the Miniglossary) before they get started. This helps students to study and prepare more efficiently, and results in better classroom participation. (What you choose to highlight will depend on the content of the course for which you are using this module, as well as on the specific concepts or issues you wish to emphasize in the classroom.)

Day One (±15 minutes): Hand Out Materials and Assign Roles

Distribute Student Handout 1: The Reading Companion, and Student Handouts 2–5: The Actor Guides, and assign each student a specific role. Students who play the role of citizen simply represent themselves. Other students are assigned a particular state, NGO, or terrorist (group) to play. When assigning roles, create an appropriate distribution of states, NGOs, citizens, and terrorists. Ideally, multiple states and NGOs should be represented in the exercise,[11] but "terrorists" can be members of the same or different groups.

Instruct students to formulate thoughtful responses to the study questions in their actor guides, to jot down some notes for use during discussion, and then to bring these to class for use in the role-playing exercise.

Day Two (±60 minutes): The Role-Play

The in-class role-playing exercise can be conducted in various ways: as an open (large group) discussion, a structured exchange between different actors, a formal debate, etc. I prefer students to work in small groups in order to collect their ideas and refine their positions before engaging the entire class in a discussion structured around the questions raised in the handouts. Throughout, my aim is to guide the exercise in a manner consistent with the principles of global civil society; that is, in a way that encourages the expression of contending views, while working to develop tolerant and inclusive understandings.

Handout 1:
The Reading Companion

Introduction

Since the September 11 attacks, public discussion of international terrorism has largely been framed in conventional terms, and policy responses have relied on traditional state-based approaches (such as military force and secrecy). This module encourages you to explore other means of understanding and addressing terrorism—to think outside the box by employing your personal values and, working within the framework of global civil society, to develop ethical responses to this contemporary global problem.

Begin by completing the assigned readings. As you read and browse, consider the following questions:

- In what way(s) does the notion of global civil society change how you think about world politics? About international terrorism?
- How is terrorism different from other "isms"? Why do disagreements persist about how to define this phenomenon?
- How have your actions and interactions with others shaped your social context? How has your social context influenced your personal identity, interests, and behaviors?

Study Questions

After reading assigned materials, reflect upon these questions:

- How important are states, nongovernmental organizations (NGOs), and individuals in world politics? How influential is each type of actor? Upon what understandings or personal experiences do you base your answers?
- Are all states significant? Are any nonstate actors more powerful or influential than state actors? How big an impact can an NGO or individual have on world politics? Explain your answers.
- Name and describe the basic goals of an NGO with which you are affiliated or have had some personal contact. How do the organization's mission and activities correspond to your personal values and ethics?
- What personal values and experiences influence your understanding of (a) world politics and (b) international terrorism? In what way(s)? How might someone who is another race or gender, lives in another country, or subscribes to another religion answer these same questions?

- How does a people-centered understanding of international politics differ from more conventional state-centered understandings? Toward which perspective do you lean? Why?
- Provide a specific example of how international politics is socially constructed. How difficult was it to come up with your example? What does this tell you about the nature of world politics?
- In what specific ways do you participate in civil society? What influence has doing so had on (a) your daily life and (b) your political activities and opinions?
- What does it mean, in practical terms, to say that global civil society's channels of opportunity are ideologically variable? Is this a good thing or a bad thing? Why? Is your response different now than it would have been before September 11, 2001? Explain.

Student Handout 2:
State Actor Guide

You are playing the role of a state in this exercise. Your task is to formulate specific policy proposals, or present a particular course of action, that will effectively address the problem of international terrorism. Toward that end, consider the following questions:

- Can you use military force to respond to international terrorism? Should you? Why?
- What alternatives to military force are available? Are any of these more effective than military force? Why?
- Is it better to act alone or in concert with other states? Why? What are the practical implications of your answer?
- Should you encourage or request assistance from nonstate actors? Why or why not? If so, which actors and in what capacity? If not, what will be your response to nonstate actors who ask to be involved?
- In what ways can you capitalize on the dynamics and processes of socially constructed IR and global civil society to help ensure your success? What aspects of these contextual environments might present problems for you, and how can you minimize any adverse effects?
- What are the one or two easiest, but important steps you can take to effectively address international terrorism? Why?
- What are the one or two most difficult, yet necessary steps you can take to effectively address international terrorism? Why?

Student Handout 3:
NGO Actor Guide

You are playing the role of a nongovernmental organization (NGO) in this exercise. Your task is to formulate specific policy proposals, or some particular course of action, that can be implemented to effectively address the issue of international terrorism. Toward that end, consider the following questions:

- Should military force be used to respond to international terrorism? Why?
- What alternatives to military force are available? Are any of these more effective than military force? Why?
- Is it better to act alone or in concert with other NGOs? Why? What are the practical implications of your answer?
- Should you encourage or request assistance from state actors? Why or why not? If so, which states and in what capacity? If not, what will you do when state actors become involved—or, more likely, take the lead—in responding to terrorism?
- In what ways can you capitalize on the dynamics and processes of socially constructed IR and global civil society to help ensure your success? What aspects of these contextual environments might present problems for you, and how can you minimize any adverse effects?
- What are the one or two easiest, but important steps you can take to effectively address international terrorism? Why?
- What are the one or two most difficult, yet necessary steps you can take to effectively address international terrorism? Why?

Student Handout 4:
Citizen Actor Guide

You are playing yourself—an ordinary citizen—in this exercise. Your task is to formulate a specific course of action to help ensure that—when it comes to the issue of international terrorism (or the "war on terrorism")—your political voice will be heard and your interests properly represented. Toward that end, consider the following questions:

- Should military force be used to respond to international terrorism? Why?
- What alternatives to military force are available? Are any of these more effective than military force? Why?
- Is it better to act alone or in concert with other individuals? Why? What are the practical implications of your answer?
- Should you encourage your government's involvement in response to international terrorism? Why or why not? If so, in what capacity? How will you accomplish this? If not, what do you propose in lieu of state action?
- In what ways can you capitalize on the dynamics and processes of socially constructed IR and global civil society to help ensure that your political voice is heard?
- What are the one or two easiest, but important steps you can take as an individual to help ensure that international terrorism is addressed effectively? Why?
- What are the one or two most difficult, yet necessary steps you can take as an individual to help ensure that international terrorism is addressed effectively? Why?
- What will you (personally) do now? Why? How?

Student Handout 5:
Terrorist Actor Guide

You are playing the role of a terrorist in this exercise. Your task is to formulate a specific course of action that can be implemented to effectively realize your demands. Toward that end, consider the following questions:

- Do you expect military force to be used in response to your actions? Why?
- What alternatives to political violence are available? Are any of these more effective than political violence? Why?
- Is it better to act alone or in concert with other terrorists? Why? What are the practical implications of your answer?
- Should you encourage or request assistance from other actors? Why or why not? If so, which actors and in what capacity? If not, what will you do when other actors engage in activities or pursue an agenda similar to yours?
- In what ways can you capitalize on the dynamics and processes of socially constructed IR and global civil society to help ensure your success? What aspects of these contextual environments might present problems for you, and how can you minimize any adverse effects?
- What are the one or two easiest, but important steps you can take to effectively realize your objectives? Why?
- What are the one or two most difficult, yet necessary steps you can take to effectively realize your objectives? Why?

Debriefing

Students come away from this exercise able to do the following:

- Clearly articulate their personal values and ethics, particularly as they apply to contemporary global issues such as terrorism;
- propose specific strategies and/or policy suggestions, grounded in ethical values, that address international terrorism without overreliance on states or conventional state-based approaches;
- describe the roles of individuals, NGOs, and social relations in shaping contemporary world politics;
- discuss the usefulness of constructivism, global civil society, and similar frameworks for making sense of contemporary world politics.

Any or all of the following questions may help to facilitate these goals:

- How significant or influential are (a) states, (b) NGOs, and (c) individuals in the grand scheme of world politics? Explain.
- How useful are constructivism, global civil society, and similar notions for making sense of contemporary world politics? Justify your position.
- What insights into global terrorism can be gleaned from the concept of global civil society? How might the widespread adoption or application of this concept, by various actors, influence the political dynamics and effectiveness of international terrorism?
- Which of your personal values or ethical principles proved most instrumental in helping you develop policies or strategies to address international terrorism?
- What personal values and ethics did the 9/11 terrorists articulate? How do these differ from your own?
- Are terrorists like the 9/11 hijackers inherently amoral or unethical, or are they simply rational actors whose values differ from our own? How does your answer influence your understanding of international terrorism and how to respond to it?
- Is terrorism ever justified? Under what circumstances, or why not?
- Imagine a world filled with civil actors that represent only your values or theirs. What would such a world look like? How would it differ from what we see today?
- Is communication between people and groups with radically different values possible? Why or why not? What are the implications of your answer for efforts to address global problems such as terrorism?
- What should be done with uncivil actors (such as international terrorists) in the context of global civil society? How would a truly civil society respond to terrorism? Explain your answers.

• In what ways did participating in this exercise (a) support and (b) contradict what you previously knew or believed?

Selected Bibliography

In Print

Ba, Alice, and Matthew J. Hoffman, "Making and Remaking the World for IR 101: A Resource for Teaching Social Constructivism in Introductory Classes," *International Studies Perspectives* 4: 1 (2003): 15–33.

Martin, Gus, *Understanding Terrorism: Challenges, Perspectives, and Issues* (Thousand Oaks, CA: Sage Publications, 2003).

Warkentin, Craig, *Reshaping World Politics: NGOs, the Internet, and Global Civil Society* (Lanham, MD: Rowman & Littlefield Publishers, 2001).

Related Web Sites

www.oswego.edu/reshaping/flies *Flies in the Ointment:* Created to support this module, this site contains links to relevant Web sites, an extended bibliography, additional resources for instructors, and downloadable handouts for easy printing and distribution.

www.pbs.org/wgbh/pages/frontline/shows/network *Inside the Terror Network:* This companion site for a PBS *Frontline* documentary focuses on the personal lives of three 9/11 hijackers, and includes excerpts from an al-Qaeda training manual and handwritten instructions for the attacks.

www.terrorismanswers.com *Terrorism: Questions & Answers:* Maintained by the Council on Foreign Relations, this site offers a wide range of information about terrorism and related issues, presented in an accessibly written question-and-answer format.

Endnotes

1. See Alice Ba and Matthew J. Hoffman, "Making and Remaking the World for IR 101: A Resource for Teaching Social Constructivism in Introductory Classes," *International Studies Perspectives* 4, no. 1 (2003) for a lecture template that also can serve as an accessible reading assignment. Additionally, note that IR textbooks increasingly include some discussion of constructivism. If you are using one of these texts, or have otherwise addressed constructivism in your course, a brief review may be all that is needed to employ this module effectively.

2. See www.pbs.org/wgbh/pages/frontline for a complete program list.

3. Craig Warkentin, *Reshaping World Politics: NGOs, the Internet, and Global Civil Society* (Lanham, Md.: Rowman & Littlefield Publishers, 2001), 174. In *Reshaping World Politics*, I examine ways in which nongovernmental organizations (NGOs) contribute to global civil society, drawing on eight NGO case studies to argue that "people make politics" and—through their ongoing interactions with international actors and each other—"reshape" the dynamics and processes of international relations (IR). This module is based on the concepts and arguments presented in the book, but extends that discussion by focusing on "uncivil" actors (terrorists) and explicitly incorporating a constructivist perspective.

4. Warkentin, *Reshaping World Politics*, 18.

5. NGOs can be domestic (or national) in character in that they sometimes operate within the boundaries of a single community, province, or state. As used in this module, however, the term "NGO" only refers to transnational groups.

6. Ba and Hoffman, "Making and Remaking," 15.

7. Ba and Hoffman, "Making and Remaking," 21–22.

8. So defined, each state has "legal personality" under international law. In practical terms, this means that states are expected to follow certain rules (or laws) when interacting with other states and international actors. For further discussion, see Chapter 2 of William R. Slomanson, *Fundamental Perspectives on International Law*, 4th ed. (Belmont, CA: Wadsworth, 2003), 53–100.

9. US Department of State, "Introduction," in *Patterns of Global Terrorism: 2002* www.state.gov/s/ct/rls/pgtrpt/2002/html/19977.htm, April 2003 (4 August 2003).

10. Joshua S. Goldstein, *International Relations*, 5th ed. (update) (New York: Longman, 2004), 214.

11. Students interested in researching their roles can be referred to the appropriate country description in the *CIA World Factbook* (available at www.cia.gov/cia/publications/factbook) or their assigned NGO's Web site.

OTHER QUESTIONS OF
SOCIAL JUSTICE

Blood Diamonds in Africa

Peter Lucas

About This Module

As a professor of peace education I stress the "positive peace" aspects of education, whereby students learn that human rights are the underlying values needed to support a culture of peace. I use human rights as a conceptual framework or a set of core organizing ideas that emphasize the process of understanding the value of these rights and the interrelationships between all human rights standards in a holistic way. In the long run, this process perspective is more important than the actual content of the curricular units, because of the many potential themes one has to negotiate as a student of peace education and human rights.

This particular module focuses on the relationship between human rights and the diamond trade. In it, my primary goal is to increase students' critical consciousness about the role of resources in global violence. A secondary goal is to see if we can move beyond educational awareness to initiate some degree of student activism. Because I often work with graduate students majoring in education, who will one day be designing their own curricula, I also want this module to demonstrate that today's human rights curriculum is flexible, ephemeral, and downloadable; that it is built around current news clippings, as well as decades-old legal standards; and that group exercises, Web sites, documentary films, photo-reportage, and acts of activism enrich opportunities to find meaning in the subject matter.

The core activity in this module turns the tables on students by having *them* teach specific human rights dimensions of the African diamond trade to the rest of the class. After a general introduction to the topic, students work in groups to research their topics. They compile their findings and reflections in scrapbooks or portfolios. Then they present a lesson based on their research to the class as whole. The multiple presentations give the class a more layered understanding of the complexity of the issues. Finally they write letters to public officials expressing their opinions on this subject. At least five in-class days are needed to complete this module;

substantial time is also needed outside of class for students to conduct research, design lesson plans, and prepare their presentations. The learning value of this module is not limited to education majors or to those specifically interested in human rights. As Toolkit 1 demonstrates, when students teach others material, their retention rates soar. The diverse active learning opportunities involved also empower them to find meaning in the material and to do something about the situation.

I prepare students for this module by first introducing them to basic human rights standards, such as those found in the Universal Declaration of Human Rights (www.un.org/Overview/rights.htm) and the Convention on the Rights of the Child (www.unicef.org/crc/crc.htm). Familiarity with the contents and politics of such primary legal instruments enables students to readily recognize abuses of these rights throughout their research into blood diamonds. Ultimately, it also prepares them to answer these questions:

1. Which specific human rights standards are most frequently and consistently abused in the diamond trade? Which treaties and treaty provisions outlaw these abuses?
2. Who are the key players in the diamond trade? How do the costs and benefits of the diamond market affect them differently?
3. What can be done to decrease the human rights abuses involved in blood diamonds? What obstacles to this are likely to surface and how can they be overcome?
4. What are the necessary elements of an effective letter to a public official on a controversial public issue?

Miniglossary

Problematization The strategy of problematization has little to do with "problem-solving." Problematizing a situation concerns posing questions in order to more deeply explore a given set of issues. In the case of blood diamonds, students problematize and pose inquiries about resources in order to understand the complexity of the situation and why the competition over valuable resources leads to conflict and human rights violations.

Critical consciousness The development of critical consciousness is to become aware of and evaluate one's own existence within an environment. Following Paulo Freire,[1] critical consciousness strives to develop analytic habits of thinking, listening, reading, writing, and speaking, which discover the deep and hidden meanings of texts, images, and events. Along with care, critical consciousness is one of the baseline values of peace education and human rights. Helping students develop their capacities of critical consciousness for themselves and for others is another primary objective of this module.

Step-by-Step Directions

I frequently teach classes that span the better part of a weekend. Educators with more traditional class periods of 50 or 75 minutes in length may want to reorganize the activities below to suit their scheduling needs.

Module Preparation

Familiarize students with contemporary human rights standards under international law. As core documents, I emphasize the Universal Declaration of Human Rights; the International Covenant on Political and Civil Rights; the International Covenant on Economic, Social, and Cultural Rights; the Convention on the Rights of the Child; and the Genocide Convention (www.unhchr.ch/html/menu3/b/p_genoci.htm), among others.

Day 1: Introduction to the Topic and Class Discussion

Divide the class into three groups. Distribute to each group one of three articles on the Democratic Republic of Congo (DRC):

- Somini Sengupta, "Innocence of Youth is Victim of Congo War." *New York Times*, June 23, 2003.
- Adam Hochschild, "Chaos in Congo Suits Many Parties Just Fine." *New York Times*, April 20, 2003.
- "Plunder of DRC Resources Denied." *Agence France Presse*, April 17, 2001. www.globalpolicy.org/security/issues/congo/2001/0417deny. htm.

Allow the class to quietly read these articles. When ready, groups discuss among themselves the human rights issues highlighted in these depictions of the DRC. Each group then reports back to the class what they learned. At this point, ask the students if they have any questions or ideas about what fuels the conflict in the DRC. The idea is to problematize the situation. An open discussion format ensures that students pose inquiries about resources, markets, trade routes, and supply competitors. This is important, because underneath the conflict in the DRC, there is a battle for a vast treasure of mineral wealth between competing Congolese warlords, military leaders from neighboring countries, and Western corporations. As explained in the articles, at stake is the trafficking in valuable timber, coffee, ivory, gold, diamonds, copper, and most importantly, coltan (columbium-tantalum), the mineral now used in the production of mobile phones and computers.

An important element in any human rights curriculum is geography. In order to help students realize that conflicts leading to human rights violations are a global phenomenon, I then pass out copies of select maps from *The Penguin Atlas of War and Peace*[2] and *The State of Women in the World*[3]. Each map is color-coded for specific themes, such as war deaths, human rights atrocities, refugees, landmines, child soldiers, small arms trade, peacekeeping forces, peacemaking processes in the works, and so on. Students return to small groups in order to study the maps and report back to the class with additional questions, surprising finds, and comments about the relationship between conflict/human rights violations and resource wars.

At the close of this day, I project the West African States map and the specific map of the DRC.[4] Together we explore the relationships between minerals, armed conflicts, refugee camps, rape statistics, HIV infection rates, child soldiers, etc. The war and peace maps present a useful setup for blood diamonds, because they begin to establish in students' minds the complex consequences of fighting over resources.

Day 2: Film and Discussion

In preparation for this day, students read three items:

- Michael Renner, "The Anatomy of Resource Wars," PDF version online from the World Watch Institute at www.worldwatch.org/pubs/paper/162
- "Resource Wars: An Interview with Michael Klare," online at www.alternet.org/story.html?StoryID=10797
- Richard Dreyfuss, "The Thirty-Year Itch." www.motherjones.com/news/feature/2003/03/ma_273_01/html

You may choose to assign additional articles or resources as well. In class, give each student five index cards and allow them to write six thoughts about resources. Then ask the students to tape their cards to the front blackboard. Once all the cards are up on the board, assign a couple of student facilitators to rearrange the cards by themes; this creates interesting clusters of shared thoughts and—just as interesting—lone ideas. Together these can form the foundation for an interesting group discussion on how natural resources fuel conflict.

Next, show the National Geographic documentary, *Diamonds of War* (available at: www.nationalgeographic.com/channel/contact.html). Set in Sierra Leone, the 1-hour special follows the correspondent Dominic

Cunningham-Reid as he tracks the flow of illegal diamonds that are smuggled out of the country. Cunningham-Reid begins with the legitimate government diamond exchange in Freetown, but as he heads into the interior under the guise of purchasing diamonds, things become more shadowy and dangerous to the point that his cameraman has to use a hidden pinhole camcorder to secretly film their encounters with dealers and smugglers. Along the way, the film captures the difficult labor conditions of mining, the environmental degradation that extensive search for diamonds causes, and the many human rights atrocities associated with conflict diamonds.

After the screening students brainstorm in groups, and generate their own questions about diamonds and the effects/dangers that valuable resources play in a war. Here is where students begin to understand why blood diamonds are also known as conflict diamonds.

In closing, assign this homework: Write a page on how your life would be different if you lived in an area where valuable minerals were mined and smuggled. Tell students to save this journal entry for inclusion in the scrapbooks they are about to begin.

Day 3: Group Research

Invite students to report back to the class on how their lives would be different if they were living in an area where valuable minerals were mined and smuggled. After everyone has spoken, open up the discussion and ask the students for their thoughts on *Diamonds of War. Specifically ask for their thoughts from a human rights perspective.* If necessary, students can refer back to the Universal Declaration of Human Rights or the Convention on the Rights of the Child to make connections.

At this point, the class breaks up into four or five research groups. Instruct each group to choose a distinct aspect of the African trade in blood diamonds to report on when the module is complete. Since diamonds can lead to various human rights issues, each group selects a different theme, such as resource wars, child soldiers, small arms and disarmament, rape as a war crime, human rights of women, dismemberment and torture, ecological violence and sustainable development, internal displacement and international refugees, contemporary slavery and economic human rights, and globalization and domestic consumer choices. All of these issues will have been introduced in the previous assigned readings.

Let's assume the class breaks into four groups: child soldiers, small arms and disarmament, displacement and refugees, and global consumer choices. This last theme holds particular interest for young adults, since diamonds—known as "Bling Bling" in Hollywood lingo—are such an important status symbol in popular culture. These themes also allow students to move beyond the confines of Sierra Leone, Angola, and the DRC as the usual case studies for conflict diamonds. One of the challenges of these reports is to not create stereotypes or project that all of Africa is mired in clandestine gem smuggling and brutal violence.

Once the groups' research topics are defined, guide each group to one lead online research link. I use the National Geographic page on Diamonds at magma.nationalgeographic.com/ngm/data/2002/03/01/html/ft_20020301.1. html, which includes an interview with the film correspondent Dominic Cunningham-Reid. This lead story on diamonds has multimedia slide shows, additional video, maps of diamond conflict areas to enlarge, audio commentary by reporters and photographers in the field, interactive forums where students can voice their opinions, and excellent links to additional Web sites that focus on diamonds. These sites not only include human rights organizations working to end the trade in conflict diamonds, but also coverage of the world's biggest diamond merchants in Antwerp, such as De Beers, so that students can ponder the business and allure of diamonds on a wider scale.

Emphasize that students will need to go well beyond this initial Web site to conduct adequate research for their presentations. By this point, students have usually caught on that one human rights Web site usually leads to others. *It's important to leave a bit of uncertainty in the mix to see how creative student investigations can become.* In fact, the chosen lead does not have to be the most obvious one.

Scrapbook Compilation

As an extended research project this stage is the longest section of the module, as students gather articles, pictures, clippings, and other media items which relate to their themes. Instruct students to gather this material into a group scrapbook that they will turn in, after the presentations and letter-writing, to demonstrate the depth, breadth, and quality of their research. This scrapbook will contain the journal entry from Day Two, as well as other reflections or original artworks they choose to include. It may also include specific treaty passages and whatever other material they deem relevant. Thus these research portfolios include items students find, as well as items they may create themselves specifically for this project. The goal is for the scrapbook to document the evolution of their thought processes over the course of their research.

Your role throughout this stage is to keep each group on task and centered on the human rights issues inherent to each theme. This is an important role. *Whatever the students come up with, it should go full circle back to human rights.* By using the Universal Declaration of Human Rights and the Convention on the Rights of the Child, the students will understand how the conceptual framework of human rights can relate to whatever theme they choose. You may find it useful to set aside some class time during this research phase in order to see what everyone is doing. You must ensure that everything the students do is documented in journal entries and scrapbooks (or portfolios). The research phase allows students creative time to fill up their scrapbooks/portfolios and reflect on how the process of researching their theme has changed their perspectives on human rights.

Day 4: Group Presentations

(Depending on class size and period length, additional class days may be necessary to complete this stage of the module.)

On this day, each group teaches the rest of the class a specific aspect of the relationship between human rights and blood diamonds. Student teachers are encouraged to use multimedia to make their topics come alive for the class. There's no telling what students will come up with. This is the X factor and part of the fun. Given the nature of this module, it's assumed—and hoped—that each group will include an interactive component in their presentations. Groups may make their scrapbooks available to the rest of the class for brief viewing at this time as well.

Day 5: Student Activism: Voicing Opinions Beyond the Classroom

After students present their research projects and the class reflects upon the material presented, the class moves into the final stage of the module. It highlights current international efforts to prevent conflict diamonds from entering the global marketplace. These efforts are well documented online. Students can view some of the Web sites and, if they so choose, pledge support against the illicit trade in conflict diamonds. Typically, during this step, students come to appreciate that living in a democracy entails certain rights, and come to understand that for a democracy to be effective, citizens must express their views and concerns.

The key scaffolding here is the guidance provided on how to write letters to public officials, a skill that pervades much political activism. Detailed tips on how to write effective letters expressing political opinion on controversial topics can be found at:

www.readingrecovery.org/sections/home/letters.asp

Noting international efforts already in place, such as the Kimberly Process and the UN resolutions on conflict diamonds[5], students write letters to public officials or to the editors of newspapers they select, in order to lend their opinions and voices to the growing international debate over the role of diamonds and valuable resources in fueling conflict and war.

Given creative free reign, my experience is that students also create e-cards, ink-jet postcards, and posters to add more creativity to the activist process. All of this material is included in the ongoing scrapbooks. Students may use original artwork or search for appropriate images, such as fine jewelry, diamond mines, child soldiers, and refugee camps, to add to their scrapbooks. *By layering text directly over images, students create critical and ironic juxtapositions in order to call attention to specific aspects of conflict diamonds that hold meaning for them.* After adding documentation of their contributions to the public discourse on blood diamonds to their scrapbooks, students turn these portfolios in.

Debriefing

Finally, students evaluate this module in a group discussion, pointing out which sessions they liked the most and what they would change the next time this unit is taught. I stress this future tense, because peace education is about helping students become self-learners. Students realize they now have the capacity to experience the world with an engaged, critical consciousness and create change on issues of interest, beyond blood diamonds and beyond the support structure of the classroom. Once they appreciate this point, students tend to leave the curriculum with an expanded notion of what global citizenship means in the human rights and peace education movement.

Selected Bibliography

In Print

Freire, Paulo. *Pedagogy of Freedom: Ethics, Democracy, and Civic Courage* (New York: Rowman & Littlefield Publishers, 1998).

Hochschild, Adam. *King Leopold's Ghost: A Story of Greed, Terror, and Heroism in Colonial Africa* (New York: Mariner Books, 1999).

Klare, Michael. *Resource Wars: The New Landscape of Global Conflict* (New York: Owl Books, 2002).

Tamm, Ingrid. *Diamonds in Peace and War: Severing the Conflict Diamond Connection* (Cambridge, MA: World Peace Foundation, 2002).

Related Web Sites

www.amnesty.org; www.hrw.org; www.crimesofwar.org For more news of
    human rights violations concerning resources and Africa, refer to
    Amnesty International, Human Rights Watch, and Crimes of War.

http://magma.nationalgeographic.com/ngm/data/2002/03/01/html/ft_2002
    0301.1.html Contains the National Geographic online article,
    "Diamonds: the Real Story" by Andrew Cockburn and related links.

http://news.nationalgeographic.com/ Contains "Reporter Discusses Dark
    Side of Diamonds" from *National Geographic News* (Feb. 12, 2003).

Endnotes

1. Paulo Freire, *Pedagogy of Freedom: Ethics, Democracy, and Civic
Courage* (New York: Rowman & Littlefield Publishers, 1998).

2. Dan Smith, *The Penguin Atlas of War and Peace* (New York: Penguin
Books, 2003).

3. Joni Seager, *The Penguin Atlas of Women in the World* (New York:
Penguin Books, 2003).

4. For the West African States map, I use the maps in the *Atlas of War
and Peace,* pages 88–89. For the DRC, use pages 90–91.

5. See the following Global Witness Web site for information about the
Kimberly Process, recent news on the UN resolutions on conflict diamonds,
and the latest ongoing campaigns: www.globalwitness.org/campaigns/
diamonds/diamond_pledge.php

The Pursuit of a Green Global Conscience: A Debate in Distributive Justice and Global Environmental Governance

Vivian Bertrand

About This Module

It is often difficult for those of us who live in North America to see environmental issues from the perspectives of people living in developing countries. Compared to North America, environmental issues and policies may take on different proportions in the developing world. An issue seemingly small to us could appear life threatening to a person living in the developing world, and vice versa. The purpose of this module is to help students consider environmental issues from the perspectives of people living in the developing world, and to understand the concept of distributive justice. This active learning module will also help expand students' understanding of global environmental issues and the challenges of global governance in relation to international environmental politics. This module uses the problem of air pollution in Delhi, India as a basis to explore the dilemmas involved in balancing local concerns with the concerns of international organizations or treaties.

When the module is complete, students should be able to:

1. explain some of the dilemmas involved in mitigating international environmental issues.
2. identify classic issues surrounding global governance questions such as sovereignty.
3. analyze the concept of international distributive justice and how it relates to international environmental issues.

Miniglossary

Distributive justice The concept of distributive justice relates to a moral assessment of the division of resources between people or countries. It can also refer to a moral assessment of institutions and systems of social rules in light of how they affect resource distributions. Some scholars use the term still more broadly to consider how markets, the production system, trade policy, international trading regimes, and the monetary system influence who gets how much of what. In a planetary context, we can speak of *global distributive justice* as concerned with an ethical evaluation of the distribution of wealth, goods, or resources among all people on Earth. In environmental politics, distributive justice also relates to intergenerational equity, because it involves the allotment of natural resources and pollution to present and future generations.

Global governance Global governance refers to a set of rules and systems established by private and public actors, such as the United Nations, quasi-governmental organizations (e.g., the World Trade Organization), and non-governmental organizations (NGOs) as a means of managing their common affairs. With respect to environmental issues, global governance refers to the sum of multilateral conventions and agreements on relevant topics as well as other formal and informal institutions and arrangements. Some of the major players in global environmental governance include United Nations organizations, such as the United Nations Environment Program (UNEP) and the Commission on Sustainable Development (CSD); NGOs, such as the World Conservation Union (IUCN) and the India-based Centre for Science and Environment (CSE); and business organizations, such as the World Business Council for Sustainable Development (WBCSD). International agreements, such as the Convention on International Trade in Endangered Species of Wild Fauna and Flora (CITES), and international programs, such as Agenda 21 (the environmental plan adopted by 178 countries at the United Nations Conference on Environment and Development [UNCED] in 1992) are two of the most common tools used in international environmental governance.

Step-by-Step Directions

In preparation for the class, students read the Student Handout and other assigned literature listed on it. When introducing this section of the class, explain that the core of this activity centers on an in-class debate. Tell students they will all be responsible for representing different groups in the debate; no one gets to sit this activity out. In order to know how they should behave true to their given roles in the debate, they must read and consider the assigned readings ahead of time. Since they may be assigned to articulate perspectives with which they disagree, the process of digesting the readings may require some effort. Either before the class or when they arrive on the day of the debate, divide them into four different groups (factory workers from India, Indian politicians, representatives of multinational corporations, and members of international environmental organizations). Give students approximately 15 minutes to formulate their strategies within their groups. Remind them that, regardless of which group they represent, they are to speak and behave in ways that are true to their roles, rather than their personal opinions.

The debate begins with one student from each group stating the group's position (some may choose to do more dramatic presentations, while others will simply state the facts). Four students speak until each group's policy preferences are stated to the entire class. Next, a second person from each group follows with an extemporaneous response to the other groups; he or she must also remain in character. No person from any group may speak more than twice (or once, depending on the class size), and students are encouraged to voice only their actor's opinions, rather than speak on behalf of others. This prompts everyone to find his or her own voice. The position-response cycle forms the structure of the debate, which usually continues for about two-thirds of the class. After it's over, each group votes on the proposal to create a new international environmental organization as a means of preventing future Bhopals. Announce the result; then immediately guide students to step outside their roles as they discuss the experience and its relevance to class themes. Use the debriefing questions to help build a thorough discussion of the issues.

You will have to determine in advance how long each person has to address the class, based on the number of students and the length of the class. Be sure to leave sufficient time to debrief after the decision. Some teachers find that using an egg timer, which everyone can see and hear helps students honor the time limit, so that no one is left out.

Student Handout

A Debate on a Proposal to Create a New International Environmental Organization

You have been called to a roundtable of stakeholders including factory workers from India, Indian politicians, representatives of multinational corporations, and members of international environmental organizations, such as United Nations Environment Program, Centre for Science and Environment, Greenpeace, etc., to debate the following question: Should an international environmental organization be created? The organization could be similar to the World Trade Organization or the International Court of Justice; you decide what form it might take.[1] As you debate, in keeping with the views of the stakeholder whose views you represent, you may consider questions such as:

- Would such an organization be able to meet the needs of both the developed and developing world?
- Is an equitable distribution of resources and power an appropriate goal of global governance? Why or why not?
- How much power should such an organization have?
- What do you think it could achieve?
- What are the pros and cons of this proposal?

At the end of your meeting, you must reach a final decision as a group (based on a majority vote). Before the in-class debate, read and reflect on the essays that follow to see how the information provided there might influence various positions the actor you will represent may take. Then read and consider the additional outside sources listed below to help you expand your preliminary debating points:

1. Usha Ramanathan, "From Bhopal to Toulouse." *Frontline*, vol. 18, issue 25, Dec. 8–21, 2001. www.flonnet.com/fl1825/18250540.htm
2. Amita Baviskar, "The Politics of the City." www.india-seminar.com/
3. Daniel C. Esty and Maria H. Ivanova, "Making International Environmental Efforts Work: The Case for a Global Environmental Organization" (Yale Center for Environmental Law and Policy. Working Paper Series: Working Paper 2/01. May 2001). http://sedac.ciesin.org/openmeeting/downloads/1004391079_presentation_mivanova_riopaper1.doc
4. Calestous Juma, "The Perils of Centralizing Global Environmental Governance" in *Environment* 42:9 (Nov. 2000), 44. www.findarticles.com

Background: The Bhopal Incident Raises International Awareness of a Potential Problem

In the early hours of December 3, 1984, while the people of Bhopal, India were in bed asleep, 40 tons of methyl isocyanate (an intermediate chemical used in the production of pesticides) leaked from a Union Carbide pesticide plant.[2] With burning eyes and lungs, people struggled out of their houses trying to escape the gas, but it was everywhere they went. By morning, the streets of Bhopal were full of corpses.[3] About five thousand people were killed in the immediate aftermath.[4] By the third day, approximately eight thousand people had died from direct exposure to the gas.[5] Since the accident approximately sixteen thousand people have died, and an estimated one hundred twenty thousand to one hundred fifty thousand survivors are chronically ill.[6] The soil and groundwater resources of several neighborhoods in Bhopal are still contaminated.[7] The most seriously affected people were those living in the densely populated settlements surrounding the plant. In India, many factory workers live in settlements or slums that they build adjacent to factories, because they cannot afford any mode of transportation other than walking and must therefore live within walking distance of their workplace.

One year later, another accident in Delhi, India—an oleum gas leak at an Indian-owned fertilizer plant—injured thousands of people and precipitated an Indian Supreme Court case (*M.C. Mehta v Union of India* AIR 1987 SC 1086).[8] This accident reminded Indians of the grave risk that residents living close to factories face on a daily basis. In 1996 and 2000, partly in response to these two disasters, the Supreme Court of India directed "noncompliance" industries to relocate outside of Delhi. Most of these industries were hazardous industries operating in residential areas. In the 1996 closures, 168 industrial units were shut down. The closures resulted in loss of employment for tens of thousands of desperate factory workers. One of the main problems with the directive was the lack of a social security safety net for workers who lost their source of livelihood.[9] Most workers who lost their jobs were not compensated. Since they had been hired on a contract basis, they were not eligible for any kind of compensation. In addition, some were unable to relocate, or when they did relocate they found that the factories had not relocated or refused to rehire them.

After the Indian Supreme Court's closure directive in 2000, riots broke out in Delhi and continued for three consecutive days. Outraged factory owners and laborers took to the streets and started a general strike to protest the decision to close factories.[10] The city ground to a halt, and people were killed in the violence that ensued. Some Indians argued that the government's intention was not to fight pollution, but to move pollution away from Delhi's elite.[11] They argued that if the government was as intent on reducing pollution as it was on eliminating slums, it would have been concerned for those working and living near the relocated industries. Yet the government did not ensure that the areas where industries were relocated would not become residential areas. Furthermore, the government's decisions regarding which factories were closed and which were relocated seemed arbitrary to many. Some factory owners followed the authorities' directions and installed expensive pollution control equipment, only to be told to close their factories.[12] The poor organization of the government, the underfunding of the responsible agency (the Central Pollution Control Board), and corruption probably helped determine which factories were closed and which were relocated.

The company that operated the Bhopal pesticide plant was Union Carbide India, which the Union Carbide Corporation (an American company) owned at that time. Indian citizens ran the plant in Bhopal. No global organization required the Union Carbide plant in Bhopal to adhere to a set of international environmental standards. It was only required to comply with Indian environmental standards. The chemical that the Bhopal plant produced, methyl isocyanate, was also produced by Union Carbide at its West Virginia plant; however, the plant in West Virginia had a computerized warning and monitoring system, while the Bhopal plant relied on manual gauges and human senses to detect gas leaks.[13]

Workers in the Bhopal factory underwent periodic health examinations. The results were sent to the US headquarters, but never reported to the workers. Doctors trying to treat Bhopal victims were not prepared to deal with the emergency. On the morning of the accident, when they asked the doctor at the Bhopal plant how to treat the victims, he told them to rinse the victims' eyes with water.[14] Although some victims have received compensation from Union Carbide, the amount most victims received was negligible compared to their medical costs and losses.[15]

The Proposed Solution Response: Creation of an Environmental International Organization?

Although these incidents were generally contained environmentally within state boundaries, other environmental issues, such as air pollution, water pollution, climate change, and trade in endangered species, are not as easily contained within national boundaries. Some say an international effort is needed to address such transborder issues. For example, air pollution originating in the United States often travels across parts of Canada, eventually depositing pollutants in the Arctic. An international treaty called the Convention on Long-range Transboundary Air Pollution is dedicated to reducing transboundary air pollution. This convention recognizes that emissions of many persistent organic pollutants travel across international boundaries, landing in countries far from their site of origin.[16]

The location of environmentally hazardous industries is a similar transboundary issue, especially when companies based in the developed world choose to run hazardous operations in the developing world. Multinational companies often locate their production facilities in areas where costs are lowest: where wages are low and environmental standards are not enforced.[17] The location of multinational corporations in areas where environmental regulations are either weak or poorly enforced is an important transboundary environmental issue and, as the Bhopal incident illustrates, often presents an issue of distributive justice by raising these questions: Should developing countries bear the burden of pollution from the production of items sold primarily in the developed world? Is this morally correct? Or is the division of costs and benefits of such a system askew? Why or why not?

Although there are numerous multilateral environmental agreements such as the Convention on Long-range Transboundary Air Pollution, there is no legal framework that forces countries to be a party to these agreements. Developing countries are not always members of these conventions. Even when they are, there is no global organization that enforces compliance with the agreements. Therefore, even if India were party to an international agreement that could have prevented the Bhopal leak by requiring factories to protect workers from environmental accidents, there would have been no global organization to enforce India's compliance.

Neither is there an international environmental court that could try Union Carbide for its alleged crimes. Instead, the Supreme Court of India was responsible for the Union Carbide trial, and although arrest warrants were issued for Union Carbide employees—including Warren Anderson, the former CEO of Union Carbide—they never appeared in court.

What You Must Do: Debate and Vote

After reading and reflecting on the additional information contained in the outside sources listed at the top of this handout, you will be given the role of a stakeholder who has vested interests to represent in the upcoming debate. Once you know who you represent, you must decide:

1. Will you argue in favor of or against the creation of an international environmental organization?
2. How is this position consistent with your stakes? After the debate, you must vote for or against the proposal.
3. Will you vote for or against it? Why or why not?

Debriefing

When the debate is over and the students have reached a decision, discuss some of the following questions:

- Are environmental issues more difficult to address in developing countries than in developed countries? Why or why not?

- How can governments address local conditions, such as poverty, while also taking actions necessary for mitigating international environmental problems?

- Do you think Bhopal would have happened if there had been an international environmental organization? Could an international environmental organization prevent these types of tragedies?

- Could this type of accident happen in the United States? What if something like Bhopal happened in upstate New York tomorrow? How do you think this would play out in the United States? Would the outcome be different in the United States (in terms of the court case and the victims' compensation)?

- Is it fair for multinational corporations to locate their industries in developing countries? Could it be more equitable if certain changes were made? What types of changes? How does this relate to the concept of distributive justice?

- Would a global environmental organization be a useful solution to today's environmental problems?

- Would a global environmental organization impinge on a state's sovereignty? If so, how?

- What are the implications of framing discussion of this issue as a two-sided debate? Is this a realistic representation of the spectrum of perspectives on this issue?

Assign students specific values and ethical standards from Toolkits 2 and 3 to apply to the Bhopal incident. Tell them to craft an ethical solution to the resolution of this case. How do their solutions differ from one another and to the actual outcome? Which are most and least popular across the class? Why? How does the introduction of these values change the dynamics of the solution-seeking process?

To give students a further incentive to reflect on what happened in the debate, you may have them write up the arguments they presented for or against a global environmental organization from the perspective of one of the four stakeholders chosen for the debate. You may also ask them to compare and contrast this perspective with their own. This simple assignment can be turned in for a participation grade.

Selected Bibliography

In Print

Caney, Simon L. R., "Entitlements, Obligations and Distributive Justice: The Global Level," from Daniel Bell and Avner de-Shalit, eds., *Forms of Justice: Critical Perspectives on David Miller's Political Philosophy* (Lanham, MD: Rowman & Littlefield, 2002), 287–313.

Frankena, William, "Ethics and the Environment," from Kenneth E. Goodpaster and Kenneth M. Sayre, eds., *Ethics and Problems of the 21st Century* (Notre Dame, IN: University of Notre Dame Press, 1979), 3–20.

Gleeson, Brendan and Nicholas Low, eds., *Governing for the Environment: Global Problems, Ethics and Democracy* (Hampshire: Palgrave Publishers, Ltd, 2001).

Hurrell, Andrew and Benedict Kingsbury, "The International Politics of the Environment: An Introduction," from Andrew Hurrell and Benedict Kingsbury, eds., *The International Politics of the Environment* (Oxford: Clarendon Press, 1992), 1–47.

Shue, Henry, "The Unavoidability of Justice," from Andrew Hurrell and Benedict Kingsbury, eds., *The International Politics of the Environment* (Oxford: Clarendon Press, 1992), 373–397.

Van den Anker, Christien, "Global Justice, Global Institutions and Global Citizenship," from N. Dower and J. Williams, eds., *Global Citizenship*, (Edinburgh: Edinburgh University Press, 2002).

Related Web Sites

www.yale.edu/environment/publications/geg/toc.html This site provides links to all chapters of an excellent publication called *Global Environmental Governance: Options and Opportunities.*

www.earthrights.org/bhopal/index.shtml EarthRights International.

www.bhopal.net/oldsite/backwhy.html and www.bhopal.net/oldsite/icjb. html Bhopal Net.

www.bhopal.com This is Dow Chemical's Bhopal site, with its perspectives of the 1984 accident. Dow Chemical acquired Union Carbide in 2001.

Endnotes

1. There exists an International Court of the Environment Foundation, which has proposed the creation of an International Court for the Environment (see www.xcom.it/icef/about.html).

2. Union Carbide India Limited, a subsidiary of the American parent company, Union Carbide Corporation, owned the plant. Since the American parent company owned 50.9% of the stock in the company, it had majority ownership over the Indian company (see www.ucaqld.com.au /community/bhopal/).

3. Bhopal Net, "The Union Carbide Disaster." www.bhopal.net/background. html

4. EarthRights International. www.earthrights.org/bhopal/index.shtml

5. Greenpeace, "Bhopal: Continuing the Fight for Health and Justice." www.greenpeaceusa.org/media/factsheets/bhopal.pdf

6. Bhopal Org, "Survivor's Testimonies." www.bhopal.org; Usha Ramanathan, "From Bhopal to Toulouse." *Frontline* 18, no. 25, (Dec. 8–21, 2001). www.flonnet.com/fl1825/18250540.htm.

7. Usha Ramanathan, "Business and Human Rights: The India Paper" (The International Environmental Law Research Center. Published in IELRC Working Paper No. 2001–2, part I). www.ielrc.org/Content/W01021T_2.html; www.bhopal.net/asianage.html

8. Shyam Divan and Armin Rosencranz, *Environmental Law and Policy in India* (Oxford: Oxford University Press, 2001).

9. Jayati Ghosh, "Pollution and the Rights of Citizens." *Frontline* 17, no. 25, (Dec. 9–22, 2000). www.flonnet.com/fl1725/17251180.htm.

10. Onkar Singh, "Industrial Workers on Rampage in Delhi." Rediff.com (Nov. 20, 2000). www.rediff.com/news/2000/nov/20onkar.htm; Onkar Singh, "Violence continues as Dikshit meets PM." Rediff.com (Nov. 21, 2002). www.rediff.com/news/2000/nov/21onkar.htm.

11. Aditya Nigam, "Industry Closures in India." Revolutionary Democracy, 7, 2 (September 2001). revolutionarydemocracy.org/rdv7n2/ industclos.htm

12. K. Ahmed, C. Khanduja and N. Sethi, "Master Plan for Anarchy," *Down to Earth*, 9, 15 (December 31, 2000). www.cseindia.org/html/ dte/dte20001231/dte_srep1.htm.

13. TED Case Studies (Trade and the Environment Database), "Bhopal Disaster." http://gurukul.ucc.american.edu/ted/bhopal.htm

14. The Uniting Church in Australia. www.ucaqld.com.au/community/ bhopal/recent_news/ucletter/ucletter.html.

15. Greenpeace. www.greenpeace.org/international_en/features/details? features%5fid=22089

16. Executive Body for the Convention on Long-Range Transboundary Air Pollution, 31 March 1998. Special session. www.mem.dk/aarhus-conference/issues/Heavy-metals/heavy2.htm

17. For more on this dynamic and its ethical implications, see Module 10: Corporate Social Responsibility for Human Rights: The Case of Burma/ Myanmar.

Truth Commissions

Julie Mertus

About This Module

One of the most pressing and interesting questions that arises in human rights, peace studies, ethics, international relations, and political science courses is the "truth versus justice" debate. Questions within the debate itself include:

- To what extent should a society emerging from conflict demand that those responsible for human rights abuses and other forms of violence be prosecuted in a court of law or otherwise held accountable?

- Does the punishment approach serve to publicize truth and promote justice, or does it encourage the hiding of truth and ultimately diminish justice?

- As an alternative to prosecution, should societies emerging from violent conflict establish commissions that encourage truth telling through offering amnesty from criminal prosecution and civil liability to perpetrators who tell the truth and confess their guilt?

- Under what conditions and to what extent do such "truth commissions" address the concerns of victims and promote the need for social healing? To what extent are truth commissions both preventative and restorative?

I had great difficulty teaching the topic of truth commissions until I developed this module. Excellent teaching material exists describing the record of truth commissions in various parts of the world. However, students are unable to fully engage in the "truth versus justice" debate by simply reading that material.

In particular, they have a hard time exploring the dimensions of the amnesty issue and appreciating its relationship to reconciliation. Also

American students tend to see this issue as something applicable only to other places. To address these teaching concerns, I devised this simple simulation and based it in the United States. However, it could be revised and used in other countries as well. You are free to modify it as necessary to suit the number of students in your class and the topical issues you discuss.

The simulation works best with a minimum of twelve and a maximum of twenty-five students, but I have used it with success in classes as large as thirty-six students. I suggest that Steps 1 and 2 of the exercise be conducted in a class period prior to the other two steps. In any event, prepare your students well before handing out the hypothetical problem.

Having completed this module, students are able to discuss the merits and limitations of truth commissions, and consider the potential applicability of truth commissions to deep and long-standing controversies in their own countries. In particular, they can answer the following questions:

1. What are the arguments in support of the establishment of truth commissions?
2. What are the arguments in opposition to forming truth commissions?
3. In your opinion, is there an ideal truth commission? Explain. Make a list of Things to Do when setting up a truth commission, and another list of Things to Avoid.
4. Why do some commentators call truth commissions "more-or-less truth commissions"? Why do some commentators see truth commissions as an illustration of the tension between justice and peace?

Miniglossary

Amnesty A decree enacted by authorities that states that the authorities will disregard one or more category of offenses and cancel any penal consequences that would normally result from being convicted of such acts.

Commissions of inquiry Nonlegal institutions established to investigate and establish a record of human rights abuses in a country or related to a conflict. While some people use the term "commission of inquiry" synonymously with "truth commission" (see definition below), others refer to commissions of inquiry as being even more narrowly circumscribed by duration, location and/or individuals involved.

Truth commissions (alternatively, truth and reconciliation commissions [TRCs]). Committees created, vested with authority, sponsored, and/or funded by governments, international organizations (or both), with the mandate of creating a record of what happened in a particular country or in relation to a particular conflict. The goals of such commissions are to account for and contribute to the end of abuses of authority, to promote national reconciliation and/or bolster a new political order or legitimize new policies.

Unlike courts, truth commissions exist only for a designated period of time and have a specific and narrow mandate. While they may be guided by international human rights principles, the commissions are not legal institutions. Rather than focusing on punishing individuals, truth commissions seek above all to raise the voices of victims and to produce a final report with recommendations for moving beyond the past and into a more just future.

Step-by-Step Directions

Step 1: Introduction to Topic

Time: 45–90 minutes (I recommend that this step be done in a class period prior to the actual simulation.)

Because students' prior knowledge about truth commissions varies considerably, it is useful not only to assign readings on the topic (see the Selected Bibliography), but also to show all or part of a video on the topic prior to beginning the simulation. The film, *Long Night's Journey Into Day,* a profile of specific cases before the South African truth commission, serves this purpose well. Student Handout 1 provides students with a brief written definition of the issue. Whatever material is used to introduce TRCs, distribute Handout 2 to discuss in small groups (three to six members each). Then come together in a large group discussion to share, compare, and analyze student responses with the class as a whole.

Step 2: Assign the Hypothetical Problem

Time: 15 minutes (I suggest you do this in a class period prior to simulation. Depending on the length of the class, this step can be combined with Step 1.)

Provide the class with a hypothetical problem in which a town council votes to establish a truth commission. Student Handout 3 provides an example you may wish to use.

Step 3: Role Group Meetings

Divide the class into the following four groups:

1. Truth commissions (have at least three members, but not more than six)
2. Police officers
3. Members of the Caucasian community
4. Members of the African-American community

To avoid self-selection and to add to the excitement of the simulation, divide the class into the groups randomly through use of the role descriptions in Student Handout 4. Photocopy enough of each; for example, if you have twenty-five class members and you want to divide up the roles equally, make five copies of each description. Cut out and paste the roles on cardboard, shuffle them, and have students pick them as from a card deck.

Note that for each category of actor, the students meeting as members of that group have the option of further subdividing the role; for example, within the category of police officers, they may play the specific role of a police officer who committed a specific crime, the police chief, the police bystander who covered up the crime, etc.

Alternatively, students can speak as a group about what competing interests would be at stake in their group. This method of assigning roles allows for maximum flexibility and is most sensitive to students who would find playing certain roles offensive or harmful.

Step 4: Separate Group Meetings

Time: 20–30 minutes (Note that this can be done prior to class.)

Have each group meet separately to work on its assigned task. Members of the group designate one main spokesperson to be the key figure representing their concerns in the town meeting (but all individuals may speak).

Step 5: Town Meeting

Time: 40–60 minutes (Depending on the length of the class, this step may need to be conducted in a separate session from Steps 3 and 4.)

1. Arrange chairs in a big circle for the town meeting. All students attend the meeting, acting in their roles. Should students attend class without a role (because they missed the earlier session during which roles were distributed or they are otherwise unprepared), they are given the role of "journalist" and are encouraged to ask questions from this perspective.

2. The truth commissioners go first and present their suggested rules on amnesty and their overall strategy to the group. The group asks questions, interrupting the truth commissioners when necessary. The truth commissioners may decide to take some comments under advisement, and hold open the possibility of modifying their rules once they have heard all concerns.

3. The police officers go next, presenting their concerns and indicating any divisions within their ranks. They are followed by the Caucasian and African-American communities. All groups are asked questions.

4. After a short break, the truth commissioners come back with any revisions to their rules and solicit further comments.

Student Handout 1:
Introduction to Truth Commissions

The failure to hold perpetrators of human rights atrocities accountable for their crimes is among the root causes of violent conflicts. At the same time, violent conflict is perpetuated by the inability of individuals and groups to reconcile with those responsible for human rights violations and other forms of violence. Societies emerging from conflict weigh the often-competing goals of punishing violators and of reconciliation and forgiveness.

What measures can best promote social healing and justice? Courts can punish perpetrators, but only if functioning court systems and the political will to use them exist. Moreover, because courts are designed to punish perpetrators, they focus on the elements of specific, legally defined crimes. The stories of victims and bystanders and the goal of promoting social healing are sidelined. For this reason, some societies emerging from conflict have established truth commissions as a complement to (and, in some cases, a substitute for) formal judicial proceedings.

At its core, a truth commission seeks to answer questions that, unanswered, will impede the country's movement to a less violent and more just era. While courts are punitive in nature, truth commissions seek to be restorative and preventative. In many cases, truth commissions are created after a civil war and/or after an authoritarian regime has been replaced by one seeking to be more democratic. Thus the specific scope of a commission's mandate is generally defined by the government, which in democratic societies should take its direction from the local population. In some cases, however, the truth commission derives its mandate less from local concerns and more from third parties, such as the international body monitoring the peace.

Truth commissions often use the potential offer of amnesty to induce violators to come forward and confess their crimes. A grant of amnesty usually covers only crimes defined as political in nature; common crimes, such as robbery for material gain, are excluded. In addition, some types of crimes may be deemed inappropriate for amnesty, such as genocide, and the commission may specifically provide that international crimes be excluded. Truth commissions may include measures for reaching out to victims of violence and their families, permitting them to speak publicly, demand answers, contest or agree to amnesty applications, and meet, confront, and, in some cases, forgive their abusers.

Student Handout 2:
Initial Questions for Discussion

1. To what extent should a society emerging from conflict demand that those responsible for human rights abuses and other forms of violence be prosecuted in a court of law or otherwise be held accountable?
2. Does the punishment approach serve to publicize truth and promote justice, or does it encourage the hiding of truth and ultimately diminish justice?
3. As an alternative to prosecutions, should societies emerging from violent conflict establish commissions that encourage truth telling through offering amnesty to perpetrators who tell the truth and confess their guilt?
4. Under what conditions and to what extent do such truth commissions address the concerns of victims and promote the need for social healing?
5. To what extent are truth commissions both preventative and restorative?

Student Handout 3:
The Hypothetical Problem—
Truth Commission or Not?

Jonesville Junction USA has been divided on racial and ethnic lines for as long as anyone can remember. The city, which is 35% Caucasian, 50% African American, and 15% Asian and Hispanic, is dominated by the Caucasian minority, which controls the police force (90% Caucasian, Caucasian police chief), court system (judges 100% Caucasian), city council, (55% Caucasian), and local media (the one city paper and one local radio station is Caucasian-owned and -operated).

The police force in Jonesville has a reputation for discriminating against non-Caucasians, stopping them for random police checks and treating them roughly upon arrest and in detention. Three years ago Ben Fields, an African-American man, died from beatings he suffered during a police interrogation. Fields was a 24-year-old insurance agent who was being held on suspicion of drug charges. He had no prior police record. No officer has ever been prosecuted in connection with the incident. The city attorney launched an investigation, but dropped it soon afterwards for lack of evidence.

Two years ago Sarah Workman, a young African-American social worker, told the press that she had been raped by a police officer, while his partner stood by watching and encouraging him. She could not identify the officers. Police records indicate that on the night in question, Sergeants Blakesley and Jones stopped Ms. Workman on suspicion of prostitution, but did not detain her or charge her with any crime. No serious investigation has ever been made into Ms. Workman's charges.

The same year Felix Yates, an unemployed 39-year-old Hispanic man, and Peter Benjamin, a 32-year-old African-American laborer, were found dead in their jail cells. Police reported these incidents, which happened only days apart, as suicides. The local chapter of the NAACP, however, called the deaths suspicious and demanded an investigation. Police chief George Butts conducted an internal investigation that confirmed the earlier reports of suicide.

Jonesville is a violent place. In addition to street violence (robberies and assaults), there is a high rate of domestic violence and gang warfare in the high school. Most violence of this sort is intraracial, but racial tensions are mounting, and members of all communities have easy access to guns and ammunition.

Faced with this growing crisis, the members of the city council have voted to establish a truth commission to investigate allegations of police violence and other unsolved, racially motivated crimes in Jonesville. They issue a statement to the community media asserting that "the tribunal will help expose the truth, and in doing so promote reconciliation and healing." The truth commission, which is composed of former judges and other prominent community members (representative of all sectors of the community), is to meet to determine its rules for granting amnesty and develop a strategy for encouraging perpetrators to come forward with the truth. The police officers are to meet to determine if they should cooperate with the tribunal and decide what the nature and extent of that cooperation will be. Religious leaders of the minority Caucasian and African-American communities call for separate town meetings about their respective stances on the tribunal.

Student Handout 4:
Role Descriptions

Truth Commissioners

Who are you? You represent all racial groups and a range of political beliefs. You may wish to declare subroles as truth commissioners belonging to certain communities or just discuss the concerns likely to come up for this diverse group.

Your Task: To determine rules for granting amnesty and develop a strategy for encouraging perpetrators to come forward with the truth. Choose one person to present the rules and strategy at a public meeting.

Police Officers

Who are you? You represent the diversity of interests in the police force. You may wish to subdivide into the roles of police chief Butts, the police officer who killed Ben Fields, Sergeant Blakesley, Sergeant Jones, or the police officers in charge of Felix Yates and Peter Benjamin.

Your Task: To determine whether you should cooperate with the tribunal and decide the nature and extent of that cooperation. What rules do you want to see on amnesty? Discuss, and prepare a spokesperson to bring concerns to a town meeting.

Members of the Caucasian Community

Who are you? You are interested Caucasians who live in Jonesville. You may wish to subdivide into specific roles, such as religious leader, business leader, witness to police violence, victim of domestic violence, and victim of intraracial violence.

Your Task: To identify the various concerns members of your community have about the truth commission and consider these questions: How will it promote or obstruct your interests? What rules do you want to see on amnesty?

Discuss, and prepare a spokesperson to bring concerns to the town meeting.

Members of the African-American Community

Who are you? You are interested African Americans who live in Jonesville. You may wish to subdivide into specific roles, such as religious leader, business leader, witness to police violence, victim of domestic violence, and victim of intraracial violence.

Your Task: To identify the various concerns members of your community have about the truth commission and to consider these questions: How will it promote or obstruct your interests? What rules do you want to see on amnesty?

Discuss, and prepare a spokesperson to bring concerns to the town meeting.

Debriefing

The members of the class fall out of their roles, and you conduct a discussion of the exercise and the issues it raised for broader class themes. You may want to pose the questions below or develop your own:

- Was it easy to come up with rules for a truth commission?
- What were the sticking points?
- Whose interests are most represented by the commission?
- How do victims feel about the offer of amnesty? Perpetrators?
- Does the truth commission address all forms of violence in the community?
- Would the proposed commission promote truth? Justice? Both? Neither?
- How is this commission like real-life commissions, such as the one in South Africa?
- How does it differ?
- How realistic is this exercise?
- Would your community support a "truth commission"? Why or why not?
- Are there issues that such a community could address in your community?

Selected Bibliography

In Print

Cooper, Belinda, *War Crimes: The Legacy of Nuremberg* (New York: TV Books, 1999).

Hayner, Priscilla B., *Unspeakable Truths: Confronting State Terror and Atrocity* (London, UK: Routledge, 2001).

Minow, Martha, *Between Vengeance and Forgiveness: Facing History after Genocide and Mass Violence* (Boston: Beacon Press, 1998).

Related Web Sites

www.irisfilms.org/longnight Homepage of Iris Films, source of more information on the film, *Long Night's Journey Into Day*, which won the Grand Jury Prize for Best Documentary at Sundance Film Festival 2000.

www.csvr.org.za Center for the Study of Violence and Reconciliation (CSVR). The CSVR, affiliated with the University of the Witwatersrand, Johannesburg, provides expertise in building reconciliation, democracy, and human rights cultures. See in particular the links to its Project on Truth and Reconciliation.

www.usip.org/library/tc/tc_coi.html United States Institute of Peace List of Truth Commissions. Superb, short list, with succinct explanations and links to additional resources.

Drafting a Convention on the Human Rights of People with Disabilities: A Treaty-Negotiation Simulation

Nancy Flowers and Janet E. Lord

About This Module

On December 19, 2001, the UN General Assembly adopted by consensus a resolution calling for the establishment of an Ad Hoc Committee mandated to consider proposals for the drafting of an international convention on the human rights of persons with disabilities. This important development resulted from many years of advocacy by people with disabilities and their representative organizations, who argued that a legally binding convention specifically addressing the rights of people with disabilities was necessary in order to (i) create a mechanism of legal accountability based on the latest developments in disability rights; (ii) prompt shifts in national laws and policies; (iii) encourage the UN system, as well as development and humanitarian institutions, to mainstream disability into their work; and (iv) to ensure that the rights of disabled people are understood as part and parcel of the human rights movement in general. The first meeting of the Ad Hoc Committee took place in New York at UN Headquarters in the summer of 2002. In keeping with other international human rights treaty processes, the Ad Hoc Committee's work will continue for a number of years, until government representatives can agree on the text of an international convention.

This activity simulates a meeting of the drafting committee for a United Nations Convention on the Rights of People with Disabilities. The committee's purpose is to formulate an article on a specific disability issue to be included in the convention. Students play the roles of representatives of governments, intergovernmental organizations (IGOs), and nongovernmental organizations (NGOs). Each role holds a particular perspective on the issue that students research between the first and second class meetings of this module. During the simulation, students put forward proposed language for the convention, which reflects the probable positions of the actors they represent. The committee then struggles to reach a consensus on the final wording of the article from among the many proposals presented.

A discussion following the simulation analyzes the process of treaty drafting and the implications of an international human rights treaty for rights enforcement and advocacy. The in-class negotiation lasts 60 minutes, although additional class time is needed both beforehand (to explain the activity and assign roles) and afterward (to debrief the negotiation). Students also need additional time between the first and second meetings to research and prepare their draft articles, as well as to form alliances and possibly share text with others.

This simulation places students directly in the process of forging international human rights law. By representing governments, IGOs, and NGOs with conflicting agendas and widely differing resources and priorities, they are confronted with the complexity and difficulty of achieving international consensus. The process of formulating the language in a legal document underscores the far-reaching importance of precise language. It also demonstrates the politics of international law and the interrelationship between domestic and international goals.

To prepare for the simulation, students learn about the culture, history, current events, and economic and political climates of different countries; and the mission, policies, and initiatives of important IGOs and NGOs. They must then interpret the position of a government, IGO, or NGO regarding a major disability issue and advocate specific treaty language with this goal in mind. Students also grapple with key issues regarding people with disabilities and come to understand them in the context of universal human rights. The concluding discussion raises questions about the role of law, governments, and advocates in the promotion and protection of human rights. At the end of this module, students should be able to answer these key questions:

1. How does international human rights law come into being?
2. What are the major obstacles to the establishment of new human rights in international law?
3. How and why do the roles of governments, IGOs, and NGOs differ in the development of human rights law?
4. How and why do the goals of these actors vary in the development of key human rights issues concerning people with disabilities?

Miniglossary

Convention A legally binding, multilateral agreement between states. Many conventions have been developed under the auspices of the United Nations or regional intergovernmental organizations. The only comprehensive, legally binding convention addressing the human rights of people with disabilities is the Inter-American Convention on the Elimination of All Forms of Discrimination against Persons with Disabilities (1999), an international treaty established by the Member States of the Organization of American States that provides a regional system of human rights protection for the Western Hemisphere. The UN Convention on the Rights of the Child (1989), which sets forth a full spectrum of civil, cultural, economic, social, and political rights for children, includes in Article 23 a provision specifically relating to the rights of disabled children. More general international human rights conventions applicable to people with disabilities are the International Covenant on Civil and Political Rights (ICCPR) and the International Covenant on Economic, Social and Cultural Rights (ICESCR) of 1966, which in binding form include many of the human rights contained in the UN Universal Declaration of Human Rights (UDHR, 1948). Because they are all legally binding agreements between states, the terms "convention," "treaty," and "covenant" are used synonymously in this module.

Declaration A document, such as the Universal Declaration of Human Rights, that articulates agreed-upon standards or principles, but is not legally binding.

Intergovernmental organizations (IGOs) Organizations, sponsored by several governments, that seek to coordinate state collaboration. These organizations have states as their members; their missions vary widely. Some are geographically based and consider a range of issues (e.g., Council of Europe, the African Union); some are defensive military alliances (e.g., NATO); and some are dedicated to specific functional purposes, including the promotion of health, education, and well-being (e.g., the International Labour Organization [ILO], the World Health Organization [WHO], UNICEF).

Nongovernmental organizations (NGOs) Organizations formed by people and groups outside the government to advance particular causes. These organizations typically have nonstate actors as their members. Some are large and international (e.g., the Red Cross, Amnesty International, the Girl Scouts); others may be small and local (e.g., an organization to advocate for people with disabilities in a particular country). Some NGOs play influential roles in shaping UN policy, and many have official consultative status at the UN. Some NGOs monitor the proceedings of human rights bodies, such as the UN Commission on Human Rights, and serve as watchdogs of the human rights that fall within their mandates.

Treaty-making process A UN treaty is formulated in a multiple-stage process that begins with negotiations among authorized representatives of UN Member States. These representatives meet, usually over an extended period, to forge a document that reflects their consensus on a particular topic. They actively invite the attendance and contributions of IGOs and NGOs with UN consultative status (or otherwise accredited), although only the representatives of UN Member States may vote on the language of the treaty. Once finalized, the draft document is submitted to the UN General Assembly for adoption. After adoption the treaty is open to the different domestic ratification procedures of each Member State. At this stage, a government must decide whether or not to give formal consent to become legally bound by the new treaty. If it does, a state is said to have *ratified* and to have become a *state party to* the treaty. Treaties *enter into force* and become legally binding upon ratifying states through various means expressed in the treaty itself, usually when the requisite number of Member States have ratified the treaty.

This module captures the negotiation stage of the treaty-formulation process at an international conference.

Step-by-Step Directions

The negotiation simulation is completed within one 60-minute class period, but you need to prepare students for the actual simulation by devoting at least some of one or two prior classes to explain how the simulation will proceed, distribute handouts, select or present the focal issue, assign roles, and provide time for students to make plans to work together outside of class, if desired, or begin working together during class.

Prepare Students for the Simulation

1. Introduce the simulation: Explain that during two upcoming class sessions focused on disabilities, students will participate in a simulation of a conference working to draft a UN Treaty on the Rights of People with Disabilities. Students will represent the interests of one of the following roles, to be assigned: a government, an IGO, or an NGO.
2. Assign prereadings as general background:

- National Council on Disability, *A White Paper—Understanding the Role of an International Convention on the Human Rights of People with Disabilities: An analysis of the legal, social, and practical implications for policy makers and disability and human rights advocates in the United States* (Washington, DC, June 12, 2002). Read Parts I–IV. Available online at www.ncd.gov/newsroom/publications/2002/unwhitepaper_05-23-02.html

• Student Handout 1: Focal Disability Issues

Day One

Select a Focal Issue

Define the selected disability issue the conference will be addressing during the simulation or ask the class to select an issue from Student Handout 1.

Assign and Select Roles

Distribute Student Handout 2 and review it with the class. Assign half the class to be governmental representatives. Assign the remaining half of the class to be representatives of IGOs and NGOs. Within each of these broad categories, students choose specific actors they want to represent. If class size permits, ensure that at least one student assumes the identity of each of the roles. In larger classes you may assign additional representatives to each category, so that students work together to represent the interests of a particular actor. In any event, be sure that students are distributed evenly among the three groups of roles.

After roles have been assigned, prepare a class list indicating everyone's role, so students can identify their potential allies and engage in presimulation negotiations. Before the simulation, prepare signs on which the names of each representative are clearly printed for easy identification during the simulation.

Explain How the Simulation Will Proceed and Assign Responsibilities

1. Tell students they will be responsible for drafting a treaty article on the chosen issue that reflects the actual or likely position of the representative they have been assigned to play. If possible, they should write their proposed treaty article on a transparency for use on an overhead projector.
2. Explain that part of the assignment for the next session will be for students to research the positions their assigned representatives would be likely to take on the chosen issue and/or draft article. Emphasize that Student Handout 2 provides a starting point for researching each role, as well as other factors students should consider.

3. Assign students to complete a second general prereading by the day of the simulation: National Council on Disability, *A White Paper—Understanding the Role of an International Convention on the Human Rights of People with Disabilities: An analysis of the legal, social, and practical implications for policy makers and disability and human rights advocates in the United States* (Washington, DC, June 12, 2002). Read Parts VI and VII. Available online at: www.ncd.gov/ newsroom/ publications/2002/unwhitepaper_05-23-02.html

4. Point out that in order to strengthen their positions, representatives at such meetings typically form alliances and agree in advance on language they can all support. Encourage students to seek such alliances with one another prior to the simulation. However, these alliances should be true to the likely positions of the countries and organizations they are role-playing. Forming such alliances in advance is especially important to limit the number of articles put forward. Provide a class list with assigned roles and some class time for representatives of the different roles to meet and explore the process of negotiating alliances and drafting common treaty articles.

5. Explain that during the simulation, each student will be expected to speak in the voice of the assigned representative, lay out the position of the government or organization she or he speaks for, and argue against others' positions.

6. You may choose to provide students with copies of actual treaty language on disability issues, on which they can model their drafts. If you do, distribute Student Handouts 3–6 below, which contain excerpts from relevant UN human rights treaties.

Day Two: The Simulation

The process for the simulation is as follows:

- Arrange the seating so that the governmental representatives are seated in an inner circle and IGO and NGO representatives are outside this circle. Make sure each student has a sign identifying the entity he or she represents.
- Act as a moderator for the discussion, calling on representatives and explaining and limiting the amount of time they speak.
- Timing: Only 60 minutes is allowed for the simulation, regardless of whether the representatives complete work on the article or not. Generally representatives are given no more than 3 minutes to make their points. Rebuttals or questions are given no more than 2 minutes.

- Although equal time is given to each group to make amendments or additions, only government representatives may vote on the final wording, with one vote per country. Explain that this provision simulates the actual process of such treaty-drafting conferences; IGOs and NGOs are free to testify and suggest, but only government representatives are able to vote. (This is because only governments will ultimately ratify and implement the resulting treaty.)
- Ask first for any government drafts and work through these as follows, with contributions from NGOs and IGOs coming as amendments and additions:

  1. Start by calling on government representatives for any draft articles. Ask whether the draft is the submission of a single government or an alliance. Read the draft aloud and show it on an overhead projector.
  2. Ask for any other governmental drafts and repeat step 1 for each.
  3. Ask all representatives for a show of hands to choose which draft to use as a working model. Do not allow discussion, but encourage everyone to vote according to the interest of the country or organization they represent.
  4. Call on IGOs and NGOs respectively to make interventions. Allow only 2–3 minutes per intervention. Allow only 1–2 minutes for questions or counter arguments.
  5. Have government representatives vote on the wording of that sentence.
  6. Repeat the process for each subsequent sentence or group of related sentences. Go as far into the draft article as you can in 60 minutes.
  7. At the end of 60 minutes, government representatives vote on whatever text(s) are before them.

Student Handout 1:
Focal Disability Issues

The following issues represent some of the most far-reaching and urgent concerns of advocates for the human rights of people with disabilities.

The Right to Life for People with Disabilities

The right to life is the most fundamental of human rights protecting human existence and the integrity of the person, and is a standard provision in major international human rights documents, including the International Covenant on Civil and Political Rights.

The right to life under international human rights law has numerous links to disability. For example, the right to life is implicated in the context of the practice of euthanasia, which in many instances takes the form of withholding life-saving treatment to a newborn child with physical and/or mental disabilities. Many disability organizations have invoked the right to life to challenge cases where children or adults with disabilities have died at the hands of medical practitioners or caregivers who have decided that their lives were "not worth living." In other cases, disability organizations have invoked the right to oppose physician-assisted suicide and related legislative initiatives. The right to life is therefore a core right invoked frequently by disability organizations in their advocacy. In developing countries, the mortality rate of children with disabilities is frequently higher than that of nondisabled children, because children with disabilities may not receive adequate care.

Family and Reproductive Rights for People with Disabilities

The international human rights framework recognizes the importance of the family unit in human life and the need for legal protection of the family. Unfortunately, the main human rights conventions do not explicitly link protection of the family to people with disabilities, meaning that people with disabilities do not currently enjoy the highest levels of protection with regard to their rights to live with their families, marry, have intimate relationships, and start their own families. People with disabilities in many countries are barred from marrying; prohibited or prevented from having children or, when they do, face having their children taken away from them; and are frequently denied the right to stay in their own families and may be forced into an institution.

The Right to Be Free from Slavery, Servitude, and Forced Labor/Nonexploitive Conditions of Employment

Freedom from slavery was among the first human rights to become a subject matter of international law, and the prohibition against slavery and related practices is a standard provision in the general international human rights treaties. The provisions concerning slavery generally cover four different practices: slavery, the slave trade, servitude, and forced (or compulsory) labor. Contemporary forms of slavery and servitude have tended to focus on trafficking in women and children, as well as human organ trafficking. International human rights law continues to develop in this sphere.

A UN Working Group on Contemporary Forms of Slavery addresses these issues and has recognized that disabled people are subjected to these practices. People with disabilities—intellectual disabilities in particular— are at risk for a variety of exploitative labor practices, many of which are found in unregulated settings or in "sheltered workshops," some of which may rise to the level of prohibited practices under the slavery, servitude, and forced labor rules of international human rights law. Organizations of women with disabilities have exposed the bondagelike treatment of women with mental disabilities who are married to men interested in having a dependent wife to control. These practices, along with others, disclose the human rights violations to which people with disabilities are so often exposed.

The Right of People with Disabilities to Participate in the Political and Public Life of Their Communities

This refers to the rights of people to participate in the governing of one's country through elections, political activities, and the holding of public office. Although these rights may frequently be restricted to those who are citizens and who do not have a criminal record, in practice people with disabilities often face many more restrictions. Many people with disabilities have no opportunity to exercise their rights in connection with political activities. For example, inaccessible voting booths prevent many people with disabilities from participating in elections; and for those who are able to vote, inappropriate efforts to improve accessibility frequently violate the disabled voter's right to privacy and a secret ballot (for example, where a voter can have access only with someone present to assist).

In addition, legislation governing who has the right to vote often dis- enfranchises those who have mental disabilities, even when the disability does not in fact hinder an individual's ability to make an informed deci- sion. Societal discrimination also prohibits many people with disabilities from holding public office, again limiting the ability of people with dis- abilities to take an active role in the governing of the societies in which they live.

Student Handout 2:
Role Reference Sheet

From the list below, choose a specific actor you want to represent. The Web sites listed after each role indicate starting points where you may begin researching your roles. Your research is not limited to the sites listed here.

Representatives of Governments

- A representative from **a Western country** with a well-developed social service system (for example, Australia, Canada, Denmark, France, Germany, Great Britain, New Zealand, the Netherlands, Norway, Sweden, etc.). For a sense of the positions taken by European countries, and the European Union (EU) countries in particular, see various EU and other government position papers at www.worldenable.org. See also Daily Summaries of Ad Hoc Committee negotiations at www.worldenable.net/rights/adhoc2meet.htm.
- A representative from **the United States.** For a sense of the position taken by the United States, see Daily Summaries of Ad Hoc Committee negotiations at www.worldenable.net/rights/adhoc2meet.htm.
- A representative from **a developing country** (for example, El Salvador, Uganda, Mexico, Jordan). For a sense of the positions taken by developing countries, see Daily Summaries of Ad Hoc Committee negotiations at www.worldenable.net/rights/adhoc2meet.htm.
- A representative from **a country with strong national legislation on the rights of people with disabilities** (for example, Australia, New Zealand, Philippines, United Kingdom, United States). For information about states with strong legislation on disabilities, see www.worldenable.net/rights/adhoc2meet.htm. For copies of national legislation, see www.dredf.org/international/lawindex.html.
- A representative from **a country with a high or rapidly growing AIDS population** (for example, Botswana, Kenya, South Africa). For information about states with high or rapidly growing AIDS populations, see www.worldenable.net/rights/adhoc2meet.htm.
- A representative from **a predominantly Communist country** (for example, China, Vietnam). For information about communist states on this issue, see www.worldenable.net/rights/adhoc2meet.htm.
- A representative from **a country where there is recent war or civil unrest** (for example, Afghanistan, Angola, Cambodia, Colombia, Congo, East Timor, Guatemala, Indonesia, Iraq, Rwanda, Sudan). To learn more about the perspectives of states recently experiencing civil unrest, see www.worldenable.net/rights/adhoc2meet.htm.

Representatives of Intergovernmental Organizations (IGOs)

- A representative from **UNICEF.** The UNICEF Web site is available at www.unicef.org
- A representative from **the International Labour Organization (ILO).** The ILO Web site is available at www.ilo.org. For ILO statements on the convention, see www.worldenable.org
- A representative from **the World Health Organization (WHO).** The WHO Web site is available at www.who.org
- A representative from **the Office of the High Commissioner for Human Rights (OHCHR).** The OHCHR Web site is available at www.ohchr.org. For OHCHR statements on the convention, see www.worldenable.org
- A representative from **the United Nations Development Program (UNDP).** The UNDP Web site is available at www.undp.org
- A representative from **a regional IGO** (for example, Council of Europe, Organization of American States, Pan-American Health Organization, African Union). See, for example, the following Web sites for background on regional intergovernmental organizations: www.coe.int; www.oas.org; www.paho.org; and www.africa-union.org
- A representative from **the World Bank or another international development bank.** The World Bank general Web site is available at www.worldbank.org. A disability-specific Web page at this site is available at www.worldbank.org/disability

Nongovernmental Organizations (NGOs)

- A representative from **an organization in which people with disabilities and their allies work for the rights of people with disabilities** (for example, Disabled Peoples' International, European Disability Forum, Landmine Survivors Network, Rehabilitation International, World Network of Users and Survivors of Psychiatry, Not Dead Yet). The leading NGOs involved in the convention process devote pages of their Web sites to the convention. For example, www.landminesurvivors.org; www.dpi.org; www.rehab-international.org; www.wnusp.org; and www.notdeadyet.org. These are organizations *of* people with disabilities, meaning that representatives speak *as* disabled people and not *about* them—a critical difference in disability rights politics.
- A representative from **a mainstream (nondisability-focused) international human rights organization** (for example, Amnesty International, Human Rights Watch). The Web site for Amnesty International is www.amnesty.org; and for Human Rights Watch is www.hrw.org

- A representative from **an international humanitarian organization** (for example, Oxfam, Care, World Vision). The Web site for Oxfam is www.oxfam.org; for Care is www.care.org; and for World Vision is www.worldvision.org
- A representative from **a charity service provider that works specifically *for* disabled people** (for example, a rehabilitation hospital, an orphanage run by a faith-based group, the Shriners). The Web site for the Shriners of North America and the Shriners Hospitals for Children is www.shrinershq.org

***

As you begin researching your role, take into consideration the following factors, as well as any others you find relevant as you develop your position for your assigned role.

For a country representative

- Culture, history, and current events; economic situation and political climate; or any other factors that are important in that country
- Other situations that would influence the state's position on that issue
- The international human rights treaties that this country has already ratified, and thus is accountable for upholding

For an IGO representative

- Special interests and mission of the IGO
- Are policies and practices already in place regarding this or related issues?
- Resources and limitations of the IGO
- How/where is disability handled by the organization?

For an NGO representative

- Special interests and mission of the NGO: Does the mission reflect a rights-based approach?
- Policies and practices are already in place regarding this or related issues?
- Resources and limitations of the NGO

Student Handout 3:
Sample Treaty Provisions on the Right to Life

International Covenant on Civil and Political Rights, G.A. res. 2200A (XXI), 21 U.N. GAOR Supp. (No. 16) at 52, U.N. Doc. A/6316 (1966), 999 U.N.T.S. 171, entered into force Mar. 23, 1976.

Article 6

1. Every human being has the inherent right to life. This right shall be protected by law. No one shall be arbitrarily deprived of his life.

2. In countries which have not abolished the death penalty, sentence of death may be imposed only for the most serious crimes in accordance with the law in force at the time of the commission of the crime and not contrary to the provisions of the present Covenant and to the Convention on the Prevention and Punishment of the Crime of Genocide. This penalty can only be carried out pursuant to a final judgment rendered by a competent court.

3. When deprivation of life constitutes the crime of genocide, it is understood that nothing in this article shall authorize any State Party to the present Covenant to derogate in any way from any obligation assumed under the provisions of the Convention on the Prevention and Punishment of the Crime of Genocide.

4. Anyone sentenced to death shall have the right to seek pardon or commutation of the sentence. Amnesty, pardon or commutation of the sentence of death may be granted in all cases.

5. Sentence of death shall not be imposed for crimes committed by persons below eighteen years of age and shall not be carried out on pregnant women.

6. Nothing in this article shall be invoked to delay or to prevent the abolition of capital punishment by any State Party to the present Covenant.

Student Handout 4:
Sample Treaty Provisions on the Right to Family

International Covenant on Civil and Political Rights, G.A. res. 2200A
(XXI), 21 U.N. GAOR Supp. (No. 16) at 52, U.N. Doc. A/6316 (1966),
999 U.N.T.S. 171, entered into force Mar. 23, 1976.

Article 23

1. The family is the natural and fundamental group unit of society and
   is entitled to protection by society and the State.
2. The right of men and women of marriageable age to marry and to
   found a family shall be recognized.
3. No marriage shall be entered into without the free and full consent of
   the intending spouses.
4. States Parties to the present Covenant shall take appropriate steps to
   ensure equality of rights and responsibilities of spouses as to marriage,
   during marriage and at its dissolution. In the case of dissolution, provision shall be made for the necessary protection of any children.

***

International Covenant on Economic, Social and Cultural Rights, G.A. res.
2200A (XXI), 21 U.N. GAOR Supp. (No. 16) at 49, U.N. Doc. A/6316
(1966), 993 U.N.T.S. 3, entered into force Jan. 3, 1976.

Article 10

The States Parties to the present Covenant recognize that:

1. The widest possible protection and assistance should be accorded to
   the family, which is the natural and fundamental group unit of society,
   particularly for its establishment and while it is responsible for the
   care and education of dependent children. Marriage must be entered
   into with the free consent of the intending spouses.
2. Special protection should be accorded to mothers during a reasonable
   period before and after childbirth. During such period working mothers
   should be accorded paid leave or leave with adequate social security
   benefits.
3. Special measures of protection and assistance should be taken on
   behalf of all children and young persons without any discrimination
   for reasons of parentage or other conditions. Children and young persons

should be protected from economic and social exploitation. Their employment in work harmful to their morals or health or dangerous to life or likely to hamper their normal development should be punishable by law. States should also set age limits below which the paid employment of child labour should be prohibited and punishable by law.

* * *

Convention on the Rights of the Child, G.A. res. 44/25, annex, 44 U.N. GAOR Supp. (No. 49) at 167, U.N. Doc. A/44/49 (1989), entered into force Sept. 2, 1990.

Article 9

1. States Parties shall ensure that a child shall not be separated from his or her parents against their will, except when competent authorities subject to judicial review determine, in accordance with applicable law and procedures, that such separation is necessary for the best interests of the child. Such determination may be necessary in a particular case such as one involving abuse or neglect of the child by the parents, or one where the parents are living separately and a decision must be made as to the child's place of residence.
2. In any proceedings pursuant to paragraph 1 of the present article, all interested parties shall be given an opportunity to participate in the proceedings and make their views known.
3. States Parties shall respect the right of the child who is separated from one or both parents to maintain personal relations and direct contact with both parents on a regular basis, except if it is contrary to the child's best interests.
4. Where such separation results from any action initiated by a State Party, such as the detention, imprisonment, exile, deportation or death (including death arising from any cause while the person is in the custody of the State) of one or both parents or of the child, that State Party shall, upon request, provide the parents, the child or, if appropriate, another member of the family with the essential information concerning the whereabouts of the absent member(s) of the family unless the provision of the information would be detrimental to the well-being of the child. States Parties shall further ensure that the submission of such a request shall of itself entail no adverse consequences for the person(s) concerned.

Student Handout 5:
Sample Treaty Provisions on Slavery, Servitude, Forced Labor/Nonexploitive Conditions of Employment

International Covenant on Economic, Social and Cultural Rights, G.A. res. 2200A (XXI), 21 U.N. GAOR Supp. (No. 16) at 49, U.N. Doc. A/6316 (1966), 993 U.N.T.S. 3, entered into force Jan. 3, 1976.

Article 6

1. The States Parties to the present Covenant recognize the right to work, which includes the right of everyone to the opportunity to gain his living by work which he freely chooses or accepts, and will take appropriate steps to safeguard this right.
2. The steps to be taken by a State Party to the present Covenant to achieve the full realization of this right shall include technical and vocational guidance and training programmes, policies and techniques to achieve steady economic, social and cultural development and full and productive employment under conditions safeguarding fundamental political and economic freedoms to the individual.

Article 7

The States Parties to the present Covenant recognize the right of everyone to the enjoyment of just and favourable conditions of work which ensure, in particular:

(a) Remuneration which provides all workers, as a minimum, with:
   (i) Fair wages and equal remuneration for work of equal value without distinction of any kind, in particular women being guaranteed conditions of work not inferior to those enjoyed by men, with equal pay for equal work;
   (ii) A decent living for themselves and their families in accordance with the provisions of the present Covenant;
(b) Safe and healthy working conditions;
(c) Equal opportunity for everyone to be promoted in his employment to an appropriate higher level, subject to no considerations other than those of seniority and competence;
(d) Rest, leisure and reasonable limitation of working hours and periodic holidays with pay, as well as remuneration for public holidays.

Article 9

The States Parties to the present Covenant recognize the right of everyone to social security, including social insurance.

Article 11

1. The States Parties to the present Covenant recognize the right of everyone to an adequate standard of living for himself and his family, including adequate food, clothing and housing, and to the continuous improvement of living conditions. The States Parties will take appropriate steps to ensure the realization of this right, recognizing to this effect the essential importance of international co-operation based on free consent.

2. The States Parties to the present Covenant, recognizing the fundamental right of everyone to be free from hunger, shall take, individually and through international co-operation, the measures, including specific programmes, which are needed:

   (a) To improve methods of production, conservation and distribution of food by making full use of technical and scientific knowledge, by disseminating knowledge of the principles of nutrition and by developing or reforming agrarian systems in such a way as to achieve the most efficient development and utilization of natural resources;

   (b) Taking into account the problems of both food-importing and food-exporting countries, to ensure an equitable distribution of world food supplies in relation to need.

Student Handout 6:
Sample Treaty Provisions on Participation in Public Life

International Covenant on Civil and Political Rights, G.A. res. 2200A (XXI), 21 U.N. GAOR Supp. (No. 16) at 52, U.N. Doc. A/6316 (1966), 999 U.N.T.S. 171, entered into force Mar. 23, 1976.

Article 25

Every citizen shall have the right and the opportunity, without any of the distinctions mentioned in Article 2 and without unreasonable restrictions:

(a) To take part in the conduct of public affairs, directly or through freely chosen representatives;

(b) To vote and to be elected at genuine periodic elections which shall be by universal and equal suffrage and shall be held by secret ballot, guaranteeing the free expression of the will of the electors;

(c) To have access, on general terms of equality, to public service in his country.

***

American Convention on Human Rights, O.A.S. Treaty Series No. 36, 1144 U.N.T.S. 123, entered into force July 18, 1978, reprinted in Basic Documents Pertaining to Human Rights in the Inter-American System, OEA/Ser.L.V/II.82 doc.6 rev.1 at 25 (1992).

Article 23, Right to Participate in Government

1. Every citizen shall enjoy the following rights and opportunities:
   a. to take part in the conduct of public affairs, directly or through freely chosen representatives;
   b. to vote and to be elected in genuine periodic elections, which shall be by universal and equal suffrage and by secret ballot that guarantees the free expression of the will of the voters; and
   c. to have access, under general conditions of equality, to the public service of his country.
2. The law may regulate the exercise of the rights and opportunities referred to in the preceding paragraph only on the basis of age, nationality, residence, language, education, civil and mental capacity, or sentencing by a competent court in criminal proceedings.

Debriefing

Depending on the length of the class for the actual simulation, the debriefing may be conducted during the same class period or a later class meeting.

1. Emphasize that the process simulated here is not limited to disabilities; it also applies to the process of drafting all treaties formulating international human rights norms and standards.
2. For an update on current treaty progress, see www.worldenable.net.
3. Discuss some of these issues:
   - How do you explain the differences between the roles played by governments, IGOs, and NGOs? Are these differences justified?
   - Who is not "at the table"? Whose voices are omitted from this debate (for example, particularly marginalized groups of people with disabilities, certain regions of the world, etc.)? What can/should be done about these omissions?
   - How does the treaty-making and enforcement process relate to other equality issues (for example, gender, race, ethnicity, class, status, political belief, etc.)?
   - Why does it matter that a treaty exists on the human rights of people with disabilities?
   - What benefits might the process of drafting a treaty have on a specific advocacy issue?
   - Assess the need for additional treaties versus the need for enforcement of existing treaties.
   - What differences between governments are likely to cause disagreements in a human rights treaty-making process? What differences between NGOs are likely to hamper coalition building in an international human rights treaty-making process?
   - Assess the position taken by the United States in engaging the international human rights process. How has the position of the United States changed over time, in terms of support for international treaties as a means of promoting international human rights? How do you feel about this?

Selected Bibliography

In Print

Disability Studies

Albrecht et al., *Handbook of Disability Studies* (Thousand Oaks, CA: Sage Publications, 2001).

Oliver, Michael, *Understanding Disability* (New York: St. Martin's Press, 1996).

Shapiro, Joseph P., *No Pity: People with Disabilities Forging a New Civil Rights Movement* (New York: Random House, 1994).

Human Rights Law

Buergenthal, Thomas, *International Human Rights in a Nutshell,* 2d ed. (St. Paul, MN: West, 1995).

Hannum, Hurst, ed., *Guide to International Human Rights Practice,* 3d ed. (Ardsley, NY: Transnational Publishers, 1999).

International Disability Rights Law

Degener, Theresia and Yolan Koster-Dreese, eds., *Human Rights and Disabled Persons: Essays and Related Human Rights Instruments* (Boston, MA: Martinus Nijhoff Publishers, 1995).

Degener, Theresia and Gerard Quinn et al., *Human Rights Are for All: The Current Use and Future Potential of the UN Human Rights Instruments in the Context of Disability* (UN Office of the High Commissioner for Human Rights, Geneva: Switzerland, 2002). Available online at www.unhchr.ch/html/menu6/2/disability.doc

National Council on Disability, *A White Paper—Understanding the Role of an International Convention on the Human Rights of People with Disabilities: An analysis of the legal, social, and practical implications for policy makers and disability and human rights advocates in the United States* (Washington, DC, June 12, 2002). Available online at www.ncd.gov/newsroom/publications/2002/unwhitepaper_05-23-02.html

NCD Reference Tool, *Understanding the Potential Content and Structure of an International Convention on the Human Rights of People with Disabilities: A Reference Tool Providing Sample Treaty Provisions Drawn from Existing International Instruments* (Washington, DC, July 2002). Available online at: www.ncd.gov/newsroom/publications/2002/understanding_7-30-02.html

Related Web Sites

www.un.org/esa/socdev/enable/ Web site for the UN's Disability Program within the Division for Social Policy and Development. It contains all disability-related UN documents and a range of other material relevant to international human rights and people with disabilities.

www.worldenable.net/rights/adhoc2meet.htm Page on the World Enable site providing useful summaries of specific oral interventions made by governments, IGOs, and NGOs on the floor of the UN ad hoc committee during its consideration of proposals for the development of an international convention on the human rights of disabled people. This is a useful way to track specific positions on convention issues by key actors in the process.

www.worldenable.net/rights/adhoc2meet.htm Page on the World Enable site containing Disability Negotiations Bulletins, a daily newspaper published by NGOs during the meetings of the UN Ad Hoc committee responsible for developing an international convention on disability rights.

www.dpi.org/en/resources/topics/topics-convention.htm Web page on the Disabled Peoples' International Web site devoted to the Disabilities Convention and containing relevant governmental and nongovernmental positions on the Convention, in addition to other relevant information.

www.sre.gob.mx/discapacidad/home.htm Official site of the Mexican government relating to the development of an international convention on the human rights of people with disabilities, containing Mexican position papers, draft texts, and other information relating to the convention process.

www1.umn.edu/humanrts/instree/auob.htm University of Minnesota Human Rights Library Web site, containing a comprehensive collection of international human rights law documents, including all human rights treaties and documents pertaining to disability.

Corporate Social Responsibility for Human Rights: The Case of Burma/Myanmar

Lucinda Joy Peach

About This Module

Increasing attention has been given to the social responsibility of corporations. Given that the one hundred biggest corporations have a combined annual revenue larger than the gross domestic product of half the world's states, and that the more than thirty-five thousand multinational and transnational corporations (hereafter referred to as MNCs and TNCs) control one-third of all private-sector assets,[1] unquestionably MNCs and TNCs have become among the most powerful organizations in the world. The greater mobility of capital in this era of economic globalization has enabled MNCs and TNCs to operate largely outside of the regulatory authority of state and national government agencies. The result has been that MNCs and TNCs have been generally free to engage in unethical conduct, including exploiting foreign labor, disregarding occupational and worker safety protections, and either directly engaging in or allowing the violation of other basic human rights.[2] In response to negative publicity surrounding these and other incidents in the last decade or so, hundreds of corporations have established corporate social responsibility (CSR) programs. Unfortunately, but perhaps predictably, these programs are often limited to developing codes of conduct.

More intense media attention and public awareness of the unethical practices of corporations in the regions where they operate has fueled the rise of campaigns to combat and prohibit such practices by a wide range of public actors in what is referred to here as the global civil society or GCS.[3] Protests by a widespread network of NGOs and citizens against the World Trade Organization (WTO) meetings in Seattle in October of 1999 are perhaps the most well-known and publicized example of such public protest against corporate activity to date. Are such informal and unofficial measures as self-regulation and public protests adequate to regulate the overseas activities of MNCs and TNCs in order to ensure, at a minimum, their noninvolvement with human rights violations and, ideally, their assistance in protecting human rights wherever they do business? This module gives each student an opportunity to answer this question first-hand by taking on the role of one of several players in the field of CSR. Since the role of corporations in human rights violations in Burma (renamed Myanmar by the military dictatorship that seized power in 1989) has received a lot of media and scholarly attention in recent years, the active learning exercise at the core of this module takes this as the focal case for consideration.

This module is designed to encourage students to grapple with the ethical issues involved in determining how best to regulate corporate social responsibility (CSR) for human rights using the example of Burma. The active learning component requires students to join together in small groups and take on a role as one of the major players in CSR to formulate a resolution proposing how CSR should be regulated and by whom. In addition, students find and review material on CSR for human rights on the Web and evaluate its accuracy and bias. This active learning module takes 3–4 days to complete.

When students have completed the module, they should be able to answer questions such as:

1. How adequate are current informal and unofficial measures, such as self-regulation and regulation by GCS, to ensure at a minimum that MNCs and TNCs are not involved in human rights violations, especially in their overseas activities?
2. Does effective protection of human rights require government regulation in addition to corporate self-regulation and global civil society watchdogs?
3. Do the forces of globalization which constrain the ability of states to regulate MNCs and TNCs further require international and even supranational regulatory mechanisms, in order to adequately protect against corporate involvement in human rights violations?

Miniglossary

Code of conduct A set of principles or guidelines that specifies ethical standards of conducting business. Codes of conduct governing CSR may be specific to a particular company, or may be industry- or profession-wide. Codes may be developed by corporations themselves, NGOs, trade and industry associations, ethics organizations, and/or governmental bodies, and so vary greatly in their uniformity, universality, and bindingness.

Constructive engagement In the context of business, this refers to a corporation's decisions to attempt to change the unethical conduct of a business partner indirectly, rather than through refusing to do business with that entity until it discontinues its unethical behavior, on the theory that this is ultimately a more effective method for getting the company to change its behavior. In the context of this module, corporations sometimes claim constructive engagement as the reason for their refusal to cease business operations in a region where human rights violations are taking place.

Corporate social responsibility (CSR) This phrase developed only in the past century as businesses have been increasingly viewed as having ethical responsibility to stakeholders in addition to their traditional obligation to maximize profits for their shareholders.

Stakeholders Those individuals or entities with a stake or claim upon a corporation. Corporate stakeholders traditionally have been mainly shareholders, but also have included management, employees, and customers. Increasingly, a number of others have been recognized as potential stakeholders, including the corporation's business partners, contractors, suppliers, affiliates, joint venturers, and competitors; residents of the local communities in which the corporation is based or does business; the state and national governments in which the business is incorporated and/or does substantial business; consumer groups; and most recently and as yet not clearly defined, the entire global community, including the environment, nonhuman beings, and future generations.

Global Civil Society (GCS) An umbrella of consumer protest and boycott groups and organizations, religious and civic organizations, human rights groups and other NGOs, associations for professional and business ethics, and, increasingly, investors and other members of the public.[4] The Seattle Protests in 1999 are perhaps the most well-known and publicized example of GCS opposing corporate activity to date.

Step-by-Step Directions

Day One: Preparation (approximately 15–20 minutes)

Provide students with the handouts below, which give them three types of background information:

1. **Theoretical background** on the ethical issues involved in corporate regulation for human rights
2. **Descriptive background** on the human rights abuses in Burma and how corporations have been implicated in the perpetration of such

abuses. (If you prefer, there are a number of other cases of corporate involvement in human rights abuses that might be substituted instead, such as BP Oil Company in Nigeria, Dupont Chemical in Bhopal, India, or Nike in Indonesia. The instructions for the class exercise and the debriefing questions included here could then be adapted as necessary for the other case.)

3. **Information about the significant stakeholders involved in CSR for human rights in Burma.**

Divide the class into small groups, each of which will play one of the following: i.) multinational and transnational corporations; ii.) governments; iii.) global civil society; iv.) intergovernmental organizations; and v.) trade and industry associations. As described in the handouts, variations in several of these groups can be made to accommodate the number of students in the class and the desired complexity of the exercise.

Next, provide all students with Student Handout 1 and each group with the handout for the role it will be playing (Student Handouts 2–6).[5] Tell students that their assignment is to read these handouts and review the Web sites relevant to their roles prior to the next class meeting. They should review these materials in preparation for their group's meeting, during which they will formulate their actor's position on CSR in Myanmar for presentation and debate at a CSR Congress. The Congress is an imaginary global body convened by the United Nations to bring together the parties with the greatest stake in CSR for human rights, in order to attempt negotiating a consensus on human rights standards for MNCs and TNCs doing business overseas.

Day Two: Groups Negotiate Resolutions on CSR within Assigned Roles (at least 1 hour)

Students meet in their groups to:

1. discuss the case and how their assigned roles influence their group's interests and perspectives on the issue (in other words, students begin to embody the roles they are playing in the class exercise).
2. draft a proposed resolution for their group on the issue of CSR in Burma, *including an ethical justification or rationale.*
3. establish a division of labor for finalizing and typing a one-page draft resolution for their group to present to the CSR Congress. The resolution must include an *ethical* argument in favor of the group's position, *including a defense of the reliability and accuracy of materials found on the Internet to support the resolution.* (You may require that

a minimum number of Internet resources be used in preparing the resolution.)

4. establish which group member will be the spokesperson for the group during the CSR Congress.

Day Three: Present, Debate and Vote on Group Resolutions (at least one hour)

1. Arrange the classroom in a circle, so that the spokespeople are in an inner circle. Members of their groups should be clustered closely behind, so they can communicate with one another during the Congress.

2. Introduce the session, reminding the class of the purpose of the Congress and the desired outcome of the deliberations: a unamimously acceptable resolution establishing CSR standards for human rights for MNCs and TNCs conducting business overseas.

3. Have each group distribute a copy of its proposed resolution to all members of the class. The selected spokesperson presents the proposed resolution for his or her group within a strict time frame (5 minutes for each group is more than sufficient).

4. After the presentation of each draft resolution, lead a discussion of the merits and disadvantages of each proposal, encouraging members of the groups to point out how they would defend or argue against the proposals of other groups, given the roles they are playing. It is helpful to write a summary of the pros and cons of each proposal on the board.

5. In the last 5 to 10 minutes allocated to the congressional meeting, ask all members of the class/congress to vote on the proposal that they think is fairest to *all* parties involved.

Student Handout 1:
Overview of CSR for Human Rights
and the Case of Burma/Myanmar

Overview

We can debate the extent of corporate social responsibility for violations of human rights. On one end of the spectrum, some people will agree that multinational corporations (MNCs) and transnational corporations (TNCs) should be responsible for the direct involvement of their officers and agents in committing human rights abuses, such as the exploitation of cheap labor in sweatshop conditions, maintaining unsafe workplace environments, paying salaries inadequate to provide a living wage, or imposing significant restrictions on workers' mobility and rights of association.

On the other end of the spectrum, some people will disagree about whether MNCs should be morally responsible for the human rights violations committed by the governments of the foreign territories in which these corporations conduct business, such as China's lack of due process protections against arbitrary arrest and indefinite imprisonment, its exploitation of prison labor, and its persecution of members of religious groups, such as Falun Gong and Tibetan Buddhists.

Despite these areas of disagreement, many will agree that corporations are responsible, morally if not also legally, for the violations of human rights that are committed by their officers and agents in the due course of conducting business. This principle of moral responsibility is premised on the foundational, ethical, and legal principle requiring persons to refrain from committing direct harms to others to whom they owe a duty of care. Corporations, which are defined as "artificial persons" for constitutional purposes in US law, are thus responsible for failure to uphold their duty of care, at least to the same extent that natural persons are.

Hence, while corporate responsibility for harms that the corporation has not directly caused is debatable, corporate responsibility for harms directly and proximately caused by corporate conduct is well established in both law and ethics. Nevertheless, MNCs and TNCs have been able in large measure to evade sanctions for failure to conform to ethical responsibilities in several areas.

Even in the areas where we might gain relative consensus about corporate responsibility for human rights abuses, however, there is no consensus about *who* is or should be responsible for holding corporations responsible when they violate their obligations to avoid direct harms. In the wake of increasing economic globalization, effective governmental control over

MNCs and TNCs has been, in large part, missing. The combination of increased power and freedom from government regulation has, paradoxically, both facilitated the ability of corporations to evade government regulation, while simultaneously imposing more responsibility on corporations themselves for behaving ethically with respect to human rights, among other areas.

Within this context, the situation of corporate social responsibility in Burma presents an interesting case for assessment for several reasons. First, the totalitarian regime that has held power there since 1989 has been taking even more repressive measures against the civilian population recently, especially against members of the pro-democracy movement. Many Burmese people have fled the country; and many Burmese women and girls have "chosen" to be trafficked for sex work in Thailand and other countries, rather than be raped by and made slave laborers for members of the Myanmar military.[6] Second, while many MNCs and TNCs have ceased to do business in the country, mainly after being pressured to do so by actual or threatened adverse publicity from GCS groups, others have continued to do business with the ruling regime. Third, governmental efforts to ameliorate political, social, and economic conditions in the country have been piecemeal and, to date, ineffective in creating a better human rights environment for the Burmese people.

The Case of Burma/Myanmar

Burma is one of the poorest countries in the developing world, with only one in four Burmese children graduating from primary school and a national income under $300 per year. The State Law and Order Restoration Council (SLORC), a military junta, seized power in 1988 and denied the democratically elected National League for Democracy (NLD) leader Aung San Suu Kyi the right to take leadership in 1990, despite overwhelming public support for her.[7]

When Suu Kyi was released from house arrest in July 1995, she declared she was still dedicated to the restoration of democracy in her country, and called for dialogue on political reform between the SLORC, the democracy movement, and ethnic groups. She also urged businessmen to refrain from investing in Burma. In November, she withdrew the NLD from the National Convention, saying it was not representative of the wishes of the people. Twice in September 2000, Suu Kyi was held to keep her from travelling outside the capital. For much of the time since then, she has been kept confined to her residence, and access to her has been strictly controlled.

On May 30, 2003, during a tour to the north, Suu Kyi was taken into custody again, along with about two dozen senior NLD members, after clashes between her supporters and members of a pro-military group. The United States said it suspected the clashes were staged by "government-affiliated thugs."[8] Her detention raised fresh international concern, and several world leaders condemned the junta for Suu Kyi's detention. The United States, Britain, and the European Union threatened more economic sanctions against the military-ruled country.

The military government's violation of human rights is widespread and egregious. The repressive ruling regime (which renamed itself the "State Peace and Development Council," or SPDC, in 1997) has forced civilians into involuntary, unpaid labor for military initiatives; development of infrastructure for tourism and foreign business investment; allowed members of the military to rape and sexually assault women with impunity; and has engaged in massive relocations of the civilian population for infrastructure projects. Despite concern about these abuses expressed by, among others, the International Labour Organization (ILO),[9] the UN General Assembly, the UN Commission on Human Rights, and the UN Committee on the Elimination of Discrimination against Women (CEDAW), the SPDC has failed to put a stop to its violations of human rights.

Since foreign ownership of companies operating in Burma is prohibited, nearly all large foreign investment in the country is carried out through joint ventures with the military regime. Despite the widespread reporting of the government's violations of human rights, the number of new investors has increased significantly over the past several years, according to Burmese news sources. European and US corporations have dominated oil and gas investments.[10] According to the Burma Project Web site, "foreign oil companies have provided at least 65% of all foreign investment since 1988 and are therefore the main source of foreign revenue for the SPDC regime. In addition, from 1995 to 1999, apparel imports to the U.S. were up 272%."[11]

The most controversial of foreign investments relates to the US$ one billion plus Yadana oil investment project in the southern Tenasserim region, led by Total/Unocal of France (over a 31% share), and joined by Unocal of the United States (28%+ share), PTTEP of Thailand (25%+ share), and Burma Oil and Gas Enterprise (15% share).[12] The project both provides financial support to the Burmese government and contributes to human rights violations. These violations include abuse of civilian populations by military personnel who provide security, use of civilians as forced labor to build infrastructure support, and forcible relocation of civilian populations along the pipeline route.

For Further Research on Human Rights Violations in Burma

The following sources are merely starting points for further research. Students are expected to become active researchers, finding and evaluating further relevant sources.

http://web.amnesty.org/web/ar2002.nsf/asa/myanmar!Open   Amnesty International Web site, 2002 Report on Myanmar.

www.soros.org/burma/index.html Burma Project.

www.freeburma.org/ Free Burma Web site.

www.hrw.org/wr2k2/asia2.html Human Rights Watch Web site, "Burma," in World Report (2002).

www.ncgub.net/index.htm National Coalition Government of the Union of Burma (NCGUB) Web site.

Schermerhorn, John, "Terms of Global Business Engagement in Ethically Challenging Environments: Applications to Burma," *Business Ethics Quarterly*, Vol. 9, No. 3 (1999), 485–505.

Student Handout 2: Actor Guide for Multinational and Transnational Corporations

It is important to recognize that there are several potentially competing stakeholders within MNCs and TNCs, including CEOs and managers, shareholders, and nonmanagerial employees. Each of these stakeholders may have significantly different interests with respect to corporate social responsibility (CSR). The following section addresses primarily how corporate managers and CEOs have responded to the CSR challenge of human rights violations in Burma.

Mostly in response to pressures of various kinds from global civil society, a number of MNCs and TNCs, including Amoco, Texaco, ARCO, and Petro-Canada, have withdrawn business dealings and/or disinvested from Burma. Although Unocal decided to stay, it was forced to de-Americanize by selling its service stations and refineries in the United States, eliminating the segment of its business most vulnerable to public action. It was also forced to open another corporate headquarters in Malaysia.

Other corporations that have exited Burma voluntarily include Levi Strauss, Liz Claiborne, J. Crew, Oshkosh B'Gosh, Colombia Sportsgear, Seagram's, Wente Vineyards, Apple Computer, and Carlsberg.[13] Other corporations, including PepsiCo, Apple, Motorola, and Kodak, have disinvested from Burma only after targeted pressure from protest groups or selective-purchasing laws. Sara Lee Corporation, which makes clothing under various brands, is one of the latest in a string of companies to pull out of Burma, making the move in September 2001, just a few weeks after the Free Burma Coalition condemned the firm on its Web site.[14]

However, some MNCs have refused to withdraw or disinvest, including the Total/Unocal consortium, Asia Pacific Breweries, and Acer Computer. Some of these companies have claimed that their continued presence in the country constitutes "constructive engagement" that is more likely to further the cause of human rights than could be accomplished by withdrawing. For instance, Unocal's Web site defends the company's policy of "engagement versus isolation" against opposing positions, and suggests that activists have misrepresented the company and "have resorted to spreading false and hurtful allegations about Unocal and the Yadana natural gas project."[15]

Total Oil has likewise claimed that it is the victim of a "disinformation campaign," and that its presence in Burma is a positive one, as it has provided relatively high wages to its Burmese workers, compensated them for acquired lands, and funded a "socioeconomic program" in support of the local population.[16] (In developing a resolution as a corporation, you will need to consider whether such justifications are valid, or mere pretexts for continuing to profit from a country where human rights violations are rampant.)

On the other side of the debate, shareholder groups have been filing shareholder resolutions for consideration at the annual meetings of MNCs and TNCs. Although shareholder resolutions seldom result in garnering a majority vote to the effect that the company is responsible for MNC violations, they have often been successful in getting management's attention; these corporate managers are now considering changes in corporate practices that will enable them to become more socially responsible. As one group's Web site states, "They use the power of persuasion backed by economic pressure from consumers and investors to hold corporations accountable."[17]

***

In drafting your resolution, consider the type of MNC or TNC you represent; its needs and interests in doing business in Burma; its needs and interests in remaining self-regulating; its needs and interests in maintaining good public relations; and similar matters.

For Further Research

Corporate Web Sites

The following are just a few of the corporate sites that deal with CSR and/or human rights issues, including those of several companies that have had dealings with the Myanmar government. You will need to research other companies than those listed here.

www.exxonmobil.com/Corporate/Notebook/Citizen/Corp_N_Citizen
    Details.asp Exxon-Mobile Web site, "Being a Good Corporate Citizen."

www.levistrauss.com/responsibility/ Levi Strauss Web site.

www.unocal.com/responsibility/ Unocal Web site (on CSR).

www.unocal.com/myanmar/ Unocal in Myanmar

Shareholder and Investor Groups

www.iccr.org/about/index.htm Interfaith Center on Corporate Responsibility (ICCR) Web site. This group is an international coalition of 275 Protestant, Roman Catholic, and Jewish institutional investors, including denominations, religious communities, pension funds, healthcare corporations, foundations, and dioceses, that merges social values with investment decisions.

www.irrc.org/ The Investor Responsibility Research Center Web site provides a "Burma Information Package" that gives institutional investors, government purchasing offices, and law firms quarterly updates on US and non-US companies engaging in activities or production in Burma.

Student Handout 3:
Actor Guide for Governments

Determine whether your group represents a *host government* (one of those officially recognized governments operating in the territory where the corporation does business abroad) or a *home government* (the official governmental entities in the territory or territories where the corporation is incorporated). In the United States, incorporation is within a particular state; in other countries, businesses may be incorporated nationally. Think about the different interests of and pressures on home and host governments as you prepare your draft resolution.

Whereas some national governments, including the United States, have imposed some restrictions on their corporations doing business in Burma, others, such as Japan, have not taken any such measures.

US government sanctions enacted in May 1997 forbid *new* investment in Burma by American companies, but are silent regarding existing investments. Other states have acknowledged similar lack of political will and/or boundaries to their authority to regulate. However, on June 11, 2003, the US Senate passed a bill (by a 97-to-1 vote) that would ban exports from Burma and freeze assets of the Myanmar regime in the United States, with indications being favorable that the House of Representatives would pass a similar bill. For current developments on US laws regarding Burma, see the US State Department Web site.

In Roe v. Burma, a case brought by fifteen Burmese villagers, a US federal circuit court ruled on September 2, 2002 that Unocal Corporation and its partners knew of and benefited from forced labor on the Yadana natural gas pipeline between Burma and Thailand; and that this evidence was sufficient to prevent the case being dismissed before the plaintiff's claims—that Unocal is liable for aiding and abetting practices of forced labor by the Myanmar military under the Alien Tort Claims Act—were heard.

Local governments in the United States have taken greater direct action than the federal government toward ending corporate complicity in human rights violations in Burma. Since 1995, many local governments, including Boulder, Colorado; Berkeley and Los Angeles, California; Madison, Wisconsin; New York City, and several cities in Massachusetts, have passed legislation prohibiting investments in Burma.[18] However, on June 19, 2000, in the case of Crosby v. National Foreign Trade Council,[19] the US Supreme Court unanimously rejected a Massachusetts state law that would have penalized companies investing in Burma, ruling that Congress had preempted state regulation by establishing a sanctions policy.[20] This ruling has severely limited the ability of local governments to effectively regulate how MNCs do business overseas.

For Further Research

A few useful Web sites are included below. You will need to conduct further research to find others.

www.usitc.gov United States International Trade Commission Web site.

www.state.gov United States Department of State Web site.

www.ibiblio.org/freeburma/boycott/sp/bsp_faq.html Free Burma Web site, "Burma Purchasing Laws: Frequently Asked Questions."

http://europa.eu.int/comm/external_relations/myanmar/intro/ European Union Web site, "The EU's relations with Myanmar/Burma."

Student Handout 4: Actor Guide for Global Civil Society

This actor on the corporate social responsibility (CSR) stage is actually an umbrella composed of a number of nongovernmental organizations (NGOs) and citizen groups. As with other relevant groups, this player in the CSR arena can also be easily subdivided into:

1. **confrontation-oriented groups** involved in public protests and consumer boycotts of corporate violations of human rights, such as Ralph Nader's Citizen Watch, the Free Burma Coalition, etc.
2. **engagement-style groups** working to encourage MNCs and TNCs to be more socially responsible, such as Social Accountability International (included under Web sites below).
3. **traditional human rights organizations,** such as Amnesty International and Human Rights Watch.

Actions taken by participants in global civil society in opposition to continued MNC and TNC involvement in Burma in the wake of the latter's massive human rights violations have included investigation and documentation by human rights groups, protests and boycotts by consumer and citizen groups, and local community initiatives. Strong advocacy efforts to restrict imports of Burmese-made garments into the United States evoked pledges from many leading retailers and designers not to buy from Burma. Human rights and other watchdog organizations provide information on why and how to avoid investing in Burma.

For Further Research

Only a few of the many Web sites of groups included within GCS are included below, grouped into the general categories specified above. You will need to conduct further research to find others that are relevant to your particular role and interests.

Confrontation-Oriented Groups

www.citizen.org/trade   Global Trade Watch (GTW) is a division of Ralph Nader's Public Citizen. GTW's executive director, Lori Wallach, was one of the prime organizers of the protests against the WTO in Seattle, Washington in September 1999.

www.nlcnet.org   The National Labor Committee (NLC) Web site. The NLC is an independent not-for-profit organization dedicated to promoting and defending human and worker rights in the global economy. The organization exposes human and labor rights abuses committed by US companies producing goods in poor countries and organizes campaigns to put an end to these abuses.

www.sweatshopwatch.org/ Sweatshop Watch Web site. Founded in 1995, Sweatshop Watch is a coalition of over 30 labor, community, civil rights, immigrant rights, women's, religious, and student organizations and many individuals committed to eliminating the exploitation that occurs in sweatshops and focused on the needs and interests of the workers themselves.

www.usasnet.org United Students Against Sweatshops (USAS) Web site. USAS is an organization of students and community members at over two hundred campuses across the United States and Canada supporting the struggles of working people and challenging corporate power.

Engagement-Style Groups

www.ethicaltrade.org Ethical Trading Initiative (ETI) Web site. The ETI is an alliance of companies, NGOs, and trade unions committed to working together to identify and promote ethical trade—good practice in the implementation of a code of conduct for good labor standards.

www.cepaa.org Social Accountability International (SAI) Web site. SAI is a charitable human rights organization dedicated to improving workplaces and communities by developing and implementing socially responsible standards.

www.nd.edu/~ethics/ The University of Notre Dame Center for Ethics and Religious Values in Business is a university-based organization that incorporates religious and other ethical perspectives into considering CSR.

Traditional Human Rights Organizations

www.amnestyusa.org/business Amnesty International (AI) is a worldwide movement of people who campaign for internationally recognized human rights.

www.antislavery.org/homepage/antislavery/about.htm Anti-Slavery International, founded in 1839, is the world's oldest international human rights organization, and the only charity in the United Kingdom to work exclusively against slavery and related abuses.

http://hrw.org/corporations Human Rights Watch (HRW) is the largest human rights organization based in the United States. HRW researchers conduct fact-finding investigations into human rights abuses in all regions of the world, which are then published, generating extensive coverage in local and international media. This media coverage helps embarrass abusive governments. HRW then meets with government officials to urge changes in policy and practice.

Student Handout 5:
Actor Guide for
Intergovernmental Organizations (IGOs)

IGOs include such entities as the United Nations, Organization for Economic Cooperation and Development (OECD), International Labour Organization (ILO), World Bank, World Trade Organization (WTO), International Monetary Fund (IMF), etc. Each of these stakeholders may have a somewhat different perspective on CSR for human rights. Since about 1972, the United Nations and other IGOs, including the ILO, OECD, and the WTO, have promulgated human rights and other guidelines regarding the conduct of MNCs and TNCs. In 2001, the ILO issued a major study on forced labor in Myanmar, pointing to the abuses of Burma in several instances, and establishing guidelines for employers to avoid violating the human rights of their workers.[21]

Given the lack of direct international jurisdiction over corporations, however, these guidelines are voluntary in the absence of a decision by a particular state to implement them into domestic law, or be bound to uphold them under a treaty agreement. The European Union recently took a harder line with respect to imposing limitations on European-based companies doing business in Burma. However, the Association of Southeast Asian Nations (ASEAN) admitted Burma to its membership in July 1997, despite opposition from human rights groups worldwide and Western governments.[22]

For Further Research

The following are a few of the most important IGOs involved with CSR for human rights. You will need to conduct further research in order to discover others, as well as how such IGOs have been criticized or commended for their positions on CSR.

www.ilo.org/public/english/employment/multi/promact/ The International Labour Organization (ILO) Web site. ILO is a tripartite organization representing governments, business, and labor. It has promulgated several sets of standards bearing on CSR for human rights.

www.oecdwash.org/ Created in 1961, the Organization for Economic Cooperation and Development (OECD) is the international organization of the industrialized, market-economy countries. It established *Guidelines for Multinational Enterprises* (1976) and *Principles of Corporate Governance* (1999).

United Nations

Several aspects of the United Nations' work bear on CSR and human rights, including:

www.unctad.org Conference on Trade and Development (UNCTAD) Web site.

www.unhchr.ch/ Commissioner for Human Rights (UNCHR) Web site.

www.un.org/partners/business/ Global Compact.

www.wto.org/ World Trade Organization (WTO) Web site.

Student Handout 6:
Actor Guide for Trade and Industry Associations

This category is also an umbrella of sorts, encompassing both groups that are primarily business oriented, but have CSR as part of their agendas; as well as those groups whose primary function or purpose is business ethics, with CSR being a significant dimension of their work.

Many of the trade, industry, and professional groups and organizations that MNCs and TNCs are members of (a few of which are listed below) have developed codes of social responsibility that contain human rights provisions. On the opposite side, an association of corporations with investments in Burma—called USA Engage—is opposed to the US government's sanctions campaign against investments in Burma, claiming that it hurts US businesses and enables foreign companies to take advantage of the breach.

For Further Research

Only a few of the many trade, industry, and professional organizations working on CSR for human rights are included here. Many others are out there on the Internet, waiting for your discovery and analysis!

www.bsr.org/ Business for Social Responsibility (BSR) describes itself as "a US-based global resource for companies seeking to sustain their commercial success in ways that respect people, communities and the environment."

www.web.net/~robrien/papers/sri/players/cep.html The Council on Economic Priorities (CEP) is a nonprofit public interest organization that was founded in 1969 to research corporate social responsibility. CEP publishes corporate reports, gives yearly corporate responsibility awards, started the Campaign for Cleaner Corporations, and provides corporate social responsibility research for investors.

www.iccwbo.org The International Chamber of Commerce (ICC) is probably the most powerful association of MNCs and TNCs, composed of business executives of major corporations from the United States, Europe, and Japan. It opposes government-mandated codes of conduct at the international level, and argues in favor of corporate self-regulation.

www.uscib.org/ The US Council for International Business (USCIB) was founded in 1945 to promote an open world trading system. Members include more than three hundred multinational companies, law firms, and business associations. It opposes linking human rights issues to trade talks in the WTO, arguing that such matters are more appropriately being addressed by other organizations, such as the ILO.

www.usaengage.org/ In USA Engage-concerned organizations, companies and individuals work together to assure that unilateral sanctions initiatives are examined rigorously to determine the potential for accomplishing their stated objectives and for damaging US competitiveness and jobs. The coalition promotes responsible alternatives that advance US security, and diplomatic and economic goals.

Debriefing

After the congressional session, debriefing provides students with an opportunity to reflect on and discuss the simulation. The following list of questions may be used for class discussion, small group work, or individual writing assignments. These questions may be given to students as a separate handout. Some of them can be assigned as follow-up or one-step-further activities, or as extra-credit projects.

1. What are the benefits and drawbacks to having CSR regulated by each of the actors participating in the CSR Congress? (It may be helpful to list the pros and cons of each actor.) Which actor or combination of actors represents the best one(s) to be responsible for regulation? Why?
2. What incentives do different actors have to promote CSR and why? Are these all acceptable?
3. What do you think of the corporate defense of constructive engagement? Is this a legitimate means for promoting CSR in the foreign territories where a company does business, or is it merely a cover or pretext for continuing to do business in states where human rights (and other ethical) violations are taking place?
4. In your opinion, who are the worst offenders of CSR abuses? Is this likely to change? How and why? Who are the heroes? (Support answers with specific acts or quotes.)
5. Does anything in either Toolkit 2 or Toolkit 3 justify accepting inequality across cultures, especially given that we have taken coercive action to root out inequalities in our own society? Does anything in your own value system justify acceptance of intercultural inequality?
6. Stepping outside of your role-playing perspective, how should we grapple with CSR?
   - Globally, regionally, locally, or per individual corporations?
   - By focusing on governments, NGOs, or businesses?
   - By focusing on individual or mass psychology?
   - By appealing to grassroots folks or elite decision-makers?
   - By emphasizing religious beliefs, international law, or professional conduct?
   - By using "hard power" or "soft power"?[23]

If you were designing a solution, who would your audience be? Would adapting values in either Toolkit 2 or Toolkit 3 help create a solution here, or is another toolkit needed, perhaps one on business ethics? Would employment of a value from your personal value system be helpful? How so?

7. What is the value of CSR? Is it just a buzzword or does it matter?

8. How useful were the Web sites you reviewed in preparation for your group's resolution? What kinds of checks can and should you use before relying on the accuracy and validity of information you find on the Web?

9. Who makes the athletic wear and university logo clothing that your campus bookstore sells? How much are their employees paid? Does your university have a CSR policy? If so, where is it written? How do you know if the university adheres to it or not? Having done this active learning exercise, do you think this policy is adequate?

Selected Bibliography

In Print

Behrman, Jack, "Adequacy of International Codes of Behavior," *Journal of Business Ethics* 31:1 (2001): 51–64.

Carroll, Archie, "Corporate Social Responsibility," *Business and Society* 38:3 (1999): 268–95.

Cassel, Dougless, "Human Rights and Business Responsibility in the Global Marketplace," *Business Ethics Quarterly* 11:2 (2001): 261–74.

DeGeorge, Richard, "Ethics in International Business—a Contradiction in Terms?" *Business Credit* 102:8 (2000): 50–52.

Gereffi, Ronie Garcia-Johnson, and Erika Sasser, "The NGO-Industrial Complex," *Foreign Policy* (July–August 2001): 1–5.

McWilliams, Abigail and Donald Siegel, "Corporate Social Responsibility: A Theory of the Firm Perspective," *The Academy of Management Review* 26:1 (2001): 117–27.

Related Web Sites

www.filmstransit.com/behind.html Films Transit International provides information on a 45-minute 2001 film entitled, "Behind the Labels: Garment Workers on U.S. Saipan." Saipan is a US island territory exempt from many labor and immigration laws that apply throughout the United States; here clothes are made by primarily Chinese and Filipina women, but carry the "Made in the USA" label.

http://news.bbc.co.uk/1/hi/programmes/panorama/archive/970385.stm This Web site presents the transcript of the 2001 BBC Panorama documentary entitled "Gap, Nike, No Sweat." This undercover investigation of a Cambodian factory making clothes for Gap and Nike allegedly found violations of both companies' policies. The documentary itself can be seen regularly on LinkTV. For viewing schedule, go to www.worldlinktv.com/programming/programDescription.php4?code=gap

Endnotes

1. Linda Mabry, "Multinational Corporations and U.S. Technology Policy: Rethinking the Concept of Corporate Nationality," *Georgetown Law Journal* 87 (1999): 563–673, at 569.

2. The international law documents that provide protections of these human rights include the UN Charter, the Universal Declaration of Human Rights, the UN Covenant on Civil and Political Rights, the UN Covenant on Social and Economic Rights, treaties of the ILO, and other international and regional treaties as discussed in the section on International Governmental Agencies in Student Handout 5.

3. Thomas Dunfee and Patricia Werhane, "Report on Business Ethics in North America," *Journal of Business Ethics* 6, no. 14 (1977): 1589–95.

4. Dunfee and Werhane, "Report on Business Ethics."

5. Alternatively, you may provide the entire class with a complete set of handouts so that each student has an overview of all the players in the simulation.

6. Human Rights Watch, "Burma," in *World Report* (2002), www.hrw.org/wr2k1 /asia/burma.html.

7. Human Rights Watch, "Burma"; John Schermerhorn, "Terms of Global Business Engagement in Ethically Challenging Environments: Applications to Burma," *Business Ethics Quarterly* 9, no. 3 (1999), 485–505, at 486–88.

8. Reuters Alertnet Country Profile Web site, www.alertnet.org/thefacts/countryprofiles/218938.htm. Provides facts and statistics on Myanmar.

9. Burma/Myanmar became a party to the International Labour Organization (ILO) Convention No. 29 in 1955, and has been subject to scrutiny by the ILO for several years.

10. Schermerhorn, "Terms of Global Business," 488–49.

11. Burma Project Web site, www.soros.org/burma/index.html.

12. Schermerhorn, "Terms of Global Business," 490.

13. Burma Project Web site, www.soros.org/burma/index.html.

14. Free Burma Coalition Web site, Press Release: "Country's Top Undergarment Brand Vows No More Business in Burma" (Sept. 4, 2001), www.freeburmacoalition.org/frames/home.htm

15. UNOCAL, "Unocal in Myanmar," www.unocal.com/myanmar/

16. Schermerhorn, "Terms of Global Business," at 488–89.

17. Interfaith Center on Corporate Responsibility (ICCR) Web site, www.iccr.org/about/index.htm.

18. However, European countries, both individually and as part of the European Community, have been taking greater steps in recent years to step up regulation.

19. www.soros.org/burma/index.html.

20. 530 U.S. 363 (2000). Alternative strategies, including divestment from companies doing business in Burma, are being pursued in Massachusetts and by some city governments.

21. International Labour Organization (ILO), "Business and Social Initiatives Database," http://oracle02.ilo:6060/vpi/vpisearch.first

22. Schermerhorn, "Terms of Global Business," 486–88.

23. In international relations, hard power typically refers to a state's tangible, quantifiable resources. It encompasses dimensions of power such as the number of nuclear weapons a state possesses, the percentage of annual economic growth a country enjoys, and the educational accomplishments of a nation's labor force. Soft power is more subtle and difficult to quantify. Among other qualities, it includes diplomatic skill, strength of national values, and a population's willingness to go to war. See Joseph S. Nye, "The Changing Nature of World Power," *Political Science Quarterly* 105:2 (Summer 1990): 177–192.

NOTES ON CONTRIBUTORS

Kristin Andrews is assistant professor of philosophy at York University in Toronto and director of York's B.A. program in Cognitive Science. She specializes in the philosophy of psychology, and has research interests in moral psychology and comparative cognition. Recent publications include "Knowing Mental States: The Asymmetry of Psychological Prediction and Explanation" in Quentin Smith and Aleksander Jokic (eds.), *Consciousness: New Philosophical Essays* (Oxford University Press, 2002) and "Why Bush Should Explain September 11th" in Patrick Hayden, Tom Lansford, and Robert P. Watson (eds.) *America's War on Terror* (Ashgate Publishing, 2003). She received her PhD in Philosophy from the University of Minnesota in 2000.

Vivian Bertrand is a policy researcher and analyst, primarily consulting with the Canadian federal government. Her work focuses on environmental policy, environmental health, and infrastructure policy. Before consulting full-time, she coordinated an international project, *Understanding Values: A Study of Values in Environmental Policy Making in China, India, Japan and the United States*, at the Carnegie Council on Ethics and International Affairs. Prior to joining the Council, she administered an environmental mentoring program for high school students, and served as an environmental researcher and policy analyst in the Canadian federal government and at Resource Futures International and Stratos, Inc. In addition to policy and social science research, Bertrand's experience includes ecosystem health research at the University of Guelph and wolf population research at the University of Waterloo. Bertrand received her MA in environmental policy from Carleton University in Ottawa, Canada and her BS in environmental science from the University of Toronto. She was a Salzburg Fellow in 2001, and recipient of the Ian MacDonald Prize for her MA thesis on endocrine-disrupting chemicals in 2000.

Nancy Flowers spent 25 years as a human rights activist and secondary school teacher. She now combines these interests as a consultant for human rights education to governments, NGOs, and UN agencies. She has worked to develop Amnesty International's education program, and is a cofounder of Human Rights USA, a national human rights education coalition. She has trained activists, professionals, and military and police personnel in Africa, Asia, the Middle East, Eastern Europe, and the Balkans. She is the author of numerous articles and books on human rights education, most recently, *Local Action/Global Change: Learning About the Human Rights of Women and Girls* (UNIFEM, 1999) and *The Human Rights Education Handbook* (University of Minnesota, 2000). She also is editor of the University of Minnesota Human Rights Resource Center's *Human Rights Education Series*.

Richard J. Harknett is associate professor of political science at the University of Cincinnati (UC) and professorial lecturer at the Diplomatic Academy, Vienna, Austria.

He received the Edith C. Alexander Award for Excellence in Teaching at the McMicken College of Arts & Sciences at UC. He is author of the Web book, *Lenses of Analysis: A Visual Framework for the Study of International Relations* and some twenty publications in the area of international security studies.

Meredith A. Heiser-Durón is a professor of political science at Foothill College in Los Altos Hills, California and a lecturer at Stanford University. She specializes in German Studies, European Studies, and International Organizations (NATO and EU expansion in particular). She also serves as the Director of Foothill College's Overseas Studies Program in Prague and Berlin. A graduate of Johns Hopkins' School for Advanced International Studies, she is the author of numerous articles concerning the evolving party system and identity in East and West Germany. She is presently working on a comparative article on state government in Brandenburg /Berlin, as well as an article on Germany's view of ESDI. She has been an NEH Fellow (1998/2001), Fulbright Scholar in Germany (1995/2002), and has won Partnership for Excellence Awards (2001–2003) and Teaching Excellence Awards at Foothill College.

Janet E. Lord joined Landmine Survivors Network (LSN) in 2001. In her role as Legal Counsel and Director of Advocacy, Ms. Lord is responsible for designing and implementing human rights advocacy programming, including LSN's Convention Initiative related to the development of a UN Convention on the Rights of Persons with Disabilities. Prior to joining LSN, Ms. Lord served as an attorney with the World Bank Group, where she practiced international administrative law. She has served as consultant to the UN Disability Program, the Office of the High Commissioner for Human Rights, the National Council on Disability, and a number of NGOs. She has taught international law at the University of Edinburgh, American University, School of International Service, and University of Baltimore School of Law, and has published widely in the area of human rights law. Ms. Lord earned two law degrees from the University of Edinburgh, an LLM in international and comparative law from George Washington University, and a BA from Kenyon College.

Peter Lucas is a faculty member in the Department of International and Transcultural Studies at Teachers College, Columbia University. His research and teaching focus on peace education, human rights curriculum for schools, school violence and school safety in New York, international human rights education, the role of photography and film in human rights witnessing, small-arms disarmament education, and violence and popular peace movements in Rio de Janeiro. His recent work includes a study on the relationship between school violence and peace education in high school. He is currently writing a new book entitled, *The Mural of Pain: The Visual Representation of Violence and Peace in the Brazilian Human Rights Movement.*

Colette Mazzucelli, MALD, PhD, DDG, Senior Lecturer and member, "Conseil Scientifique," Rotary Center for International Studies in Peace and Conflict Resolution, Sciences Po, Paris, is a founding faculty member and Provost of the OnLine Training

(OLT) College. A Da Vinci Laureate, Mazzucelli was cited as International Educator of the Year in 2003 for pioneering work, with Roger Boston, to develop multimedia pedagogy for active learning. She is the author of *France and Germany at Maastricht* and numerous other publications.

Julie Mertus is assistant professor at American University's School of International Service. She is codirector of the MA program in Ethics, Peace, and Global Affairs. A graduate of Yale Law School, her work focuses on ethnonational conflict, human rights, refugee and humanitarian law and policy, gender and conflict, and postconflict transition. She has been a United States Institute of Peace Senior Fellow, MacArthur Foundation Fellow, a Harvard Law School Human Rights Fellow, a Fulbright Fellow, Counsel to Human Rights Watch, a Law and Religion Fellow at Emory University, and a Rockefeller Foundation visitor at Dartmouth College. She has also served as a consultant on human rights and humanitarian issues to UNCHR, the Watson Institute for International Affairs, Oxfam, the Soros Foundation, and many NGOs and IGOs. Professor Mertus is the author or editor of over thirty-six academic articles and book chapters. Recent books include *Looks Can Be Deceiving: Human Rights and American Foreign Policy* (Routledge, 2003) and *Human Rights and Conflict* (with Jeffrey Helsing; USIP, 2003). In 2003 she received the SIS Faculty Award for Outstanding Curriculum Development and the SIS Faculty Award for Outstanding Scholarship and Professional Service.

Helena Meyer-Knapp has been teaching political and international studies at The Evergreen State College for 20 years. Teachers there are encouraged to develop carefully considered pedagogy, and are particularly committed to connecting theory with real-world experiences. Meyer-Knapp's research centers on peace-making, specifically on the processes by which warring communities decide it is time to end their fighting. Her book, *Dangerous Peace-Making*, was published in 2003. Her work in this field has received support from the Carnegie Council on Ethics and International Affairs and from the Bunting Institute (now called the Radcliffe Institute for Advanced Study) at Harvard University.

April Morgan, PhD, Georgetown University, is assistant professor of political science at the University of Tennessee. She specializes in international relations theory and international law. Her research interests include the changing nature of state sovereignty, ethics and global politics, the war on terror, and pedagogy. In 2000 Morgan received the Chancellor's Award for Excellence in Teaching. In 2003 the National Alumni Association named her Outstanding Professor of the Year. Georgetown University's Class of 1995 gave her the Edmund A. Walsh Honored Faculty teaching medal. A volume on teaching, coedited by Dr. Morgan and Dr. Marilyn Kallet, is forthcoming (University of Tennessee Press, 2005).

Gabriel Palmer-Fernandez, PhD, Harvard University, is director of the Dr. James Dale Ethics Center and professor of philosophy and religious studies at Youngstown State University, where he teaches a number of ethics courses, including bioethics.

He has published and lectured widely on such topics as ethical issues in DNA research, fairness in selection of research subjects, questions concerning just wars, and problems of justice. Recent books include *Deterrence and the Crisis in Moral Theory; Moral Issues: Philosophical and Religious Perspectives;* and *Encyclopedia of Religion and War* (Routledge, 2004).

Lucinda Joy Peach is associate professor in the Department of Philosophy and Religion at American University, where she teaches courses in the areas of applied ethics, moral philosophy, and women's studies. She earned her PhD from the Department of Religious Studies at Indiana University (1995) and holds a JD degree from New York University School of Law (1982). She has published widely in areas at the intersection of law, religion, ethics, and gender; her works focus on topics such as the impact of religious lawmaking on women's rights, the ethics of women in military combat, corporate social responsibility for human rights, and women's human rights, especially in the area of sex trafficking. She was recently a Rockefeller Fellow in Gender and Globalization in the Women's Studies Program at the University of Hawaii, Manoa, where she researched the moral discourse surrounding sex trafficking and prostitution; and a Fulbright lecturer in Women's Studies at the Women's Studies and Development Centre, University of Delhi.

Craig Warkentin is an associate professor at the State University of New York, Oswego, where he teaches courses in international relations. His primary research interests are in the areas of international organization, Internet politics, and global gender issues. He has published academic articles and book chapters on NGOs, global civil society, Chilean women's movements, the United Nations, women in development, and the role of culture in multilateral diplomacy. His book, *Reshaping World Politics: NGOs, the Internet, and Global Civil Society* (Rowman and Littlefield, 2001), was awarded the 2002 Chadwick F. Alger Prize by the International Studies Association.

INDEX

 Also from Kumarian Press...

Humanitarianism, Ethics, Civil Society

Human Rights and Development
Peter Uvin

The Humanitarian Enterprise: Dilemmas and Discoveries
Larry Minear

Nation-Building Unraveled? Aid, Peace and Justice in Afghanistan
Edited by Antonio Donini, Norah Niland and Karin Wermester

Patronage or Partnership: Local Capacity Building in Humanitarian Crises
Edited by Ian Smillie for the Humanitarianism and War Project

Progress of the World's Women 2002, Volume One
Women, War, Peace: The Independent Expert's Assessment on the Impact of
Armed Conflict on Women and Women's Role in Peace-Building
Edited by Elisabeth Rehn and Ellen Johnson Sirleaf, published by UNIFEM

War's Offensive on Women
The Humanitarian Challenge in Bosnia, Kosovo and Afghanistan
Julie A. Mertus for the Humanitarianism and War Project

Worlds Apart: Civil Society and the Battle for Ethical Globalization
John D. Clark

World Disaster's Report, 2003: Focus on Ethics and Aid
Edited by Jonathan Walter, Published by International Federation of Red Cross and Red
Crescent Societies

Global Issues, Development, Conflict Resolution

Buddhism at Work
Community Development, Social Empowerment and the Sarvodaya Movement
George D. Bond

Southern Exposure
International Development and the Global South in the Twenty-First Century
Barbara P. Thomas-Slayter

War and Intervention: Issues for Contemporary Peace Operations
Michael V. Bhatia

Visit Kumarian Press at **www.kpbooks.com** or
call **toll-free 800.289.2664** for a complete catalog.

Kumarian Press, located in Bloomfield, Connecticut, is a forward-looking, scholarly press that promotes active international engagement and an awareness of global connectedness.